THE
GREAT EXHIBITION

London's Crystal Palace Exposition of 1851

GRAMERCY BOOKS
New York • Avenel

INTRODUCTION

ondon's Crystal Palace exposition of 1851 was the first world's fair, organized to stimulate trade, elevate popular taste, display the best designed examples of manufactured objects, and promote international peace through commerce. The Great Exhibition of the Industry of All Nations was ceremonially opened by Queen Victoria in May 1851 and closed by Prince Albert six months later. Visited by more than six million people, it was a huge success—and came to be considered one of the most important cultural events of the nineteenth century.

England in the mid-1800s was engaged in a major cultural revival, based on technical progress and domestic and public virtue. In 1837, the year of Queen Victoria's coronation, the government established the School of Design to promote "the direct practical application of the arts to manufacture." Shortly after his marriage to the queen three years later, Prince Albert was appointed president of the Select Committee "for the promotion of the fine arts in this country in connexion with the rebuilding of the Houses of Parliament." It was Prince Albert who proposed the idea of a mammoth international exposition. In a speech at the Lord Mayor's Banquet in October 1849, he lauded the purpose of the undertaking: "The great principle of the division of labour which may be called the moving power of civilisation is being extended to all branches of science, industry, and art.... The products of all the quarters of the globe are placed at our disposal.... Gentlemen, the Exhibition of 1851 is to give us a true test and a living picture of the point of development at which the whole of mankind have arrived in this great task, and a new starting point from which all nations will be able to direct their further exertions." In July 1850, the title Commissioners for the Exhibition of 1851 was incorporated, followed a month later by the granting of a charter for the project.

No less significant was the exposition hall itself, erected over twenty-one acres in Hyde Park. The startling design of the Crystal Palace symbolized the industry and progress of the age. Designed by architect Joseph Paxton, the building was constructed of iron and glass and owed little to the prevailing architectural atmosphere that borrowed eclectically from the past. Owen Jones, who a few years later published his *Grammar of Ornament*, one of the most famous color-illustrated books of the nineteenth century, was responsible for the exhibition's much-praised color scheme. Henry Cole, who had introduced the *Journal of Design and Manufacture* in 1847, was one of the chief organizers of the Great Exhibition; he acquired many of the objects from the exposition as the basis for a museum collection, and in 1857 formed the South Kensington Museum and School, which later became the Victoria and Albert Museum. Matthew Digby Wyatt, the Crystal Palace's architectural supervisor, was involved in the design of Paddington Station, a building directly influenced by the exposition hall's style. It was completed in 1854, the same year that the Crystal Palace itself was relocated—under Paxton's supervision—to a two-hundred-acre park at Sydenham, a few miles from London, where it became an exhibition and amusement center famous for its fireworks. Ironically, a fire destroyed the building in 1936.

This facsimile edition of the catalogue of the Industry of All Nations exposition has more than three hundred pages of engravings of the most representative objects displayed at the Crystal Palace in 1851. Included are illustrations of glass chandeliers, Wedgwood pottery, fine carriages, rich embroideries, and ornately carved furniture, as well as clocks, ironwork, fireplaces, silverware, pianos, carpets, wallpaper, mirrors, statuary, and jewelry—beautiful Victorian objects that attest to an era's faith in industry, progress, and artistry.

GEORGE PALMER BLAKE

New York, 1995

Copyright © 1995 by Random House Value Publishing, Inc. All rights reserved.

This edition is published by Gramercy Books,
distributed by Random House Value Publishing, Inc., 40 Engelhard Avenue, Avenel, New Jersey 07001.

Random House
New York • Toronto • London • Sydney • Auckland

Printed and bound in the United States of America

Library of Congress Cataloging-in-Publication Data
The Great Exhibition: London's Crystal Palace Exposition of 1851.
p. cm.
Reprint. Originally published: Bounty Books, 1970.
ISBN 0–517–12209–X
1. Great Exhibition (1851: London, England) 2. Crystal Palace (London, England)
T690.B1G74 1994
907.4´421—dc20   94–32563
                                                    CIP

8 7 6 5 4 3 2 1

Publisher's Note: This is a facsimile of the *Art Journal Illustrated Catalogue of the Industry of All Nations,* which commemorated London's Great Exhibition of 1851. All of the engravings and the text of the original book are reproduced in this edition, with the exception of the inserted plates of individual sculptures and four essays on science, machinery, taste, and "the vegetable world."

THE TABLE OF CONTENTS

ENGRAVINGS OF WORKS EXHIBITED.

TABLE OF CONTENTS.

TABLE OF CONTENTS.

TABLE OF CONTENTS.

PREFACE.

E submit this Volume to the public in full assurance of its success. It will be obvious that neither cost nor labour has been spared to render it, in all respects, a worthy record of the great gathering of Works of Art and Industry to which an illustrious Prince invited all the Nations of the World—and to which there was a cordial and grateful response.

We have studied to introduce into this Catalogue, engravings, the most interesting and the most suggestive, of the various objects exhibited; to include, as far as possible, all such as might gratify or instruct; and thus to supply sources of after-education to manufacturers and artisans of all classes, and of all countries; rendering the Exhibition practically beneficial, long after its contents have been distributed. From the Exhibitors, universally, we received zealous aid and encouragement; and the result has been, we hope and believe, to satisfy them, generally, as to selection and manner of execution.

We have obtained from high and experienced authorities, Essays, such as might be permanently useful, in illustrating the leading objects of the Exhibition; and we close the Volume with the Prize Essay, for which we have awarded the sum of 100 Guineas. To the accomplished Professors who have thus co-operated with us, our best thanks are due: we are also bound to express our acknowledgments to Messrs. Dalziel, the eminent engravers, who superintended the engravings, and whose duty has been discharged with great ability, punctuality, and care; to Messrs. Nicholls and other artists by whom we have been assisted; to the Printers, Messrs. Bradbury and Evans, to whose exertions we are largely indebted for having placed at our entire disposal no fewer than thirty presses during a period of eight months, and who may refer to this publication as evidence not only of their skill in wood-block printing, but of the immense resources of their establishment; and to others by whose aid we have been enabled to complete a work which involved considerable toil, anxiety, and attention, on the part of all who were engaged in its production.

It may be permitted us to state that but for its association with THE ART-JOURNAL, it would have been impossible to have published this collection at less than four times the price at which it is now issued: and, perhaps, but for the experience and machinery possessed by the conductors of that Journal, it could not have been produced at all. We commenced our labours—and announced this Catalogue—immediately after the promulgation of the plan and the appointment of a Commission: personally visiting most of the principal cities of Europe: communicating with all the chief manufacturers of Great Britain: and arranging for such aids as might enable us to complete our undertaking with regularity, and as early as possible after the opening of the Exhibition.

The results of the Great Exhibition are pregnant with incalculable benefits to all classes of the community: the seed has been planted, of which the future is to produce the fruit: among the eager thousands whose interest was excited and whose curiosity was gratified, were many who obtained profitable suggestions at every visit: the manufacturer and the artisan have thus learned the most valuable of all lessons,—the disadvantages under which they had laboured, the deficiencies they had to remedy, and the prejudices they had to overcome.

But it is to the honour of Great Britain that, notwithstanding the generous risk incurred by inviting competitors from all the nations of the world—prepared as they had been by long years of successful study and practical experience—the fame of British manufacturers has been augmented by this contest: and there can be no doubt, that when His Royal Highness Prince Albert issues his summons to another competition, British supremacy will be manifested in every branch of Industrial Art.

In terminating our labours, we may hope that a project we have repeatedly and earnestly advocated in THE ART-JOURNAL, and which we presume to regard as, in some degree, the issue of our efforts to connect the Fine Arts with the Industrial Arts (a procedure originating with that Journal, having never been attempted elsewhere in Europe, and in which for a long period we had to contend against difficulties that seemed insurmountable), will derive some of its advantages from the Report thus made in this Illustrated Catalogue. Upon this topic it is unnecessary for us to dilate: the readers of THE ART-JOURNAL are well aware of our efforts to promote the interests of the manufacturer: to induce his advance, on the one hand; and, on the other, to lead the public to appreciate his improvements: to report his progress, and to make him acquainted with the progress of his competitors: to furnish him with such information as might be gathered from the best instructors —and, by immediately connecting him with the artist, to direct him to the safest sources of Art-education.

Our exertions have been fully appreciated: THE ART-JOURNAL has obtained a success unprecedented in periodical literature: we have the happiness to contrast the state of British Art-Manufacture in the year 1846 (when our labours in this direction may be said to have commenced), with its position in the memorable year 1851; and we trust that no one who has traced our course will consider us presumptuous in feeling that in the Great Exhibition of the Industry of All Nations, we have received our "exceeding great reward."

HISTORY OF THE GREAT EXHIBITION.

WE commence this ILLUSTRATED CATALOGUE of the principal contents of the GREAT EXHIBITION with a brief but succinct History of the Building — and of the Project from its commencement up to the present time.

The experiment of an Exhibition of the Industry of all the civilised Nations of the World has been tried, and has succeeded beyond the most sanguine expectations of its projectors. It is, indeed, scarcely possible to instance any great enterprise of modern date which has so completely satisfied the anticipations which had been formed of its results. Differing from most other institutions for benefiting the great family of mankind, which have required time and experience to mature, it has sprung, like Minerva from the brain of Jove "full armed," into life and activity; resembling the goddess, however, only in her more pacific attributes; her love of the olive tree, and her patronage of the Industrial Arts. Other nations have devised means for the display and encouragement of their own arts and manufactures; but it has been reserved for England to provide an arena for the exhibition of the industrial triumphs of the whole world. She has offered an hospitable invitation to surrounding nations to bring the choicest products of their industry to her capital, and there to enter into an amicable competition with each other and with herself; and she has endeavoured to secure to them the certainty of an impartial verdict on their efforts. Whatever be the extent of the benefit which this great demonstration may confer upon the Industrial Arts of the world, it cannot fail to soften, if not to eradicate altogether, the prejudices and animosities which have so long retarded the happiness of nations; and to promote those feelings of "peace and good will" which are among the surest antecedents of their prosperity; a peace, which Shakspeare has told us—

> " Is of the nature of a conquest ;
> For then both parties nobly are subdued,
> And neither party loses."

It forms no part of our present object to enter, with any degree of minuteness, into the history of exhibitions of this class; but a brief glance at the origin and progress of such associations in France and England may not be considered irrelevant. So far back as 1756-7, the Society of Arts of London offered prizes for specimens of various manufactures —tapestry, carpets, porcelain, among others—and publicly exhibited the articles which were thus collected; and in 1761 and 1762 the artists of Great Britain formed themselves into two societies for the exposition and sale of works of art. A few years afterwards (1768), the Royal Academy of Painting was established, as a private society, under the immediate patronage of the Crown, and Sir Joshua Reynolds appointed its President. Since then, numerous institutions of a similar character have been set on foot in this country, with considerable advantage to the branches of industry they were intended to benefit. France must, however, be regarded as the originator of exhibitions which are, in character and plan, most analogous to that on whose history we are about to enter. We gather from the historical essay of Messieurs Challamel and Burat, and the pamphlet of the Marquis d'Aveze on the subject, that, shortly after that nobleman's appointment to be Commissioner of the Royal Manufactories of the Gobelins, of Sèvres, and of the Savonnerie, in 1797, he found that two years of neglect had reduced the workmen almost to starvation, whilst it had left the respective warehouses filled with their choicest productions. In this crisis, the idea occurred to him of converting the chateau of St. Cloud, then uninhabited, into a bazaar, for the exhibition and disposal, by lottery, of the large stock of tapestry, china, and carpets, on hand in these establishments. Having obtained the consent of the government to his proposal, he set about arranging the various objects in the apartments of the chateau; but, on the day fixed for the opening of his bazaar, he was compelled, by a decree of the Directory, banishing the nobility, to quit France at a very short notice, and the project fell to the ground. On his return to Paris in the ensuing year, the Marquis planned another exhibition of an even more important kind. Having collected a great many objects of taste and *vertu*, he distributed them throughout the house and gardens of the Maison d'Orsay, Rue de Varennes, with a view to their sale. In looking over the catalogue of objects of which this collection was composed, we can hardly help being struck with its aristocratical character. The richest furniture and marqueterie produced by Boule, Riessner, and Jacob; the finest clocks and watches of L'Epine and Leroy; the superb china of Sèvres, of Angoulême, and of Nast; the most elegantly bound books, fully confirming the traditional excellence of Grolier and De Thou; silks of Lyons; historical pictures by Vincent and David; bronzes, and sculpture; served to show to what class of the community French manufacture had, up to that period, been mainly indebted for support. The success which attended the efforts of the Marquis led to the adoption of his idea by the government, and the establishment of the first official Exposition, on the very spot, on the Champ de Mars, on which the army had held a triumphal show of its splendid collection of Italian spoils. Six weeks after that fête, the nation erected on the same spot a Temple of Industry for the exhibition of more pacific trophies; an edifice surrounded by sixty porticos, filled with the most beautiful objects that had been manufactured in France. The system of deciding on the comparative merits of the various exhibitors by juries, composed of gentlemen distinguished for their taste, was then, for the first time, adopted. Prizes were awarded for watches, mathematical instruments, painting china, etc. The success of this Exposition was so great, that the government resolved to repeat it annually; but, in spite of the circular of the Minister of the Interior to that effect, the political commotions of the times prevented him from repeating it, until the year 1801, and then only at the instance of the First Consul, who visited the factories and ateliers of the principal towns in France, with several men of science, for the purpose of convincing the manufacturers of the importance to themselves of supporting such an undertaking. This second display took place in the quadrangle of the Louvre, in a temporary building erected for the occasion. Notwithstanding the difficulties which had attended its establishment, 200 exhibitors were competitors for the prizes. Upon this occasion, ten gold, twenty silver, and thirty bronze medals, were awarded; one of the last having been adjudged to the celebrated Jacquard, for his now famous machine.

It must not be overlooked that even at this early period the Juries awarded prizes for improvements in the quality of wool as a raw material, and for excellence in woollen and cotton fabrics. The third exhibition took place on the same spot in 1802; and on that occasion no fewer than 600 exhibitors competed for the prizes. The popularity of these expositions led to the formation of the *Société d'Encouragement*, which aided very importantly the industrial efforts of the French manufacturers. It is a remarkable fact, however, that whilst in France the Society of Arts and Manufactures owes its origin to these public expositions of the products of its industry, we are in England wholly indebted for exhibitions of this kind to our Society of Arts. The fourth exhibition of French industrial products took place in 1806, in a building erected for the purpose in front of the *Hôpital des Invalides*; when the exhibitors had increased to 1400, and it was found necessary to keep open the doors for 24 days. Here, for the first time, were displayed the printed cottons of Mulhausen and Logelbach; silk, thread, and cotton lace; blonde, cloth and mixed goods. Among the improvements for which prizes were awarded, were the manufacture of iron by the aid of coke instead of charcoal, and that of steel by a process wholly unknown till then.

The disturbed condition of France, arising out of her wars with her European neighbours, prevented the fifth exhibition from taking place until 1819, when it was inaugurated on the fête of St. Louis, and continued open for thirty-five days. The number of exhibitors had increased to 1700. The sixth exhibition took place in 1823 on the same spot as its predecessor, and remained open 50 days. Great improvement was manifest in the manufacture of many of the articles; in machinery more especially. It was on this occasion that the model of the first French suspension bridge over the river Rhone, by M. Leguin, was exhibited by its engineer. The next Industrial Exposition occurred in 1827, when a large building was erected for it in the *Place de la Concorde*. The eighth was held in 1834; the ninth in 1839, when no fewer than 4381 competitors entered the field; the tenth in 1844, when 3960 manufacturers exhibited their productions; and the eleventh in 1849, in the Champs Elysées, when the number of competitors had increased to 4494. [Both these exhibitions were fully reported and extensively illustrated in the ART-JOURNAL.] It is true that other nations had followed the example of France, but without achieving her success. The Belgian and Bavarian governments have both had their industrial exhibitions [the Exhibition at Brussels was fully reported and illustrated in the ART-JOURNAL]; but neither of them call for especial notice.

In this country, during the last dozen years, there have been many exhibitions of this description; but, with here and there an exception, they have differed little in character from the ordinary Bazaar. Manchester, Leeds, and Dublin (the last so early as 1827) had all opened bazaars for the sale of the productions of the surrounding neighbourhood; but the first building in this country devoted expressly to the exhibition of manufactures, was that erected at Birmingham in 1849 on the occasion of the visit of the British Association. The building, on that occasion, included a space of 10,000 square feet, independently of a corridor of 800 feet, which connected the main exhibition room with Bingley House, within whose grounds it had been located; so that, including the rooms of the old mansion, the total area covered by the Exhibition was equal to 12,800 square feet. The cost of the building did not exceed 1300*l*. This and the Free Trade Bazaar, held in Covent Garden in 1845, approached nearer to the French expositions in the variety and extent of the national productions they comprised, than any of their predecessors in this country. [Both these exhibitions —that of the Free Trade Bazaar, and that held in Birmingham—were fully reported and extensively illustrated in the ART-JOURNAL.]

The idea of an Exhibition which should include specimens of the Industrial Products of various nations originated, in the early part of 1849, with M. Buffet, the French Minister of Agriculture and Commerce; and with a view to ascertain the opinions of the manufacturers on the subject, circulars were addressed by him to the Chambers of Commerce throughout France, proposing that specimens of the arts and manufactures of neighbouring countries should be admitted to the approaching exposition. The replies which were received to this suggestion were so unfavourable to its adoption, that M. Buffet was induced at once to abandon the idea. If, therefore, the merit of having originated exhibitions of her own manufactures belongs to France, it is to his Royal Highness PRINCE ALBERT that the more noble and disinterested plan of throwing open an institution of this description to the competition of the whole world, is exclusively due; and his suggestion has been carried out in a spirit every way worthy its grandeur and generosity.

The great success which attended the French Industrial Exposition of 1844 had caused representations to be made to the English government of the advantages which would accrue to our commerce from a similar exhibition in this country; but the efforts which were made to obtain its co-operation appear to have been wholly unsuccessful. In 1848, a proposal to establish a self-supporting exhibition of the products of British industry, to be directed by a

Royal Commission, was submitted by H.R.H. Prince Albert to the government, but with no better success; and it then became apparent that no reliance whatever could be placed upon the active support of Her Majesty's ministers for any such plan. They had, in all probability, no objection to see the experiment tried, but were evidently unwilling to commit themselves to any responsibility in behalf of a scheme which seemed to be beset by so many difficulties. Meanwhile, the popular feeling in favour of such an undertaking was rapidly strengthening, and the success which has attended the experiment may, in a great measure, be referred to the freedom of action which this dissociation from the timid councils of the government secured for its projectors. It may be proper, in this place, to remark that, excepting in facilitating its correspondence with foreign nations; the provision of a site for the building; and the organisation of the police; no assistance has been either sought or obtained from the government for the present Exhibition; whilst, in every case in which it has been attended by expense, the cost has been defrayed out of the funds at the disposal of the Executive Committee.

The initiative in those inquiries which were indispensable to the due consideration of the means by which the idea of an Exhibition for all Nations was to be carried out, was taken by the Society of Arts, a committee of whose members was formed in June, 1845, for the purpose; the funds for defraying the preliminary expenses of which were subscribed among themselves. An inquiry having been instituted for the purpose of ascertaining how far the manufacturers of Great Britain were favourable to such a design, with no very encouraging result, the idea was for a time abandoned. In 1847, the Council of the Society launched their pilot balloon in the shape of an Exhibition of British Manufactures, professedly the first of a series; and encouraged by its success, repeated the experiment in the ensuing year; when the intention of its executive was announced, to establish an annual competition of the same kind, with a view to the opening of a quinqennial exhibition for the industrial products of all nations to be held in 1851. As an accessory to their plan, the council

THE MEDAL OF MR. G. G. ADAMS.

THE MEDAL OF MR. LEONARD C. WYON.

THE MEDAL OF M. BONNARDEL.

sought to connect with it the various Schools of Design established in our larger towns, and obtained the co-operation of the Board of Trade, through its president, Mr. Labouchere, in that object. They also secured the promise of a site from the Earl of Carlisle, then Commissioner of Woods and Forests; who offered them the central area of Somerset House, or any other government ground at his disposal which seemed adapted for their purposes. The Exhibition of 1849, confined for the most part to works in the precious metals, several of the more important of which were contributed by Her Majesty, proved more successful than either of the two that had preceded it, and stimulated proportionably the exertions of the Council. A report on the French Exposition of the same year, by Mr. Digby Wyatt, had, moreover, strongly confirmed them in their conviction of the utility of such an exhibition in this country.

Meanwhile, H. R. H. Prince Albert was not only privy to, but entirely approved of these proceedings; and, on the termination of the Parliamentary session of 1849, took the subject under his immediate superintendence. But, indeed, for his indefatigable perseverance, his courageous defiance of all risks of failure, his remarkable sagacity in matters of business, and the influence which attached to his support, the whole project, notwithstanding the great exertions which had been made to secure its realisation, must have fallen to the ground. The maturely considered views of his Royal Highness, and the patriotic objects he proposed in making this great peace-offering to mankind, are admirably set forth in the speech delivered by him on the occasion of the banquet given by Mr. Alderman Farncomb, then Lord Mayor of London, to the municipal authorities of the United Kingdom in support of the project. "The Exhibition of 1851 would," he said, "afford a true test of the point of development at which the whole of mankind has arrived in this great task, and a new starting point from which all nations would be able to direct their further exertions." It is difficult to assign to Prince Albert the degree of praise which is really his due on this occasion without incurring the suspicion of being in some degree influenced by the exalted position he holds in the country. "It is," says Coleridge, "one of the most mischievous effects of flattery that it renders honourable natures more slow and reluctant in expressing their real feelings in praise of the deserving, than for the interests of truth and virtue might be desired." The remark applies with peculiar force to a person of His Royal Highness's rank. Rather than incur the imputation of sycophancy, his admirers have sometimes been led to do less than justice to the very prominent part he has taken in this project, and to the consummate skill with which he has smoothed down all opposition to it. In a word, for the World's Exhibition, the world is entirely indebted to the Prince Consort.

On the 29th of June, 1849, at a meeting, at Buckingham Palace, of several of the gentlemen, who afterwards became members of the Royal Commission, and Prince Albert, his Royal Highness communicated his plan for the formation of a great collection of works of Industry and Art in London, in 1851, for the purposes of exhibition, of competition, and of encouragement; when he proposed that these contributions should consist of four great divisions, namely: raw materials; machinery and mechanical inventions; manufactures; and sculpture and plastic art generally; and the best proof we could adduce of the sagacity by which his suggestions were characterised is to be found in the brilliant success which has attended their almost literal adoption. At the second meeting for the same object, held at Osborne House on the 14th July, 1849, which was attended among other distinguished supporters of the project, by the late Sir Robert Peel, His Royal Highness gave a general outline of the plan of operations he recommended, which met with the unanimous approbation of his fellow labourers. These suggestions comprised the formation of a Royal Commission, its duties and powers; the definition of the nature of the Exhibition, and of the best mode of conducting its proceedings; the determination of the method of deciding the prizes, and the responsibility of the decision; and the means of raising a prize fund, and providing for the necessary expenses which the permanent establishment of quinquennial exhibitions would involve. The amount which it was proposed to distribute in prizes was 20,000l, and the lowest estimate for a suitable building did not fall below 50,000l. He also pointed out the advantages of the site which has since been adopted, and recommended an early application to the crown for permission to appropriate it.

Impressed with the truth of the proverb, *Ce n'est que le premier pas qui coûte,* the council of the Society of Arts, after much fruitless negotiation with other parties, entered into an engagement with Messrs. Munday, the well-known contractors, by which those gentlemen undertook to deposit a prize fund of 20,000l.; to erect a suitable building; to find offices; to advance the money requisite for all preliminary expenses; and to take the whole risk of loss; on the following conditions: The 20,000l. prize fund, the cost of the building, and five per cent on all advances, to be repaid out of the first receipts; the residue to be divided into three equal parts; one part to be paid over at once to the Society of Arts, in aid of future exhibitions; and out of the other two parts all other incidental costs, such as those of general management and preliminary expenses; the residue, if any, to be the remuneration of the contractors for their outlay, trouble, and risk. Messrs. Munday subsequently consented, instead of this division, to receive such part of the surplus only, if any, as after payment of all expenses might be awarded by arbitration. An executive committee of four members, who became subsequently the executive committee of the Royal Commission, was then formed, who induced the contractors to allow them the option of determining the contract any time before the first of February, 1850. In such an event, however, Messrs. Munday's claims to compensation for their outlay and risk were to be adjusted by arbitration. After remaining out of their money more than a year, Messrs. Munday obtained very recently, an award of 5000l. with interest.

The pecuniary part of the undertaking having thus been provided for, the next object was to satisfy the government of the desire of the public for the proposed Exhibition, in order to warrant the issue of a Royal Commission for its management. With this view, a deputation from the Executive Committee proceeded to the manufacturing districts to collect the necessary information; and after visiting sixty-five of the most important towns and cities of the United Kingdom, brought back with them strong manifestations of the popular desire in the shape of documents in which nearly 5,000 influential persons had registered their names as promoters of the project. About the same time Mr. Scott Russell, having occasion to visit several of the states included in the Zollverein, found that the advantages which it offered to the commerce of the world were everywhere appreciated, and received the most cordial offers of co-operation from a great number of influential persons in those countries. On the presentation of these reports to the government, the Royal Commission was issued, and at their first meeting on the 11th January, 1850, they decided on availing themselves of the election which had been reserved for them by the Society of

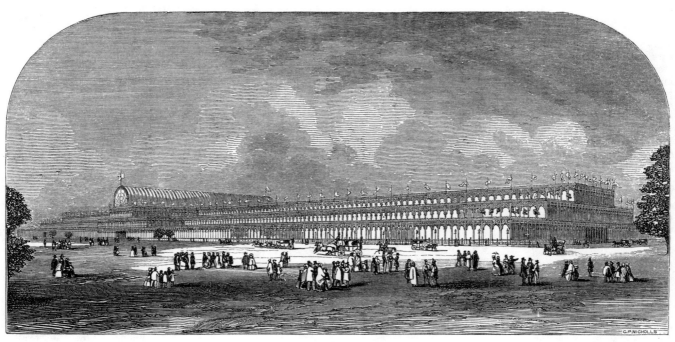

EXTERIOR OF THE BUILDING FOR THE GREAT EXHIBITION (SOUTH SIDE).

Arts, and rescinded the contract with Messrs. Munday; thus relying for their means of carrying out their views, in the first instance, wholly upon voluntary contributions.

How the appeal of the Commissioners to the country was responded to is sufficiently known. Meetings having taken place in all parts of the United Kingdom, subscriptions began to flow in, in a highly encouraging manner. On the 17th of October, 1849, the Lord Mayor of London called a meeting at the Egyptian Hall to receive a deputation of the members of the Society of Arts, charged by Prince Albert to explain the outlines of His Royal Highness's proposal for a Great Exhibition of the Industry of All Nations, to be held in London, in the year 1851. This meeting was attended by nearly four hundred of the most influential merchants, bankers, and traders, of London, and nothing could be more cordial than the spirit displayed by almost every person who assisted at it. Mr. Cole, who was the exponent of Prince Albert's views on the occasion, gave, in a speech of considerable ability, an interesting account of the reception the project had met with from the large body of manufacturers in the provinces, whose adhesion he had succeeded in obtaining. The feeling in favour of an international Exhibition appears to have been almost unanimous. Other meetings in the city, and other parts of the metropolis, were subsequently held, and a large amount of subscriptions collected. Whilst matters were progressing thus favourably, the Lord Mayor of London conceived the magnificent idea of inviting the chief magistrates of the various towns, cities, and boroughs, throughout the United Kingdom, to a grand banquet, at the Mansion-House, with the view of promoting the success of the Exhibition. The results of this *réunion* were, in the highest degree, satisfactory. Nearly the whole body of provincial Mayors accepted the invitation, and were thus inspired with something like a personal interest in the success of the undertaking. They had, moreover, the advantage of receiving Prince Albert's explanations from his own lips. Among the voices raised in favour of an international Exhibition on this occasion, were those of Lord John Russell, Lord Stanley, the Archbishop of Canterbury, the French Ambassador, and the late lamented Sir Robert Peel. On the succeeding day a meeting of the public functionaries who were present at the dinner, took place in the Egyptian Hall for business purposes, when the ball was set moving in good earnest.

The Commissioners having revised their original intention to give large money prizes, invited, by public advertisement, artists of all countries to compete for the designs for the reverses of three bronze medals intended to form the respective prizes, which should be illustrative of the objects of the Exhibition; and offered three prizes of 100*l.* each for the three subjects which should be selected for that purpose, and three prizes of 50*l.* for the three best designs which might not be accepted. In consequence of this advertisement no fewer than one hundred and twenty-nine designs were sent in, and were publicly exhibited in the rooms of the Royal Society of Arts. The judges appointed by the Commissioners were Lord Colborne, W. Dyce, Esq., R.A., J. Gibson, Esq., R.A., M. Eugene Lami, C. Newton, Esq., Herr J. D. Passavant, and Dr. Gustave Waagen; who on the 29th June decided in favour of the following gentlemen:—The first prizes of 100*l.* each, were awarded to, 1. Hyppolyte Bonnardel, of Paris. 2. Leonard C. Wyon, of London. 3. G. G. Adams, of London. The second prizes of 50*l.* each, were awarded to, 4. John Hancock, of London. 5. L. Wiener, of Brussells. 6. M. Gayrard, of Paris.

The medal of M. Bonnardel is decidedly the most ambitious of the three. It represents Britannia standing on a platform, with outstretched arms, and a crown in each hand with which she is in the act of decorating, simultaneously, the brows of Mercury, and a female he is holding by the hand, who may be presumed to be Industry. Flags of different nations make up the background. Motto—"Est etiam in magno quædam respublica mundo."

Mr. Wyon's design represents Britannia seated and in the act of placing a laurel wreath upon the head of a figure emblematical of Industry, whilst she extends her right hand as if to raise her up. Behind her are impersonations of the four quarters of the globe by whom Industry has been conducted to Britannia. To the right are emblems of the four sections: 1. The cotton plant and wheatsheaf; 2. A wheel; 3. A bale of goods; 4. A vase. Motto—"Dissociata locis concordi pace ligavit."

Mr. Adams's medal presents a gracefully modelled group of Fame crowning Industry, and Commerce looking on with approving eye. Industry has a distaff in her hand, and appears to be sitting on a cornucopia.

In July, 1850, letters patent were issued, incorporating the Commissioners under the title of "The Commissioners for the Exhibition of 1851," and the charter was accepted on the

WESTERN ENTRANCE TO THE GREAT EXHIBITION.

15th August. A guarantee fund of 230,000*l.* had been subscribed by a limited number of gentlemen, favourable to the Exhibition, one of whom opened the list with a subscription of 50,000*l.* Upon this security the Bank of England undertook to make the necessary advances. On the 21st of February preceding, the Building Committee ventured to recommend that upwards of sixteen acres should be covered in.

With a view to give Foreign nations as much time for preparation as possible, the Commissioners resolved, long before they had decided on the size and character of the building, to divide a certain large extent of space among foreign countries, amounting in the whole to 210,000 superficial feet, or rather more than the entire space which France had occupied for its two expositions of 1844 and 1849. Subsequently, the quantities of space allotted to foreign nations was increased; France obtaining 65,000 feet instead of 50,000. A definite amount of space proportioned to their presumed wants was also allotted to each of the British Colonies. With the view of avoiding, in the first instance, the confusion that would have arisen from the collection of duties for the objects imported, the government was induced to treat the Exhibition as a bonded warehouse. On the 31st of October, 1850, the last day on which applications for space could be entertained, the whole of the demands for horizontal (floor and counter) space exceeded 417,000 superficial feet; being beyond the amount of available space for the United Kingdom, by about 210,000 superficial feet. Every class appears however to have been satisfied with the final allocations, which were the best that could have been made under the circumstances.

When the time arrived for making definite arrangements for the erection of the building, the Commissioners had only 35,000*l.* in hand; and, notwithstanding the guarantee to which they had themselves largely subscribed, they must have felt themselves committed to a very deep responsibility. Nothing daunted, however, an invitation was addressed, through the public prints, to architects of all nations, to furnish designs for an edifice, the roof of which was to cover 700,000 square feet; and the area of which, including the open spaces, was not to exceed 900,000 feet. Other conditions were enumerated which

SOUTHERN ENTRANCE TO THE TRANSEPT.

showed that the whole of the details had been carefully and judiciously considered. Although the time allowed for the preparation of the drawings was only a month, there were no fewer than two hundred and thirty-three competitors, many of whom sent in designs of a highly elaborate character. Of these, thirty-eight, or one-sixth of the whole, were from foreigners; 128 from London and its vicinity; and 51 from the provincial towns of England. The duty of examining, classifying, and comparing them, devolved on Mr. Digby Wyatt, who embodied the result of his investigation in a report. After fifteen protracted sittings, the Building Committee arrived at the "unanimous conclusion that, able and admirable as many of these designs appeared to be, there was yet no single one so accordant with the peculiar objects in view, either in the principle, or detail of its arrangements, as to warrant them in recommending it for adoption." This report was presented to the Royal Commissioners on the 9th of May. The rejection of the whole of the plans of the competing architects created, as was natural, no ordinary dissatisfaction; a feeling which was in no respect diminished by the fact that the Building Committee had prepared a plan of their own; and, assisted by Mr. Digby Wyatt, Mr. Charles Heard Wild, and Mr. Owen Jones, had completed extensive working drawings which they had caused to be lithographed. Their next step was to issue invitations for tenders to erect the building; requesting from the respective competitors, in addition, such suggestions and modifications, accompanied by estimates of cost, as might seem likely to effect a reduction in the general expense. The design of the Building Committee comprehended an edifice 2200 feet long, and 450 feet wide. Into any detailed description of it, however, it is foreign to our purpose to enter; suffice it to say that this child of many fathers was condemned, not less for its extraordinary ugliness, than that it would have been unnecessarily large, cumbrous, and costly, for a purpose avowedly temporary. Meanwhile, the contractors found some difficulty in getting their tenders ready by the 10th of May. On that day, however, nineteen were sent in; but of these only eight professed to comprehend the execution of the whole of the work. The amounts of the remaining eleven competitors varied from 120,000*l.* to 150,000*l.*: and this, for the use only of the materials for the building. The Building Committee defended their edifice in an elaborate report, setting forth its economy and good taste. Public opinion was, however, decidedly against its adoption; and fortunately, a gentleman, not an architect, came "to the rescue."

Among the contractors who had accepted the invitation of the Building Committee, was the firm of Fox & Henderson, who, availing themselves of the permission to alter and amend the plan of the Committee, contained in the latter part of the report, presented a tender for a building of an entirely different character from that which had been suggested by the Committee. This, we need scarcely add, was the plan which, with certain modifications and additions, was ultimately adopted; and for which, notwithstanding all that has been said to the contrary, the public is wholly indebted to Mr. Paxton. He was, as he himself tells us, at that time occupied in erecting a house for the Victoria Regia, in the Gardens of the Duke of Devonshire, at Chatsworth, and to that circumstance the Crystal Palace may be said to owe its direct origin. The accounts which have been given by Mr. Paxton, Mr. Fox, and Mr. Barry, of their respective shares in the production of the accepted plan, are not strictly reconcileable with each other; but that the idea, in a state of maturity which demanded no great effort of mind to make it more complete, originated with Mr. Paxton, does not admit of a question. The very nature of that idea which rendered a single section of the building completely explanatory of the whole, would seem to have rendered elaborate plans of the proposed edifice, in its entirety, less a work of mind than of mechanical dexterity. A single bay of 24 feet square would,

INTERIOR OF THE TRANSEPT, AS SEEN FROM THE SOUTH ENTRANCE.

if we except the transept and its semicircular roof, supply the means of making a correct drawing of the whole; and if it be correct, as stated by Mr. Paxton at the dinner given to him at Derby, on the 6th of August, that his original sketch on a sheet of blotting paper indicates the principal features of the building as it now stands as much as the most finished drawings which have been made since, there can be no excuse for attempting to deprive him of any portion of the merit of the invention. But he appears to have done considerably more than merely furnish the idea. In nine days from that on which he had made the blotting paper sketch, he was in possession of nine plans, all, with a single exception, prepared by his own hand. And although his suggestion to Messrs. Fox & Henderson was offered so late as the 22nd June, 1850, his plan was engraved and published in the *Illustrated News* of the 6th July. There can be no doubt that the great experience of Mr. Fox enabled him, after consulting with

Mr. Cole, to adapt the drawings more to the arrangements adopted by the Committee in the plan they had themselves prepared, than Mr. Paxton had done: but in a case like this, the first idea is considerably more than half the battle. Mr. Fox prepared, he tells us, the working drawings, and made everything ship-shape; but to the fullest extent he admits that all the leading features of the plan, including each progressive improvement of any importance, were suggested by the originator of the general idea. At one of the meetings of the Building Committee, it was suggested that the transept, at the sacrifice of not dividing the building into two equal parts, should include the larger trees; but there appeared to be a good deal of difficulty in adopting such a recommendation, as at that time the whole of the roof was intended to be flat. Having promised to see what could be done in the matter, Mr. Paxton accompanied Mr. Fox to his office, and whilst he was occupied in arranging the ground-

THE TRANSEPT, FROM THE NORTH SIDE.

plan, so as to bring the trees into the centre, he "hit upon the idea of covering the transept with a circular roof, similar to that on the great conservatory at Chatsworth, and made a sketch of it, which was copied that night by one of Mr. Fox's draughtsmen." In a recent letter to the "Times" newspaper, Mr. Barry, in reference to this statement, declares that at the first presentation of Mr. Paxton's design to the Building Committee, as well as to the Royal Commission, and before he had offered any suggestion on the subject, he recommended, very strongly, the addition of a vaulted roof, not only to the transept, but also over the nave; and submitted to the Commissioners a sketch showing the effect of such an addition. The probability, therefore, is, that the two gentlemen hit upon the same idea at pretty nearly the same moment. There is, however, at all events, no pretext for imputing to either of them a desire to claim for himself a merit which does not belong to him. The Royal Commissioners themselves, in their official report, distinctly acknowledge the services which were rendered to the edifice by Mr. Barry's judicious suggestions, and whilst they compliment Mr. Paxton on the "grand effect produced by his happy idea of raising the semi-cylindrical vault of the transept above the tiers of terraces which extend on either side of it," acknowledge that, "for much of its grace of proportion and beauty of form, the building is indebted to Mr. Barry;" and that "upon the form and distribution of the arches and filling in frames, as well as of the columns, the suggestions of that gentleman exercised a happy influence." We doubt, however, if the adoption of these suggestions should be allowed to detract in any respect from the *éclat* due to Mr. Paxton as the legitimate parent of the Crystal Palace.

After consulting the iron masters, glass manufacturers, and others, on whose co-operation they were compelled, in a great measure, to depend for their means of fulfilling their proposals, Messrs. Fox & Henderson sent in their tenders, and on the 16th were verbally informed that they were accepted. On the 26th July, the Committee expressed a wish that they should commence operations; but as no Royal Charter could be obtained until the succeeding year, and as the solicitor to the Treasury was of opinion that until that had been obtained, the Commissioners could not legally act, the works must have stood still, but for the good understanding and mutual confidence, which subsisted between Messrs. Fox & Henderson and themselves. Rather than that any delay should take place, they agreed to proceed at once, and to incur the risk whatever it might be of waiting for the Royal Charter. To avoid unnecessary complication, Mr. William Cubitt was invested with absolute power to arrange with Messrs. Fox & Henderson all the details connected with the arduous task on which they were about to enter. On the 30th July, they obtained possession of the ground, and proceeded to take the necessary levels and surveys, and to fix the position of the various points. The working drawings, all of which he made himself, occupied Mr. Fox 18 hours a day for seven weeks; and as these left his hands, his partner Mr. Henderson directed the preparation of the iron work and other materials required for the construction of the building. As the drawings proceeded, calculations of strength were entered into; and so soon as a number of the important parts were prepared, such as the cast-iron girders and wrought-iron trusses, Mr. Cubitt was invited to witness a set of experiments illustrative of the correctness of these calculations. The greatest load it was possible for it to receive having been placed upon each part, it was distinctly shown that it would bear four times that weight without a fracture. As the works advanced, the safety of the edifice was much discussed in the public prints, and grave doubts of its stability having been

THE MAIN AVENUE—WEST.

suggested by Mr. Turner, the constructor of the large conservatory in Kew Gardens, and by Professor Airey the Astronomer Royal, a series of experiments was decided on which should set any such question wholly at rest. Tests had, as we have shown, been applied in the course of the work which had satisfied the scientific men who witnessed them that the iron girders would bear a strain upon them four times as great as they could ever be called upon to bear; but it was resolved to subject them to a still severer ordeal.

The first of these more elaborate experiments, which took place in the presence of Her Majesty, Prince Albert, and several scientific persons, was to ascertain the extent of oscillation that would be produced in the galleries by the regular motion of large bodies of persons. Three hundred workmen were accordingly deployed over the platform, and then crowded together as closely as possible. The load borne by the planks laid across the platform represented the degree of pressure that would be occasioned by the crowding of the bays of the galleries. The amount of deflection produced by this experiment was scarcely perceptible. The men next walked regularly and irregularly, and finally ran over the temporary floor, with little more effect. Even when packed in the closest order, and jumping simultaneously for several minutes, the play of the timbers and the wrought-iron work, was admirably developed, and the extreme deflection of any one girder did not exceed a quarter of an inch. As, however, the workmen were unable to keep military time in their step, the whole corps of Sappers and Miners employed on the ground, arranged in close order, marched several times over and around the bays without producing any other effect than is observable in a house in which dancing is going on. The crowning experiment suggested by Messrs. Maudslay & Field, the eminent civil engineers, rendered any further test wholly unnecessary. Seven frames, each capable of holding 36 cannon-balls, of 68lbs each, were constructed, and drawn with their contents over the floor. In this way a pressure on the flooring of seven and a-half tons was obtained; the probable pressure from a crowd not exceeding 95lb. The pressure of an ordinary crowd, however, at a public meeting or a theatre does not exceed 60lbs. to the square foot.

During the entire progress of the building, Mr. Fox was present daily at the works, to assign to each part, as it arrived upon the ground, its proper position, without which it would have been impossible that the building should have been completed in time; and so unlimited was the confidence displayed by his firm in the Royal Commissioners, that it was not until the 31st of October that the contract with them was completed; up to which time they had not only received no order for the building, and no payment on account of the work they had done, but had incurred the risk of expending upwards of 50,000l. without being in a legal position to call upon the Commissioners for the repayment of any portion of it. There was, however, no ground for apprehension on the score of finance; for whilst the work was yet in progress, funds were flowing in to the exchequer of the executive with a rapidity altogether unlooked for, and to an amount which was calculated to silence all further anxiety on the subject. To anticipate, in some respects, the order of our narrative, we may mention that before the Commissioners had opened their doors to the public, that is to say on the 29th of April, they had in hand 113,044l. :—namely, 64,344l. arising from public subscriptions; 3200l. from Messrs. Spicer & Clowes for the privilege of printing the Catalogues; 5500l. from Messrs. Schweppe, for the privilege of supplying refreshments; and 40,000l. arising from the sale of season tickets. The last item afforded a tolerable notion of the probable prospects of the Exhibition, in a financial point of view; nor have those expectations, sanguine as they were, been in any respect disappointed.

It is now time to enter upon the history of the building itself, and of the manner in which the contractors have fulfilled their duty to their employers and to the public at large.

The site of the Great Exhibition is the one originally

THE MAIN AVENUE—EAST.

proposed for it by H.R.H. Prince Albert. It consists of a rectangular piece of ground in Hyde Park, situated between the Queen's Drive and Rotten Row, and contains about 26 acres, being 2300 feet in length, by 500 feet in breadth. Its principal frontage extends from east to west. Several lofty trees which stretch across the centre of its length have been allowed to remain, and it is to them we are indebted for the magnificent transept and semicircular roof, suggested after the first plans had received the approval of the Commissioners. The ground although apparently level has a fall of from 1 to 250 inches from west to east. Among the most striking advantages of the spot were the facilities of access from all parts which it presented, and the ease with which it could be drained and supplied with gas and water; whilst the beauty of the neighbourhood can scarcely be exceeded within the same convenient distance from the metropolis. Indeed, however strong may have been the private objections urged against the adoption of this site, in the first instance, it is now universally admitted that a more desirable locality for the purpose to which it has been converted could not have been selected. The plan of the building forms a parallelogram 1848 feet long and 408 feet wide; independently of a projection on the north side, 48 feet wide and 936 feet long. The principal entrance is situated in the centre of the south side, opposite to Prince of Wales' gate, which forms one of the main openings into Hyde Park. After passing through a vestibule 72 feet by 48, the visitor finds himself in the transept, which is 72 feet wide, 108 feet high, and 408 feet from south to north. The roof springs in a semi-cylindrical form from an elevation of 68 feet from the ground, and occupies a diameter of 72 feet. The *coup d'œil* of the exterior of the building from the Prince of Wales' Gate is exceedingly striking. On each side of the space covered by the transept runs an aisle 24 feet wide. The nave or grand avenue, 72 feet wide by 64 feet high, occupies the centre throughout the entire length of the building, and

is 1848 feet long. On either side smaller avenues or aisles run parallel with it 24 feet in width, and at a height of 24 feet from the ground are galleries, which not only extend the whole length of the building, but which are carried completely round the transept; thus opening a direct communication throughout the whole of that floor. Beyond the nearest aisles and parallel with them at a distance of 48 feet, are second aisles of similar width, with galleries over them, which are on the same level as those by which the outside aisles are surmounted. To facilitate access from one line of galleries to the other, bridges, at frequent intervals, span the 48-feet avenues, and, at the same time, divide them into courts, most of which have been so arranged as to be open to the spectator, who may happen to be in the gallery above. The width of 48 feet thus subdivided, and the second aisles, are roofed over at a height of 44 feet from the ground. The remaining portion of the building comprises in width only one story 24 feet high, in which, of course, there are no galleries. Access to the galleries is obtained by ten double staircases, 8 feet wide. About its centre, the grand avenue, at a point determined by the position of three large trees which it was resolved to enclose, is crossed by the transept. Two other groups of trees, whose immolation was also interdicted, have rendered open courts necessary; but they are, nevertheless, included within the building. The entire area enclosed and roofed over comprises no fewer than 772,784 square feet, or about 19 acres; thus presenting an edifice about four times the size of St. Peter's, at Rome, and six times that of St. Paul's. We have already described the principal entrance at the south front. Besides this, there is one at each end, and, at convenient intervals, no fewer than fifteen places of egress. The horizontal measure of 24 feet, which formed a leading feature of the design of the Building Committee, is also preserved in the present plan. The avenues into which

THE UNITED STATES' DEPARTMENT.

the building is divided are formed by hollow cast-iron columns, 24 feet apart, which rise in one, two, or three stories respectively. In the lower story these columns are 19 feet high, and in the two upper ones 17 feet. Between the different columns short bars of iron, 3 feet in length, called "connecting pieces," from the use to which they are applied, are employed as supports to the girders in horizontal tiers, dividing the building, at its greatest height, into the three stories to which we have already referred. The girders, of which, some of cast, and some of wrought-iron, are all of the same depth, namely, 3 feet, with the exception of four; an arrangement by which the horizontal lines are preserved throughout.

The first impression conveyed to the mind of a visitor, inexperienced in the science of architecture, on entering the building, is a sense of insecurity, arising from the apparent lightness of its supports as compared with the vastness of its dimensions. But this feeling is soon dissipated when he is informed how severely the strength of every separate part has been tested, and with what extreme care the connexion of all the supports with each other has been considered, so as to present the greatest possible combination of strength. The ratlines of a ship of war, and the wires of a suspension bridge, may have little retentive power *per se*, but when judiciously connected with other supports, offer a resistance which a superficial observer would be little likely to understand. The lightness of its proportions indicates, at a glance, the nature of the material which forms the main supports of the building; and whilst those which are vertical consist entirely of cast-iron, the horizontal "connecting pieces" and girders are constructed both of wrought and cast-iron. Of wrought-iron 550 tons have been employed; but of cast-iron Messrs. Fox and Henderson have used no fewer than 3500 tons. The whole

of the roof above the highest tier or story of iron frame-work, consists of wood and glass, and the external enclosures and face-work are composed, for the most part, of the same materials. In the entire edifice there have been employed 896,000 superficial feet of glass, and, including the flooring, 600,000 of wood. In those parts of the building which are two or more stories or tiers in height, the upper tiers do not support galleries, being only intended to give additional stability to the columns. The highest tier is in all cases devoted to the support of the roof; an arrangement which forms a rather remarkable feature of the edifice. Among other striking examples of the ingenuity of the originators and constructors of the Crystal Palace is the ridge-and-furrow roof, by which the rain water is distributed into equal portions, and all ordinary chances of overflow averted; and the peculiar formation of the floor, which is a "trellised wooden pathway," with spaces between each board through which, on sweeping, "the dust at once disappears, and falls into the vacuity below." It may also be thoroughly washed without discomfort, for the water disappears as fast as the dust through the interstices; and the boards become fit for visitors almost immediately afterwards. There is one drawback on its adoption, however, of which most visitors to the Exhibition must have had experience; wherever it is laid transversely it is extremely troublesome to walk over, be the boards ever so evenly placed. Into technical minutiæ connected with the erection of the building, and the simplification of labour by its constructors, it is no part of our design to enter. Those who may be interested in such details, will find them duly set forth in the official records of the Commissioners. Many of them deserve praise for their ingenuity; and the speed enforced upon Messrs. Fox & Henderson, in the construction of the Crystal Palace, is the

THE HALL OF THE ZOLLVEREIN.

less to be deplored, as it necessitated experiments which have created important facilities for the builders of future edifices of this description. There are, however, some details yet to be recorded, without which the present sketch, although addressed to the general reader only, could hardly be considered complete. The total area of the ground floor is, as we have already stated, 772,784 square feet, and that of the galleries, 217,100 square feet. The extent of the latter is nearly a mile. The total cubic contents of the building are 33,000,000 feet; there are nearly 2300 cast-iron girders, and 358 wrought-iron trusses for supporting the galleries and roof; 30 miles of gutter for carrying water to the columns; 202 miles of sash bars; and 900,000 superficial feet of glass.

The decoration of the Exhibition of the Industry of all Nations was entrusted to Mr. Owen Jones, and some apprehensions were entertained, in the first instance, that the combination of deep blues, reds, and yellows, would produce too glaring an effect upon the eye. Mr. Jones has, however, by toning down his colours, and calculating the effect of a long perspective upon them, produced a result which has met with very general approbation. The outside of the building, which has not afforded him the advantages presented by the perspective of the interior, has not been considered quite so successful. At the east and west ends considerable spaces have been enclosed for the exhibition of objects, the weight and dimensions of which precluded their admittance within; among them, large blocks of marble, stone, slate, coal, asphalte pavements, and garden and monumental ornaments. At the western end, and considerably beyond the recognised precincts of the Exhibition, is the fine colossal model for a statue of Richard Cœur de Lion, of the Baron Marochetti. About 155 feet from the north-west angle is an engine-house, 96 feet by 24, for generating the steam which gives motion to the various machines which require to be exhibited in operation. The external appearance of this

structure is similar in character to that of the main edifice. It contains five boilers, of 150 horse power, and a large tank, serving as a balance head to the water supply. With this is connected a six-inch main, which runs completely round the Exhibition, on which, at intervals of 240 feet, are placed firecocks; and, at different points in its circuit, 16 four-inch branch pipes supply the water requisite for the purposes of the building. The mains, which run along the north and south sides of the building, are connected across the transept by a five-inch main, from which, near the centre of the building, pipes branch out for the supply of the various fountains erected on the central line of the nave; nor has the more substantial convenience of the visitors been overlooked; large refreshment rooms and counters, with corresponding waiting-rooms, have been provided around the trees at the northern extremity of the transept, and adjoining the open courts, at the eastern and western ends. The official business of the Exhibition demanding the services of a large staff of clerks, ample accommodation has been provided for them in offices placed on each side of the southern entrance; whilst, for money and check-takers, venders of Catalogues, etc., a considerable space has been appropriated at the eastern and western extremities of the building, as well as on each side of the principal entrance.

Although all objections to the use of the site in Hyde Park by the Commissioners vanished as the building advanced towards completion, they had been compelled to bind themselves by a deed of covenant to remove it, and resign the ground into the hands of the Commissioners of Woods and Forests, within seven months after the close of the Exhibition. This agreement rendered an appeal to parliament indispensable. After much discussion, in both houses, and elsewhere, a respite of one year has been granted; an arrangement which appears to have been perfectly satisfactory to all, save a few dissentients who either reside or possess property in the immediate neighbourhood. Mr. Paxton's notion from the

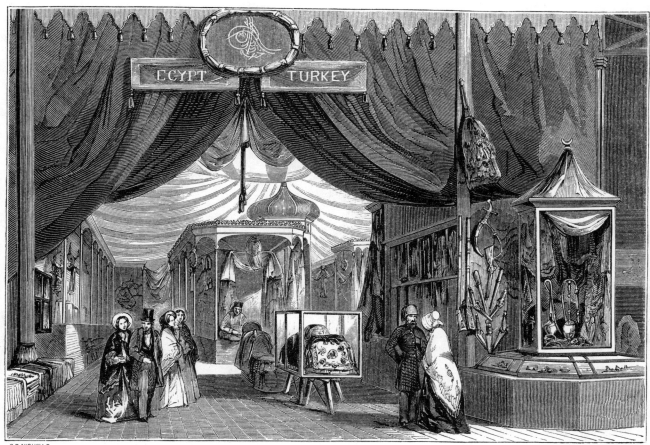

C.P. NICHOLLS.

ENTRANCE TO THE TURKISH DEPARTMENT.

first appears to have been to convert it into a winter garden when it shall have answered its present purpose.

Whatever credit may be claimed by the Executive Committee, much is due to the contractors, Messrs. Fox and Henderson, for the almost superhuman exertions which were made by them to enable the commissioners to open the Exhibition on the 1st of May. Such was the extraordinary eagerness of the public to be present at its inauguration, that upwards of 40,000*l.* of season tickets were disposed of on the 29th of April; and but for the restriction that the holders of season tickets only should be admitted to this ceremony, the place would doubtless have overflowed with visitors. It is not our intention to enter into minute details of the circumstances which attended its inauguration; they were in every respect worthy of the occasion. It was opened by Her Majesty in person, accompanied by the Royal Family, and attended by the members of her cabinet, and by all the officers and ladies of her court. So soon as the music which hailed her entry had ceased, H.R.H. Prince Albert, as President of the Royal Commissioners, read a report of their proceedings since their appointment. This manifesto mentions that "for the suggestion of the principle of this structure, the Commissioners are indebted to Mr. Joseph Paxton, and expresses a hope that the undertaking, which has for its end the promotion of all branches of human industry, and the strengthening of the bonds of peace and friendship among all nations of the earth, may, under God's blessing, conduce to the welfare of Her Majesty's people, and be long remembered among the brightest incidents of her peaceful and happy reign."

To this address, Her Majesty returned a most gracious answer, and the Archbishop of Canterbury having invoked the blessing of the Almighty on the undertaking, the ceremony terminated with the performance of the Hallelujah chorus by the united choirs of the Chapel Royal, St. Paul's, Westminster Abbey, and St. George's Chapel, Windsor. The procession included all the persons who had been officially engaged in the work; the royal and foreign commissioners, Her Majesty's ministers, the whole of the lords and ladies of the court in waiting, and the foreign ambassadors. The vast but elegant proportions of the building, the richness and tastefulness of

INTERIOR OF THE MEDLÆVAL COURT.

the costumes, and the large number (25,000) of well-dressed persons assembled on the occasion, rendered its inauguration one of the most imposing sights that had ever been witnessed in this country. But it is not in her regal capacity alone that Her Majesty has deigned to honour the Great Exhibition with her countenance. Day after day, accompanied by her children, and often at much personal inconvenience, has she flattered the various exhibitors by careful examinations of their productions; until it may fairly be presumed that there is scarcely one of her subjects who has more thoroughly inspected all that is worthy of attention within its walls than she has done. Whatever may have been the weather, or however crowded the interior, Her Majesty has devoted, almost daily, until the close of the session of parliament released her from attendance in London, several hours to visits to the Crystal Palace; inspecting each department in succession, and selecting from many of them such objects as gratified her taste, or were, for other reasons, considered to possess claims upon her attention.

On entering the building, for the first time, the eye is completely dazzled by the rich variety of hues which burst upon it on every side; and it is not until this partial bewilderment has subsided, that we are in a condition to appreciate as it deserves its real magnificence and the harmonious beauty of effect produced by the artistical arrangement of the glowing and varied hues which blaze along its grand and simple lines. After passing through the southern entrance, the whole extent of the transept, interrupted only by the magnificent glass fountain of Messrs. Osler, and the groups of sculpture and tropical plants and trees, that are intermixed throughout, flashes on the eye more like the fabled palace of Vathek, than a structure reared in a few months by mortal hands. On either side, as well throughout its centre, are ranged groups of statuary by Baily, MacDowell, Foley, Marshall, Lough, Bell, Marochetti, Wyatt, Watson, Weekes, Hollins, Legrew, Earle, and other well-known English sculptors. Forming the centre, or nearly so, of the entire building, and dividing alike the transept and the nave, rises the gigantic fountain of Messrs. Osler, the culminating point of view from every quarter of the building; whilst at the northern end the eye is relieved by the verdure of tropical plants and the lofty and overshadowing branches of forest trees.

On the right, looking from Messrs. Osler's glass fountain up the Eastern Division of the Nave, towards the American organ and its enormous eagle, a combination of splendours bursts upon the sight of overpowering magnificence. Here, as in the Transept, the objects which first attract the eye are the sculptures, which are ranged on every side; some of them of colossal size and of unrivalled beauty, by Kiss, Simonis, Monti, Du Seigneur, Duchesne, Müller, Schwanthaler, Powers, and others. The Western Division of the Nave, devoted to the products of England and her Colonies, if less showy, on a superficial view, than its rival, has much of sterling merit to recommend it. Here, too, are interspersed statues, fountains, mirrors, organs, and other large ornamental objects.

Crossing the Transept, and pursuing our course to the left, we enter the western division of the nave. We have here the Indian Court, Africa, Canada, the West Indies, the Cape of Good Hope, the Mediæval Court, and the English Sculpture Court, including works of Gibson, Baily, Mac Dowell, Foley, Carew, Marshall, Behnes, Hogan, Bell, Jones, Stephens, Thornycroft, Watson, etc. To these succeed Birmingham, the great British Furniture Court, Sheffield, and its hardware, the woollen and mixed fabrics, shawls, flax, and linens, and printing and dyeing. The long avenue leading from the Mediæval Court to the end of the building is devoted to general hardware, brass and iron-work of all kinds, locks, grates, etc.; whilst behind it, and parallel with it, but occupying three times its breadth, is the department for agricultural machines and implements. At the back of this division is the long narrow gallery occupied by the mineral products of England. Passing the small compartment of glass which runs transversely under the great organ gallery, across the nave, we have the cotton fabric and carriage courts, leather, furs, and hair, minerals and mineral manufactures, and machinery; including cotton and woollen power-looms in motion. The next is the largest compartment in the building, comprising machinery in motion, flax, silk, and lace, rope-making lathes, tools, and mills; minerals and mineral manufactures, furniture, marine engines, ceilings, hydraulic presses, steam hammers, fire engines, etc. Then follow paper and stationery; Jersey, Ceylon, and Malta, with the Fine Arts Court behind them; railway and steam machinery in motion; building contrivances, printing, and French machinery, occupying the whole of the last compartments on both sides the nave, as well as those which face the transept. Crossing to the left of the Crystal Fountain, we have Persia, Greece, Egypt, and Turkey, Spain, Portugal, Madeira and Italy, musical instruments, and chemicals; France, its tapestry, machinery, arms, and instruments, occupying two large courts; Belgium, her furniture, carpets, and machinery; Austria, with her gorgeous furniture courts, and machinery furniture; the Zollverein, with its octagon room, the most tastefully-arranged compartment in the building; North of Germany and Hanse Towns; Russia, with its malachite doors, vases, and ornaments; and the United States, with its agricultural implements, raw materials, etc., occupying all that part of the nave which terminates with its organ, if we except a small gallery on the north-east side, devoted to English paper-hangings. From this extremity of the building, and from the organ gallery more especially, the finest *coup d'œil* of the nave and its adjoining galleries may be obtained.

Crossing once more the nave on our return, we pass from the United States to Sweden, part of Russia, Denmark, another division of the Zollverein, Russian cloths, hats, and carpets, Prussian fabrics, Saxony, and the Austrian sculpture court; Austria runing back side by side with Belgium, the whole way. Next succeeds another division of France, with its splendid frontage of articles of *virtu* and ornamental furniture, its magnificent court for plate, bronzes, and china; its tasteful furniture, and carpets, its jewels, including those of the Queen of Spain; its laces, gloves, and rich embroideries; Switzerland, China, and Tunis, terminate this half of the nave.

Among the more striking objects in the south-eastern gallery, in the British half of the nave, are the silks and shawls, abutting on the transept; lace and embroideries, jewellery, and clocks and watches; and behind them military arms and models, raw produce, substances used as food, and chemicals. Traversing the gallery for naval architecture, by the organ, we have philosophical instruments, civil engineering, architecture and building models, musical instruments, anatomical models, glass chandeliers, decorations, etc.; china, cutlery, and animal and vegetable manufactures, and china and pottery above the left side of the northern part of the transept. On the opposite side, in the north-eastern gallery, are perfumery, toys, fishing materials, miscellaneous articles, wax flowers, stained glass, British, French, Austrian, Belgian, Prussian, Bavarian, and American products.

Clear passages under the galleries, of eight and ten feet broad, run the whole length of the building. Upon the extreme north and south sides, there are also longitudinal passages of similar width; the former interrupted by the offices of the commissioners and the entrances, and the latter by the refreshment rooms. With the exception of the offices, staircases, entrances, refreshment courts, and the various avenues and passages, including the transept, the whole of the ground-floor and galleries are available for exhibitors. As we have already shown, foreign countries, including the United States of America, occupy the east side of the transept above and below; whilst the United Kingdom, the East Indies, and the British Colonies are confined to the west side; with the exception of the United Kingdom, which extends into parts of the north and south galleries, on the east side of the transept. The productions of England and her Colonies occupy thirty separate sections. Of the four main departments into which it is divided, machinery occupies the north side, raw materials and produce the south side, and manufactures and the fine arts the centre. Along the central passage, to the west of the transept, a frontage on each side, of seven bays, or 168 feet, is devoted to the production of the Colonies.

In retiring from the contemplation of this magnificent edifice, the extraordinary expedition with which it was constructed must be regarded as one of the marvels of the age.

The tenders of the contractors were not, it is stated, accepted by the Royal Commissioners until the 26th of July, 1850; the possession of the site was only obtained on the 30th of the same month, and the first column was not fixed until the 26th of September, leaving only seven months for its completion. When we remember the elaborate calculations that were necessary before the iron and wood-work of the building could be put in hand, the machines for economising labour that had to be devised and manufactured, and the contracts for materials to be entered into, and the thousands of hands that had to be set to work, the celerity with which the building was completed is one of the most remarkable features of its history.

In the sketch which we have here given of the history of the Great Exhibition, from its origin to the present time, we have confined ourselves exclusively to facts; having carefully avoided making it the vehicle of opinions of any kind. This restriction, and the limited amount of space at our disposal, have prevented us from entering upon many topics which might otherwise have diversified our narrative, and relieved the monotony inseparable from the compression, into a few pages, of the great body of facts we have been called upon to enumerate. All questions inviting discussion would have been out of place in a narrative like this, which aims simply at presenting a brief, but faithful, history of one of the most splendid and remarkable undertakings that has ever been attempted in this or any other country. We have left all controversy on the plans and arrangements of the Royal Commissioners, and the officials with whom they have associated themselves, to the *Art-Journal*, without the aid of whose staff it would have been impossible for us, or, indeed, for any one else, to have produced the present volume, at anything like the price at which it is now published. With the composition of the juries, or the principle on which they arrive at their verdicts, and all the topics to which such an enquiry would of necessity conduct us, we shall have nothing to do on the present occasion. The *Art-Journal* has displayed no want of courage in dealing with such subjects, or in protecting the interests of the great body of British exhibitors from the effects of that overstrained courtesy which seems to consider that the rights of hospitality demand sacrifices on the part of their English competitors, which are alike inconsistent with reason or with justice. We have, moreover, no official knowledge of the manner in which the respective prizes have been awarded, and possess, therefore, no correct data for speculation on the subject; much will depend not only on the impartiality, but competency of the various jurors for the duty they have undertaken, and their perfect freedom from national jealousy or bias of any kind. Whether or not this great enterprise will be productive of the unmixed good which has been anticipated from its present success, its effects on the general trade and commerce of the country cannot have been as injurious as some persons profess to think; but it may be questioned if it have not benefited some classes at the expense of others. How far the glut on the English market, of all kinds of ornamental goods, when the Exhibition has closed, may be atoned for by the increased stimulus which their excellence may have given to the British manufacturer remains to be seen. The question has been often asked, what is to be done with the Crystal Palace; but the graver inquiry would seem to be, what is to be done with its contents? A very large proportion of them will, in all probability, be sold for what they will fetch; and if so, with what effect upon the trade of the British metropolis? —A partial injury at most: whilst the benefits arising out of the Exhibition are certain to prove both important and permanent. It will encourage us in the prosecution of those arts in which we are in the ascendant, and show us our weakness in those branches of industry in which we may be behind our neighbours. To be aware of our deficiencies is the first step towards amending them; and there is no maxim safer than that which teaches us not to undervalue our rivals: our Industrial Exhibition will have had this good effect at least.

The extent to which this congress of the world's genius and industry has already promoted the objects of civilisation and of peace, may be seen in the cordial feelings with which England and France are now inspired towards each other; and the noble spirit of emulation, devoid of its former rancorous prejudices, which it has generated between them. We need scarcely refer more particularly to the splendid and cordial reception given by the great body of savans and men of science of France to a large assemblage of English gentlemen (most of them identified in some way or other with the Exhibition), at the Hôtel de Ville of Paris, in the early part of August; and the strong and grateful impression it has left upon the minds of all who had the opportunity of participating in it. So noble a demonstration of mutual good feeling cannot fail to form an era in the histories of both countries; realising, as it did, so completely the language of Beranger's charming song, written when the prejudices and antipathies of the two nations were at boiling heat:—

> " J'ai vu la Paix descendre sur la terre,
> Sémant de l'or, des fleurs, et des épis,
> L'air était calme, et du dieu de la guerre,
> Elle étouffait les foudres assoupis.
> ' Ah !' disait-elle, ' égaux par la vaillance,
> Français, Anglais, Belge, Russe, ou Germain,
> Peuples formez une sainte alliance,
> Et donnez-vous la main !
>
> " ' Oui, libre enfin, que le monde respire,
> Sur le passé jetez un voile épais,
> Sémez vos champs aux accords de la lyre,
> L'encens des arts doit brûler pour la paix.
> L'espoir riant au sein de l'abondance,
> Accueillera les doux fruits de l'hymen.
> Peuples formez une sainte alliance,
> Et donnez-vous la main !' "

The Art-Journal ILLUSTRATED CATALOGUE of the INDUSTRY of all nations

THE Works of Mr. ALDERMAN COPELAND, for the manufacture of PORCELAIN and EARTHENWARE, are at Stoke-upon-Trent,—the principal town of the Staffordshire potteries: his London establishment is in New Bond Street. The artist who presides over the works is Mr. Thomas Battam, whose taste, judgment, and experience have been largely exercised to secure for this manufactory the high reputation it enjoys, not only in England, but throughout Europe, in Asia, and in America. The list of the Alderman's productions comprises all classes of "goods"—from the statuary porcelain figure and the elaborately decorated vase, to the commonest article of earthenware—manufactured for exportation by tens of thousands. The

compartment allotted to Mr. Copeland in the Exhibition cannot fail to be universally attractive,—not alone because of the grace and beauty of the articles shown, but as exhibiting our progress in a class of art upon which much of our commercial prosperity must depend. The collection will be carefully examined, and by foreigners especially, who will find much to admire, and much that will by no means suffer in comparison with the best productions of Dresden and Sèvres—always bearing in mind that at these Royal works objects are occasionally produced at national cost—such as those now to be found upon the stalls allotted to these famous factories; and that to expect private enterprise to enter into competition with them would be neither reasonable nor fair. At the same time it is only right to say, that Mr. Copeland challenges a comparison between his productions and those of either Dresden or Sèvres—in so far as concerns articles made especially for trade—and that from such comparison he does not shrink as regards either the materials, its ornamentation, or its price. We have devoted to the works of Alder-

man Copeland a larger space than we shall be able to accord generally even to manufacturers of the first order; but his works are very numerous and excellent, and although we assume to have selected the best, we have left unrepresented a mass of interesting and beautiful productions. For instance, out of forty statuettes, in statuary

man. The statuette of SAPPHO is from the

porcelain, we engrave but two—the "Sappho," after Theed; and the "Bacchus and Ino," after Foley: setting aside the "Sabrina," after Marshall; the "Indian and the Negro," after Cumberworth; the "Venus," after Gibson, and

others of great merit and beauty formed in this valuable material. The tazza, called "THE DOVE TAZZA," which commences the preceding page, is a superb ornament, peculiarly adapted for general purposes of elegant decoration; it is

original, by M. Theed,—an artist of high ability,

executed in fine porcelain: the doves, from the celebrated doves of the Capitol, together with the festoons of flowers, and the embossment generally, are richly gilt. On the same page

are a PINE-STAND, formed of the foliage of the pine, and a BRACKET, called the IVY BRACKET. The EWER AND BASIN which commence this page are in the Greek style, with outlines after Flax-

who has been for a long time resident in Rome.

The figure is, we believe, the largest yet

attempted in this style of Art-manufacture, being

about thirty-four inches high. The PANEL FOR

A FIREPLACE, is one of a series of admirable

designs in this class of manufacture, for which this house is so justly eminent: the foliated

and the outer borders enriched with chased and

extremely rich and harmonious. The concluding

scroll panels and works are enamelled on a gold ground, the centre subjects in colours on black,

burnished gold, relieved with blue: the effect is

object on the second page is a JUG of Etruscan

form, graceful in outline, and ornamented with floriated decorations and antique enrichments.

The first subject on the third page is a BRACKET, called the "Cupid Bracket." It is followed by a TRIPOD FLOWER-STAND, a very meritorious production, and one which, with reference to its size as well as merit, we have

not seen equalled in the beautiful material of which it is composed, viz., statuary porcelain; there is much classic elegance in this design, and the execution of its components is in the highest degree satisfactory. Following this is a VASE of much beauty: and on the succeeding columns are pictured, first the "Bacchus and Ino," of Foley—a very triumph of Art;

and next a GROUP OF OBJECTS FOR THE CONSERVATORY, consisting of Vases, Flower-pots, and Pedestals for the same. The uses to

which these useful ornaments are intended to be applied require no explanation; it is sufficient to point out their merits as elegant

luxuries for the wealthy. The first engraving on this page is a VASE and PEDESTAL, of blue and white porcelain, standing together

about five feet high; the proportions of the column have been well studied, and the base, of a triangular form, exhibits at each angle

a Stork of considerable dimensions. These objects are succeeded by a TAZZA in the Italian style, a kind of AMPHORA, or water-bottle, of antique form and decoration, and by a GARDEN SEAT, the latter ornamented with a bas-relief of classicly-designed figures. The last subject is a PANEL for a fireplace, simply but tastefully embellished with coloured designs: this ap-

plication of the plastic arts to domestic architecture is now becoming very general in houses of a superior class.

In all the examples here brought forward there is undoubted evidence that the mind of the artist has been at work to accomplish the task of uniting beauty with utility, by a skilful adaptation of what may be gathered from the past to the tastes and requirements of the present generation, however varied and exacting.

We engrave on this page two beautiful objects contributed by M. LE PAGE-MOUTIER, of Paris,—a FOWLING-PIECE and a SHIELD, both exquisitely wrought. The stock of the former is elaborated with designs, in which the ivy forms a prominent feature; the lock is chased, and represents a dog and a fox, and the barrel is also richly chased in vine leaves and grapes: the

work is altogether worthy of the best period of the middle ages, when offensive weapons of all kinds seem to have been made as much for ornament as for use. The shield is an extraordinary piece of workmanship, chased by the artist VECHT in metal, in the boldest and most vigorous style.

The subject represented is the "Massacre of the Innocents," and the designs are copied from some of the best works of the old masters,—Raffaelle, Poussin, &c.; it seems, therefore, almost unnecessary to dilate upon what has emanated from such sources, the fountain of all that is great and noble in Art. The theme is one calculated to elicit no other feelings than those of

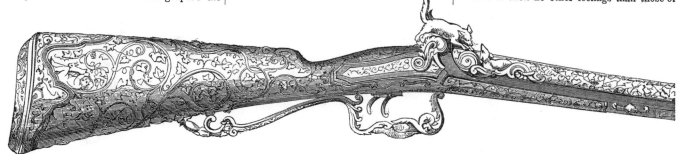

horror and detestation, but it affords abundant scope for the display of bold action and most effective grouping. Unlike a field of military combatants, where man meets man in deadly struggle, and each feels that life or death depends, perhaps, on the strength of his own right hand, the rage and fury are here on one side only, the

despair and agony on the other. Still there is no quiet submission—no resistless surrender of the little ones, to those who are executing the commands of the tyrant. It is this mingling together of men, women, and children, their variety of attitudes, induced by the difference of purpose which places them in action, the strength of arm

that emboldens the warrior, the power of maternal love that animates the mother, which make any representation of the "Murder of the Innocents" a picture such as no other historical event can furnish. M. Le Page-Moutier has acquired as a manufacturer of the most costly and excellent fire-arms, swords, &c., the reputa-

tion of being among the first, if not the very first, in France; we visited his establishment a few months ago, when a large variety of his

productions were submitted to our inspection; the only regret we felt on the occasion was, that so much talent and labour should be bestowed

on the art that destroys, instead of upon that which assists to preserve mankind, and to elevate the moral and social condition of humanity.

The establishment of Mr. Handyside, of Derby—the "Britannia Foundry"—is principally represented by the elegant iron Vase which we engrave. It is of very large size and elegant character. The body of the vase is decorated with an elaborate interlaced design, which we

Among the specimens ot excellent iron-work contributed by M. Ovide Martin, of Paris, are some beautiful Crosses, of which we engrave

have engraved above it. The base is an octagon, having eight open-work screens hanging in front of the pedestal, which give singular lightness and elegance to the entire object. As an example of the taste and improvement which characterise the iron manufactures of our own

two, chiefly as suggestions in ornamental design for our own manufacturers. They are charac-

country, we believe our readers will consider this work deserving of much attention ; it is an excellent design, as excellently worked out, and reflects credit on the establishment from which it has emanated—one that from the magnitude of its operations is second to none in England.

terised by much lightness and elegance of outline, while the main portions are "filled in" so as to add to the general richness of the design.

The appended engraving is of the plinth of a CANDELABRUM, manufactured by M. BROCHON, Paris, for the Strasbourg Railway. It is of cast iron, and will be much admired for its elegant proportions, and its artistic details; the shaft rises in gothic flutes from a floriated base, which is again followed by ornamental work of a similar character, but varied in form and design, having fruit inter-

Munich, famous for its school of PAINTING ON GLASS, contributes no example of it to the Exhibition; the fame of Bavaria in this department of Art is upheld only by Messrs. KELLNER, of NUREMBERG, who contribute a copy of the "Volkhamer Window,"—the glory of the Lorenzo Kirche, of that renowned city. It is not known who composed this votive offering of the Volkhamer family, but the general opinion seems to be that when the design was decided upon, several artists assisted in preparing it. The figure-subjects are taken from the Old and New Testa-

ments. The figures kneeling at the lower portion of the window represent the various members of the Volkhamer family. The minor divisions are filled up with florid architectural ornaments and scriptural illustrations; and in the upper compartment is represented the Holy Trinity, surrounded by a choir of angels. The dimensions are 30 feet by 12 feet; we engrave only a part of it. In this work, whether we regard its technical superiority, the richness of its composition, or the extraordinary blending of colour which it presents, all has been achieved which

mixed with the leaves. The pedestal exhibits several projecting ornaments, terminating at the top by what would seem to be the heads of the panther. The whole column shows that much artistic taste has been expended upon its construction; it is of very considerable height, and altogether reflects great credit upon M. Brochon's establishment, which is one of the most important, for ironwork of all kinds, in Paris.

could possibly be expected even from the gifted days when it was created. It was a deep sense of these excellences that induced M. Stephen Kellner to make a copy of the window, as faithful as possible, both in drawing and colour; and all who have seen the beautiful original, must consider that he has succeeded to admiration. He is one of the sons of Jacob Kellner, of Nuremberg, whose family are much renowned as glass-painters, and have produced some of the most beautiful specimens

of modern art. They are thoroughly acquainted with the style and characteristics of the middle ages, as the many excellent copies they have executed testify. Their prices are very moderate, being from twelve to fifteen florins (20s. to 25s.) per square foot, according to the nature of the design. Their establishment in Nuremberg, —which we visited in the summer of 1850—is well worthy the attention of church-builders, and, indeed, also of private gentlemen who desire to decorate their houses.

The productions of Mr. W. G. ROGERS, of London, in WOOD CARVING, are by no means new

to our readers, comprising as they do the most perfect of modern efforts in this branch of art. Mr. Rogers's fame, as it is well-known, rests mainly on his imitation and extension of the style

adopted by his great forerunner in wood-carving, Grinling Gibbons; but he has recently diversified his labours by adding to the works of the character described, such as may be truly called the *bijoux* of the art, consisting of small and

delicately finished objects, chiefly in box-wood, and in the Italian style. From among these

minute performances, executed with the co-opera-

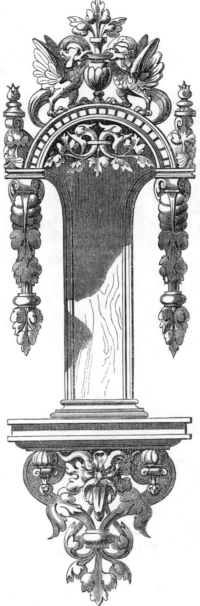

tion of his son W. Harry Rogers, as designer, we have

principally selected the illustrations of our great carver's contribution to the Exhibition; believ-

ing them to be not only interesting subjects to the general reader, but useful suggestions to the manufacturer. Upon the present page will be seen a carved Box-wood BRACKET, with canopy,

intended to receive a thermometer; two perforated PANELS belonging to a work-table, composed of the foliated ornament; a BRACKET in satin-wood; an ORANGE CUP, covered with subjects and inscriptions connected with the career

of William III.; and a box-wood SALT-CELLAR, enriched with columns and elaborate sunk panels. The last subject is accompanied by its corre-

sponding SPOON, which, from its ornamentation, we have deemed worthy of two separate views.

Continuing our illustrations of Mr. Rogers's

early Italian character, and have been converted by Mr. Rogers (for G. Field, Esq.) into BRACKETS,

by the addition of plafonds and masses of heart-shaped foliage. We introduce these four original conceptions, believing that they will prove prac-

the page, is a large oval FRAME of the Venetian

carvings, we here offer to our readers a selection of various objects, all of which are very perfect both in design and execution. The two oval MINIATURE FRAMES at the top of the page are in boxwood, and in different styles. The first is a sim-

ple border of pinks arranged round a moulding and carved literally from nature; while the second is in the quaint conventional style which is generally known as "Elizabethan." Following these are four grotesque masks, which have an

school, made for the Hon. Arthur Kerr, and kindly lent by that gentleman for exhibition. The two remaining works here engraved are GROUPS OF STILL LIFE, intended for the decoration of dining-rooms.

Both are studies from original fragments by Grinling Gibbons, restored and extended; and are favourable examples of a style of art, the prosecution of which has mainly tended to raise Mr. Rogers's reputation to its present position. One is a NET,

tically suggestive, because while in many styles of ornament the mask is a very prominent feature, it is rarely executed with the spirit and

vigour which are evinced by the present examples. The next subject, that in the centre of

in and about which fish and shells are arranged with studied negligence; as a finish to the whole, sprigs and flowers of aquatic weeds are plentifully introduced. The other is a TROPHY, consisting of a pheasant and a woodcock hung up together, and accompanied by a profusion of fruit and flowers. The feathering of the birds' plumage, produced by a remarkably few touches, is eminently successful, and the eyes and general expression of the heads afford a striking contrast to those of

some birds by the same hand, in which life is attempted to be portrayed. Mr. W. G. Rogers's most important contribution to the Exhibition (if magnitude be a criterion) is a carved frame, 11 feet high by 9 feet wide, boldly relieved in lime-tree, in the style of Gibbons. It is entirely composed of English fruits and flowers, mounted upon a moulding of polished walnut-wood. Of this frame we engrave the upper portion, which is admirably grouped, and in which appear many kinds of English flowers which Gibbons never introduced into his productions. In the centre of the page is the celebrated boxwood cradle, executed for her Majesty the Queen, and with the details of which our readers are already familiar. We conclude our selection from Mr. Rogers's works with engravings of three miniature frames of various designs. The first consists merely of a garland of different flowers, frame, intended to receive miniatures of the Royal family of this country. The design, which is surmounted by a regal crown, contains the letters V.A.R., monogrammatically arranged, and interlaced with the motto, "Dieu et mon Droit." The third and last subject is a small frame in the style of the period of Elizabeth or James I. Here the curious strap ornament, which prevailed at that epoch, is made a good use of, and happily blended with cords supporting masses of fruit. It is with much satisfaction that we find Mr. Rogers offering so excellent a display of the perfection to which England has attained in the beautiful but long-neglected art of carving in wood. This art, unquestionably, owes no small portion of the excellence it has reached among us at the present time to the success which has attended his efforts, and to the example of his energetic perseverance and ability in pursuing it. There cannot be a doubt that many of the admirable specimens that our wood sculptors exhibit in the great Exposition may be traced indirectly, if not directly, to his influence. A large share of merit is

bound by twisted ribbon, and placed round a simple bead moulding. The second is an oval the letters V.A.R., monogrammatically arranged, therefore due to a true artist who has been the means of again resuscitating an almost forgotten Art.

The COALBROOKE-DALE IRON WORKS, as might be expected, from the magnitude and high character of the establishment, are worthily represented in the Exhibition. The first of our examples is a GARDEN VASE, of cast iron, with masks and handles of novel design; it

stands on a marbled pedestal, measuring altogether about three feet in height, and is adapted for flowers or for a fountain. This is followed by another GARDEN VASE, with serpent handles, in

feet nine inches high, finished in white and gold, with branches for six lights; the pattern of this

complete with the pots in china. The first two engravings on the next page are copied from an

frame merits all commendation. Below this is an ornamental FLOWER-POT STAND four feet high,

elegant VASE and PEDESTAL, in which floriated decoration and stags'-heads form the principal

which is placed an earthen pot for flowers. The next object is an Elizabethan LOOKING-GLASS, two

features of the ornament. But the most important contribution of the Coalbrooke-dale Company is an ornamental CHIMNEY-PIECE and GRATE,

and the mouldings are of imitation marble; the grate consists of burnished steel fronts and ornaments in bronze electro-gilt, and the whole is so

seven feet high and four feet wide, with decorations illustrative of deer-stalking, boar-hunting, and hawking. The figures are of cast iron gilt,

arranged that the ornamentation connects in one design the fender, ash-pan, and grate. The fire-brick for the back is in one piece, including the bottom of

the grate on which the fire rests, and is constructed to give the greatest heat with a small fire. The fender, ash-pan, and grate are removed in one piece, to afford greater facilities for the operation of sweeping the chimney. The entire work is a beautiful example of manufactured Art.

The Coventry "Town Ribbon," of which we append an engraving, is the result of a town subscription, and may, we presume, be accepted as an example of the combined skill of several workers in the ancient and venerable city, famous for the fabric of ribbons since the commencement of the sixteenth century, or from even an earlier date. This specimen is exceedingly effective, creditable not alone to the designer, but to the various workmen engaged in its production; it "tells" well in black and white, a severe test for an article of this kind; but the reader will be pleased to imagine a large number of colours, harmoniously combined into a production of much grace and beauty. The ribbon is designed by M. CLACK (a pupil of the Coventry School of Design), and draughted by R. BARTON, requiring in its manufacture 24,000 cords and 10,000 cards.

An IRON BEDSTEAD, and CHILD'S COT, also of iron, contributed by M. DUPONT, of Paris, will attract attention from the rich and elaborate designs which they exhibit, especially the former object. This has a kind of frieze in basso-relievo, running round one of the sides and the end, representing a hunting party; the flat terminating pillars are also similarly ornamented. The whole is of cast-iron, produced from a mould that brings out the figures and details of the design with remarkable sharpness and decision. The framework of the cot is very light and elegant, and the introduction of a young angel at its foot, as if keeping watch over the little sleeper, is a pretty idea: the basket and fringe are made of netted wool. We may, perhaps, be allowed to take an objection to the practical convenience of the bed, although we may unequivocally express approbation of its ornamental design.

Etruria—the celebrated establishment founded by JOSIAH WEDGWOOD, and where the knowledge of Bentley and the classic taste and genius of Flaxman, combined with his own ability, gave a world-wide reputation to its founder—has sent its *quota* of beautiful works through its present occupants, Messrs. WEDG-

WOOD & BROWN, who have reproduced some of the best articles originally designed or executed by its famous founder. There are still in the establishment many designs of high quality which have not yet been worked out, and we may instance the group of the

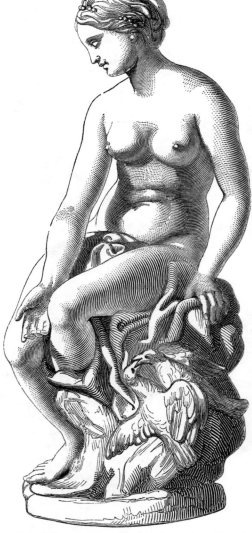

Infant Hercules strangling the Serpents, said to be the work of Flaxman, and now first made for the

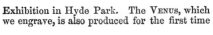

Exhibition in Hyde Park. The VENUS, which we engrave, is also produced for the first time

on the same occasion, as well as the CUPID; both charming figures The entire series of works displayed by the present firm are of the

classic form and style of decoration, so well known to connoisseurs; the ground of each

article being of a lavender tint, the figures and ornaments, in pure white clay in relief upon the surface, have the delicate and beautiful shades of the tint faintly appearing through the more

delicate parts. Many of these Vases are of large size, and some have figures directly copied from the antique; others being designed in strict accordance with those upon the Greek and Roman gems. Indeed, the Wedgwood imita-

tions of these rare and costly articles have always been highly prized. There is much

simplicity in the general character of the floral and other ornament which decorate the sur-

its position among the principal Art-manufac-

turers of the present day; attesting to the deserved character obtained for the establish-

face of these choice works; and we rejoice to see this eminent house again prepared to assert

ment by the famous Josiah Wedgwood. These

works are all carefully and beautifully executed, and deserve the high praise they will

command; and the re-awakened attention which will be insured, to one of the most famed and tasteful of

English establishments, in connection with plastic art.

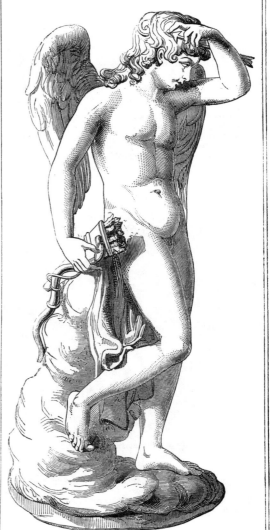

THE INDUSTRY OF ALL NATIONS.

We commence this page with a group composed of CANDELABRA, TABLE-LAMPS, and a GAS-CHANDELIER, selected from a variety of articles of a similar description contributed by Messrs. SALT & LLOYD, of Birmingham. In all these objects the designer has had recourse to nature for the ornaments with which they are enriched. It would not, probably, be very difficult to point out where these ornaments might have been more effectively and tastefully disposed; but still there is much in the general character of the designs that will meet approval, and exhibit

the advance which, within a few years, has been made by the manufacturers of Birmingham. One great error, against which it is necessary to guard British manufacturers of ornamental articles, is the too free introduction of decoration; elegance is more often united to simplicity than allied with abundance: symmetry and beauty of form must never be sacrificed to a profuse display of adornment. These remarks are not made with reference to the objects here engraved, but are thrown out as hints to our manufacturers generally. The edifices and works of Art which Greece produced, when she had reached the highest point of refinement and civilisation, were remarkable for their elegant simplicity. It was not till luxury had enervated her powers, and wealth had created an over abundance, that she lost her purity of taste and became lavish, even to prodigality, of the resources at her command. It is to the earlier periods of the history of that country one looks for all that is great in Art.

A SIDEBOARD of mahogany, selected from the contributions of Messrs. JOHNSTONE & JEANES, of London, is entitled to high commendation for the pure taste which the manufacturers have exhibited in its construction. The style is Italian, of the best period, not over-ornamented, yet showing an abundance of chaste decoration, which may be thus briefly described:—At each end is a young Bacchus; one, placed on a lion, holds up a bunch of grapes to the other, who stretches out a cup to receive it; these figures are carved with much spirit. In the centre of the back-piece is a medallion of a Bacchante, and at each corner one of a Bacchanal, the interstices being filled in with wreaths of the grape-vine and its fruit.

The WINE COOLER, exhibited by M. EICHLER, of Berlin, is of terra-cotta; it may be accepted as a proof of the great excellence so frequently given by competent artists to ordinary objects of commerce. In composition, grouping, drawing, and entire arrangement, few more perfect works than this have been produced in the precious metals; yet upon this common material, so much fine taste and intellectual labour have been expended as to give it high value as a work of pure and true Art.

A silver-mounted MEERSCHAUM, by M. HELD, of Nuremberg, representing St. George and the Dragon. We have selected for engraving this out of several drawings sent us by one of the most successful manufacturers of Germany. The article is one upon which much ingenuity is expended; it is often embellished with great skill and taste, and is not unfrequently made costly by the exercise of artistic talent; indeed, a very large proportion of the young Art of Germany is employed in modelling, carving, or decorating these meerschaums. In Germany there are few more productive articles of trade; they are exhibited in the gayest shops; and their ornamentation is generally expensive as well as beautiful.

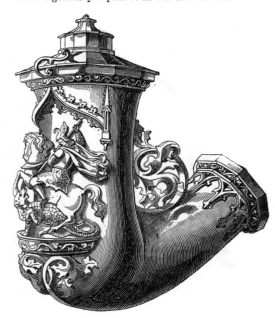

The FRAME of CARTON PIERRE, with the brackets and medallions enclosed in it, are the contributions of Messrs. GROPIUS, of Berlin. Their establishment is renowned throughout Germany; they have obtained repute or the quality and durability of their material as well as for the excellence of their models; it is known, indeed, that they are assisted by several accomplished artists. When we visited their extensive works and show-rooms, in the summer of 1850, we examined a vast variety of fine compositions in brackets, statuettes, picture and looking-glass

frames, &c.; as in all such cases of manufacture, a large portion of the merit of the manufacturer consists in the skill with which he composes his materials—the judicious mixture of the component parts; still, as in this instance, celebrity is to be obtained also by employing good artists to produce good models: the collection exhibited by Messrs. Gropius cannot fail to be appreciated; its introduction into England is desirable.

Mr. BATTAM, of Johnson's-court, Fleet-street, Enameller of Porcelain and Glass, contributes various TAZZE, VASES, &c., imitations of Etrus-

can art, in form and ornamentation. These imitations are of rare excellence; in many cases

indeed, they cannot be distinguished, except upon minute scrutiny, from the originals. The vases

are of various sizes; the third upon this column is of considerable height—nearly four feet.

The FAIR LINEN CLOTH, which commences this column, is intended for a communion-table; it is one of the contributions of Mr. GILBERT FRENCH, of Bolton, to whose manufactures of a similar description we have, on more than one occasion, referred with great satisfaction. Mr. French exhibits a pure taste and an accurate knowledge of what is essential to appropriateness of design in his various productions of church linen; and spares no expense in procuring suitable patterns, and in working them out in the finest qualities of fabric. The improvements he has effected in these articles of ecclesiastical use are such as must be manifest to all who had observed the inelegant, and often offensive, designs which formerly covered the altars of our churches; many of them better adapted for a dining-hall than a sacred temple. The cloth here engraved bears on it the symbols of its application; in the centre is the "Lamb," surrounded by the evangelists.

The TABLE-TOP, formed chiefly of the MARBLE OF DERBYSHIRE, is contributed by Mr. G. RED-FERN, of Ashford, by whom the work is manu-factured, and who has established a high reputa-tion for various admirable productions in the spars and marbles of the county in which he flourishes; these objects comprise cups, vases, chimney-ornaments, and the ordinary "toys" of the material, with articles of greater value and im-portance. The table-top here engraved is unques-tionably the best production that has been yet manufactured in Derbyshire. It is composed of various marbles—from the common limestone to the costly lapis lazuli, verd antique, malachite, &c. The groundwork is of the ordinary black marble—a marble found remarkably pure in this district, often in large slabs, without a single speck of white. The design introduces several birds of varied plumage, and ornamentation of a graceful character. As a specimen of mosaic, it may vie with examples of the costliest order that have been produced in modern Italy; the table will rank among the most satisfactory proofs of what may be achieved by British taste and skill, and will also afford evidence of the value of home materials judiciously applied.

The picturesque village of Ashford, in which Mr. Redfern has his establishment, is situated in one of the beautiful dells of Derbyshire, not far from princely Chatsworth, and in the neighbour-hood of the best quarries of the county; whence the largest variety of British marbles is obtained.

M. Vanderkelen-Bresson, of Brussels, a lace-manufacturer—who has, by his untiring ability, greatly aided the ce ebrity of the Belgian capital in this branch of the textile Arts—has contributed an exquisite specimen of patient industry in a Lace Veil, the border of which we here engrave. It possesses novelty in its design, as well as in its fabrication. We do not engrave the *fond*, or groundwork of the lace, except in some portions

of the scroll, which will better enable our readers to judge of the taste and elegance of the design. It is meritorious and more than usually suggestive.

The three Vases are from the establishment of M. Villemsens, of Paris, worker in bronze, and manufacturer of church ornaments; the latter branch of business, especially, being largely car-ried on by this house. During our visit to Paris, towards the close of the past year, we saw in his extensive show-rooms a vast variety of objects, exhibiting more or less taste in composition, and ingenuity of workmanship; these were principally executed in bronze and in brass, and were adapted as well for the embellishment of the private dwelling as for purposes of ecclesiastical

use and decoration,—statues, vases, chandeliers, candelabra, delicate rail-work, &c. The three bronze vases and dish selected from the con-tributions of this firm, are distinguished by beauty of outline and elaborate ornament, ap-proaching very closely to the best antiques.

Messrs. WATERHOUSE, of Dublin, have contributed the various specimens of BROOCHES which appear

on this page. They are all, more or less, remarkable, as well for the peculiarity of their

character as for their history, and the ability shown in their fabrication. They are, in fact, copies of

museum of the Royal Irish Academy and elsewhere. The largest and finest of the series, "the royal Tara

brooch," has been very recently discovered, near Drogheda; it is of bronze, ornamented with niello and gems,

and is the most remarkable work of the kind that has yet been procured. In these objects, Messrs. Waterhouse

The pillar engraved below is of TERRA-COTTA, the production of FEILNER & Co., of Berlin. Its height is above seven feet; it is from the design of an eminent Prussian architect. In the establishment of the Messrs. Feilner we saw many admirable examples of this beautiful art, and regretted to learn that their contributions to the Exhibition were to be limited. Their "Industry" relies for its recompence, however, less upon articles which more closely appertain

the most curious antique brooches which have been found in Ireland, and are preserved in the

have been singularly successful; the great beauty of their works cannot fail to insure their extensive popularity.

to Fine Art than to those necessaries of life, the fire-stoves, which in Germany are so frequently found beautifully and elaborately ornamented. Yet these gentlemen have produced works of far higher moment. There is in the garden of Professor Wichmann, a doorway copied from a medieval design, of which the whole of the arch and side column mouldings are of terra-cotta; it is also used for figure and arabesque bas- and alt-relief enrichments of considerable size, and with admirable effect in front of ordinary dwelling-houses.

The CENTRE-DISH and two VASES which occupy this column, are from the establishment of Mr. MELLISH, of London. They are of glass, silvered by Mr. Hale Thomson's process, described at length

in the "Art-Journal" for March of the present year, to which we would refer such of our readers as feel an interest in this truly beautiful manu-

facturing Art. There is a peculiarity in the manufacture of the glass used by Mr. Mellish in his process, which merits particular notice, from its

novelty and ingenuity; all the articles, whether goblets, vases, or others, have double sides, between which the silver solution is precipitated.

The TOILETTE GLASS and the CUP, underneath, are exhibited by M. RUDOLPHI, of Paris. His works, generally, are on a small scale, but valuable

even more for their beauty, than for the materials of which they are composed, though these are of a costly kind; gems and intaglios set in the purest gold of elaborate workmanship, and gold and silver ornaments exquisitely wrought. The

TOILETTE-GLASS is small in dimensions, about thirteen inches high; it is of silver, intermixed with enamels of various colours, to represent fruit and foliage: the object is of rare taste in conception, and of great merit in execution. The design of the CUP, though not altogether novel, is carried out with much ingenuity: the base exhibits a boy assisting another to climb a vine. The bowl is of agate, and the mounting of silver burnished and matted, with grapes of enamel: the diameter is about nine inches.

The small VASE is the contribution of Mr. HEMPHILL, of Clonmel; and is formed of ivory, in what he has termed the Elizabethan style. It is five inches in diameter, and four in height, and is turned entirely in the lathe. The intention of the designer has been to produce a work, graceful in outline, and sufficiently ornamental without being heavy. There is a commendable originality in the decoration of the lower parts.

Messrs. H. & A. HOLMES, carriage-builders, of Derby, contribute a LIGHT PARK PHÆTON, of which the accompanying is an engraving: it upholds the high reputation which these gentlemen have acquired in all parts of Europe. The phæton is elegant in outline, light and simple in construction, free from unnecessary carvings and ornamental iron-work; and, moreover, inexpensive to keep in repair, and not difficult to clean.

The IRON LETTER POST is manufactured by M. VANDENBRANDE, of Brussels. These posts serve the purposes in Belgium that a receivinghouse does in England. The letter collectors open them several times during the day, and each time affix a notice, on a tablet, of the time of the next "Levée," or taking out. They stand about three feet in height;

The CHIMNEY-PIECE and BOOKCASES, intended for the side of a library, are contributed by Messrs. HOLLAND & SONS, of London, and have been executed by them from the designs, and under the superintendence of, Mr. T. R. Macquoid, architect. The style is founded on that of the cinque-cento, with a free adaptation of natural forms introduced with judgment and taste. The work is exquisitely carved in walnut-wood, and

and are made to serve also as posts at the corners of the chief streets.

inlaid with green and red marbles; the doors are of perforated brass, and all the materials are of British growth and manufacture. The size is about twenty feet long by thirteen feet high; we engrave only the half.

Mr. Potts, of Birmingham, has long been distinguished as a manufacturer of Lamps, Clock-Stands, Candelabra, and articles of *virtu*, displaying pure taste in design, and refined skill in manufacture. It is not, perhaps, too much to say that his abilities and exertions have done much to elevate the character of the Birmingham bronze and brass works. The whole of his numerous contributions are entirely the work of English hands: we select, we believe, the best. The first engraving is from an elegant little

Hand-Bell, the handle of which introduces "Puck," seated on a snail, and directing his course. The next is a Candelabrum, which he calls the "Heron Candelabrum," from the birds

priate and well-studied design, and most careful execution. It will well bear the closest scrutiny.

from the story of Daphne and Apollo: the figures are vigorously and expressively grouped,

The centre subject at the bottom of this page is a grand Candelabrum for ten lights, designed

that support the stem. A very elegant Clock Stand claims attention from its truly appro-

displaying great artistic skill in the modeller. The last engraving on this page is from another

Candelabrum, made to hold four lights; its

principal ornaments are grotesque winged figures.

Resuming the contributions of Mr. Potts, we introduce first on this page a Tripod Flower

Stand, simple in construction, with much of the character of the antique. Following this is

a Candle Lamp, the pedestal composed of elephants' heads, very skilfully wrought. Across

the two columns, on the top of the page, is a Gas Lamp, with three burners, exhibiting considerable novelty in design; it is bold in character, yet not heavy. An exceedingly pretty

an actual copy. We have engraved the whole of the bas-relief forming the decorative part of the

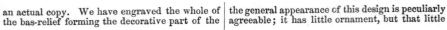

body of the vase; the subject is a youthful sylvan, "Pan," kneeling at the altar of Hymen, where he is crowned by Flora: it is termed by

the maker, "A Festival in honour of Spring." The other engraving is from a Candle Lamp:

Card Dish follows; it is of metal, and the designer has introduced birds of Paradise as supporters of the tray. Below this is a Flower Vase, formed after the antique model, yet not

the general appearance of this design is peculiarly agreeable; it has little ornament, but that little

is judiciously applied, and executed with much spirit. There are few objects of manufacturing Art which have exhibited, during some years past, more manifest improvements than the table candle-lamp, in all of its many varieties of form.

We stated, in our preliminary remarks on Mr. Potts's contributions, that no one had done so much to advance the character of the Birmingham bronze and brass works as this intelligent and enterprising manufacturer. To him must be accorded the merit of having first introduced a new combination of artistic media, which has

since been followed up by others with no little success, though Mr. Potts has still kept the lead in his hands. We allude to the application of a ceramic substance, statuary porcelain, for ornamental purposes in conjunction with metal, in

chandelier lustres, lamp brackets, and numerous other objects of utility and decoration. This introduction has given a vast impulse to the Industrial Arts, presenting as it does a valuable auxiliary, which may, in interwoven or appended ornament, minister most felicitously to elevate

and enrich the particular branch to which it may be applied. But it is requisite to use it with the utmost discrimination and judgment, inasmuch as it might otherwise lead to the perpetration of much that is offensive to the taste. The charm of novelty taxes the talent of the designer most severely, and often compels him to pro-

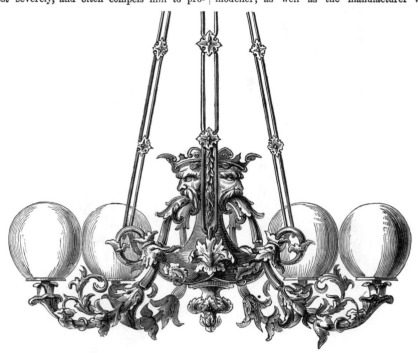

determines what is, and what is not, to be produced, should be well skilled in those principles by which such desirable ends may be attained: each should habituate himself to considering the effect of every pattern in different materials and articles. Above all, the designer should be

selected from Mr. Potts's contributions as exhibited on this page. The first is a light and elegant CANDELABRUM for two or four lights; it is designed after the best examples of the antique. By its side is a richly ornamented GAS CHANDELIER in the Italian style of decoration,

duce, for the sake of change, and to please a public too exacting on this point, that which his judgment and matured experience would impel him to withhold. But inasmuch as novelty is worth nothing without beauty and correctness of form, it is necessary that the designer or modeller, as well as the manufacturer who

taught that his principles ought to be found only in the very highest art. The designer must, in mental power, be raised to the level of the artist, and must emulate him, not only in skill, but in range of information. But we must proceed to notice the remaining objects we have

the scrolls being surmounted by grotesque masks. The two engravings below these represent another GAS CHANDELIER and its PULLIES: the style of this work displays a bold arrangement of curves and angles, and is altogether a beautiful example of metallurgical manufacturing art.

The silver works of Mr. HIGGINS, of London, are such as come within the province rather of a spoon and fork manufacturer than of a maker of

silver plate. From his very numerous contributions we select several, chiefly commending those designs which are taken exclusively from natural objects; and we may remark that

the articles which Mr. Higgins exhibits, as specimens of his best ordinary production, are worthy of more public attention than such as have been

prepared expressly for the present occasion. Our illustrations commence with an APOSTLE SPOON, surmounted by a figure of St. Peter, being one of a series of twelve, which are elevated on a rotatory pedestal. With this is a simple but graceful DESSERT-FORK, of which the stem and prongs are of silver, in imitation of twisted

branches, and the handle composed of agate. On the opposite side of the page are a DESSERT SPOON and a DESSERT-FORK taken from different sets, one composed of vine-branches and the other of conventional ornament. In the centre

column we engrave a light and elegant CREAM-LADLE, the design of which appropriately consists of stems, leaves, and flowers of the common buttercup. The plant is fashioned for its purpose

with the best possible taste, and the effect of the work is greatly enhanced by the gilding, which is only introduced in the cavities of the flowers. Underneath the cream-ladle, which, when per-

forated in the bowl, may be employed as a sugar-sifter, are two small spoons, one a TEA-SPOON, ornamented with convolvulus, and the other an EGG-SPOON, chiefly remarkable for the novel form of the bowl, which is both pleasing to the eye and agreeable to the lip. The two remaining subjects are CADDY-SPOONS, of beautiful sim-

plicity. We especially admire the shell, to which clings a sprig of weed resembling the small water-lily. The flowers and the interior of the shell are gilt. Its companion is also worthy of

much praise, though a mere wild anemone gathered in the fields, and copied with as much fidelity as its application to the form of a caddy-spoon would permit. The first group on the present page are two KNIFE-HANDLES; the first made of ivory, and decorated with vine leaves and bunches of grapes; the second of

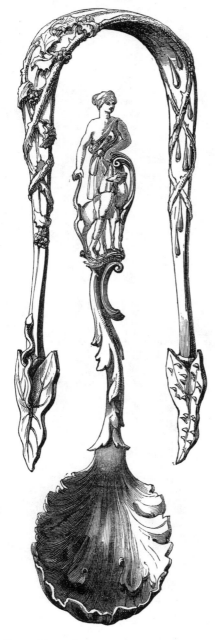

silver, with ornaments of a conventional character; both are distinguished by considerable elegance. Next follows a SKEWER-HANDLE, in the Italian style; the introduction of the birds

is very effective and graceful. On the top of the second column are a pair of ICE-TONGS and a

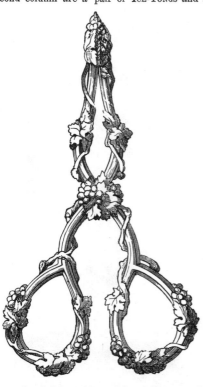

SPOON for helping this article of luxury; the form and ornamentation of the first of these objects exhibit great originality; the second, with the figure terminating the handle and its leaf-like bowl, possesses much beauty of design. A PAIR OF SUGAR-TONGS commences the third column; they are decorated with the vine-branch, its foliage, and fruit. A TAPER-STAND succeeds to this: in it the designer has also had recourse

to the productions of nature for the form and character of his subject. The page is completed by a FISH-CARVER of massive design, somewhat assimilating to the Moorish: we admire this as a deviation from the ordinary forms of such objects, as well as for its own intrinsic merit. There is not one of the subjects we have engraved in these

two pages that is not worthy of the best period of manufacturing Art wheresoever practised; an undoubted proof of the advanced state of taste and ingenuity on the part of our designers and those associated with them in carrying out their

intentions. It is gratifying to see British manufacturers taking advantage of the often inculcated maxim that "to nature alone must we look for beauty, and the nearer the approach to

her creations the more striking the success:" it is a truth ever to be remembered by the designer.

We occupy the present page with some examples of INDIAN MANUFACTURE, exhibited by Capt. H. C. JAMES, of the Bengal army. They were brought by him from India, and are curiously characteristic of Eastern taste. The papier-mâché tray was made in Cashmere, and is entirely painted by hand, in a most elaborate style, labour of this kind being of very little value there. The vase beneath is constructed of

over apartments; it was taken at the capture of

being peculiar to that country. On the opposite side of our page is the case of a small compass, carried by Mahomedans in India when travelling. It is made of a kind of bronze, inlaid with silver; the inscription contains the names of Mahomet and his two brothers. The compass within it is in the shape of a flying bird, whose head points to the west or Mecca, and tells in what direction the bearer

Lahore, and is believed to have belonged to some of Holkar's household. The brooch is used by the women of Chinese Tartary to fasten their plaid shawls over their shoulders. It is generally made of brass; its chief curiosity con-

a composition of metal and clay, called "biddur," of a very dark tint, and is inlaid with thin

sists in its size, which, in the original, is nine inches and a half by seven inches. The gold ring

ought to turn his face to pray. The magnet is, of course, in the right wing of the bird.

pieces of silver; such vessels are generally used to hold water, and are chiefly manufactured at Ninga-

The cut at the foot of the page exhibits the pattern of a Cashmere covering for a couch;

pore, in Bengal. The very elegant silver vase, with the chain attached, is used to sprinkle rose-water

is of the fashion of those commonly worn by the better class of natives in Cashmere, the pattern

the ornament is stitched over a light blue silk, which gives it a peculiarly delicate tone.

Mr. J. S. EVANS, of London, contributes two ALBUM COVERS, the work of his son, Mr. J. W. Evans. The first is a small quarto, richly illuminated in gold and various colours on brown

of the time of Henry II., of France. The interior of each cover is of white vellum, elegantly tooled in gold, from a pattern by Mr. W. Harry Rogers.

leather; and we should, perhaps, mention that while the black, which forms the field, is a positive dye, the remaining colours are enamelled. The design is taken from an original specimen

The second is a royal quarto, of brown Russia, inlaid with black kid, a novel process as applied to rich workmanship, though not unusual in

The CURTAIN-PIN and CORNICE POLE-ENDS in this column are contributed by Mr. HANDS, of Birmingham, whose manufactory is eminent for

all kinds of stamped metal goods, such as those we have engraved, door-furniture, coffin-furniture, &c. In the subjects we have selected, floral

decoration has been resorted to with considerable success, and with sufficient taste to give the flowers a true and natural position, as we see in

the blue-bells, introduced into the third design, and the bunches of hops in that which precedes it. In the manufactured articles themselves, we

simple book-binding. The design, in harmony with the colours of the materials employed, is in the Etruscan style, and is from a drawing by

Mr. Rogers. A vase occupies the centre, and the border and corners are composed of Archaic foliage, in which the honeysuckle is prominent.

find a sharpness and accuracy of detail that prove the amazing power of the stamping-machine to produce so desirable a result.

THE INDUSTRY OF ALL NATIONS.

This and the following pages are devoted to the contributions of PORCELAIN, from the ROYAL MANUFACTORY AT DRESDEN, or, rather, at Meissen, a small town on the Elbe, about fifteen miles from the capital of Saxony. The Dresden china, for it has always borne the name of the city though made at a distance from it, acquired through the past century high distinction for the beauty and variety of its fanciful decorations, and for the costliness of its workmanship; nor has its value become much lessened even at the present time, although it may, perhaps, be doubted whether its progress has kept pace with that of many other branches of manufacturing art. During our recent tour through Germany, we had an opportunity of visiting this establish-ment, and were supplied by the Director, through the Minister of the Interior, with the drawings from which our engravings are taken. We con-fess to have felt a little disappointment at the comparatively limited scale on which these royal porcelain works are conducted, and still greater surprise at the small amount of wages paid to their artists and workmen, many of whom are men of first-rate talent, who do not receive more than fifty shillings per month. If the English manufacturer, therefore, had this low rate of wages to contend against, he would stand no chance of a successful competition; but inasmuch as the monopoly exercised by the government keeps up the prices of the produc-tions both are placed, so far, on a tolerably

department. The peculiarities of manufacture which distinguish the collection of this porcelain

equal level. The total number of persons en-gaged in the manufactory at Meissen is about three hundred and fifty, and each respective room is set apart for a particular division of the process. Thus, in one apartment, the simpler vases and table-services are moulded; in another, flowers are exclusively manufactured, each leaf being inserted separately; in a third, birds and the more delicate ornaments, and so forth; while the painting and gilding form a separate

ware are relieved floral and bouquet agroupments, figures round and relieved, and many varieties of the famous hawthorn pattern, all these

which is adorned with birds, flowers, and fancy ornaments. The next two are of VASES, from four to five feet high, exceedingly elegant in

are the characteristics of the Dresden manufacture. The first engraving on the opposite page is from an enormous LOOKING-GLASS, the frame of

form, and decorated in a chaste and pure style of art. The first two engravings on this page are also of VASES, the former an imitation of

the antique Grecian, but decorated with enamelled paintings; the latter of a floral character, and filled with porcelain flowers. The group con-

tains objects of very great elegance and beauty; the contributions altogether uphold the character of modern Dresden.

THE INDUSTRY OF ALL NATIONS.

The extensive GLASS works of Messrs. BACCHUS and SONS, of Birmingham, furnish some beautiful examples of their manufacture, of which we engrave two groups, remarkable both for their novelty of form and of ornamentation. Several of these objects, it will be readily supposed, lose no little portion of their rich appearance in the engravings, where black only is made to take the

The three COAL-VASES, or, as such articles of domestic use are generally called, coal-scuttles, are from the establishment of Mr. PERRY, of Wolverhampton, who has, with much good taste, endeavoured to give a character of elegance to these ordinary but necessary appendages to our

place of the most brilliant colours; this is especially to be observed in the large vase in the first group, where, if we imagine the lozenge-shaped ornaments of a deep ruby colour, cased with white enamel, and the wreaths of green ivy, we may form some idea of the rich effect produced. There are few objects of British manufacture which have, of late years, been marked by more decided im-

"household hearths." Hitherto, in whatever room of a dwelling-house one happens to enter, the coal-scuttle is invariably thrust into some obscure corner, as unworthy of filling a place

among the furniture of the apartment, and this not because it is seldom in requisition, but on account of its unsightliness. Mr. Perry's artistic-looking designs, though manufactured only in japanned iron, may, however, have the effect of drawing them from their obscurity, and assigning them an honourable post, even in the drawing-room. It is upon such comparatively trivial matters

provement than is to be found in our "glass-houses;" and Birmingham is now a formidable rival to London in this branch of industrial art: moreover, it is rapidly, and rightly, advancing.

that art has the power to confer dignity; and, notwithstanding the absurdity—as we have sometimes heard it remarked—of adopting Greek and Roman models in things of little importance, they acquire value from the very circumstance of such pure models having been followed.

The decorative articles of various kinds in EMBOSSED LEATHER, executed by Messrs. LEAKE, of London, exhibit the applicability of that substance to very many articles of luxury and convenience used in domestic life. As a simple decoration it possesses the tone and effect of wood carving, at a considerable diminution of expense; and it may be applied to cornices of rooms, or portions of furniture as massive as cabinets and book-cases usually are, with the best possible effect. The flower-wreaths of Gibbons, or the fanciful grotesques of the *cinque cento*, may be reproduced with remarkable precision. Of course, we do not venture to say that wood-carving can be equalled in this fabric, but it may be approached closely. The process of ornamenting leather is one

of a very early date; indeed, it may be traced back some three thousand years, to the days of the ancient Pharaohs, and, singularly enough, we then find it embossed much in the same manner as practised at the present time. The extraordinary durability of leather gave it much value in the eyes of our forefathers; defensive armour was frequently constructed therefrom, and mediæval writers abound with notices of very many useful and ornamental

articles made of *cuir-boulli*, as this manufacture was then called. The cuirass of the knight and the casket of the lady were equally constructed of leather, and

ornamented with embossed work of a rich and beautiful kind. The works of Messrs. Leake are, in some instances, excellent reproductions of antique designs; and in others, equally

good original works, or adaptations of good forms. It will be seen that fruit, flowers, and the human form, are produced by this process, as well as all the varieties of orna-

ment. Great boldness and vigour, and occasionally, extreme delicacy, are visible in all the works of these manufacturers. The chair

the style of the seventeenth century. The panel, executed in the taste of the Renaissance, re-produces the vigour and fancy of the gro-

on our present page exhibits the applicability of the Art to the decoration of furniture. The picture-frame is a happy rendering of

tesque works of that period to the eye, as successfully as the fruit and flowers recall the works of the famed wood carvers of yore.

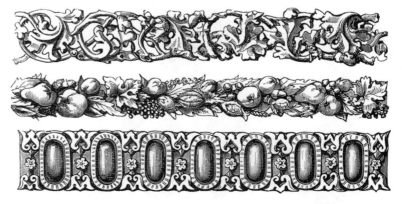

THE INDUSTRY OF ALL NATIONS.

Mr. MORANT, of London, whose reputation, and that of his father, for cabinet-work and house decoration has been established for nearly half a century, contributes a variety of

The VASE and four POKALS, or DRINKING CUPS, upon this and the succeeding page, are the contributions of the Royal Porcelain Manufactory of MUNICH; and they are nearly the only aids which the Exhibition receives from the renowned capital of Bavaria. They are designed by NEUREUTHER; and are intended to hold the famous

elegant objects—of which we have selected three. The first is the top of a CONSOLE GLASS.

The next is a small TABLE, supported by storks, | the top is of plate glass painted to imitate Floren-

and potent Beer, the favourite beverage of all classes of Bavarians. M. Neureuther is at the

tine mosaic. The last subject is also a TABLE, from a design furnished by the Duchess of Sutherland, for whom Mr. Morant executed it. The column of this table exhibits swans and aquatic plants.

head of the government establishment, and we received direct from him the drawings from which these engravings are executed, with expressions of regret that his country will not be more

worthily represented. The cups are of Por-

celain, ormed upon the old German models, and

beautifully ornamented in colours and gold, portions of the decoration being in relief.

The two FIRE-GRATES engraved on this page are from the manufactory of Messrs. STUART and SMITH, known as "Roscoe Place," SHEFFIELD, an establishment which ranks high among those of that famous industrial town. They are made upon the principal known as "Sylvester's," whose invention formed an era in domestic economy and comfort. Their superiority over the old-fashioned grates has become widely tested by their very general use ; these latter were so constructed that the larger portion of the heat passed up the chimney, from the fuel being placed so high, and, as a consequence, the lower part of the room was invariably cold, a condition

directly opposite to health and comfort ; it is obvious that the principle of construction must be best which throws the greatest heat where it is most required, and this is mainly effected by the invention of Mr. Sylvester. The first example engraved is denominated by the makers a "Trefoil Grate," from the shape of its outer frame ; it is composed partly of "dead" steel, and partly of burnished, with or-molu enrichments. The object of its ornamentation has

been to create a style of decoration rom nature, without the introduction of mere conventional forms. The other, in the mediæval style, is designed by Mr. H. Duesbury, an architect of ability, who has shown much taste and ingenuity in adapting this style to its required purpose. The extensive collections of Messrs. Stuart and Smith exhibit a large variety of this description of manufactures, displaying enterprise, taste, and clever mechanical execution.

The five engravings of KEY-HANDLES, on this column, are selections from the contributions of Mr. JOHN CHUBB, London; whose safety locks and improved keys have become famous, not only in England, but throughout Europe. He

has devoted much attention to those improvements which may be described as restorations;

taking the best antique models, and, in some instances refining even upon them : he has thus

substituted forms of much elegance for the ungainly shapes to which we have been accus-

tomed, yet in no way to lessen the ease with which the object may be used. The articles

he contributes cannot fail to augment the high reputation he has laboured for and acquired.

The CUT GLASS DISH and COVER which we here engrave are productions of M. DIERCKX, of Antwerp, and are chiefly remarkable for the peculiarity of design which they present, and which is of a novel

character. Glass is peculiarly susceptible of angular decoration; and this dish and cover are ornamented with figures designed to give the fullest amount of prismatic beauty of which the material is capable.

The establishment of MM. GAGNEAU, Fréres, Paris, has attained deserved celebrity for the manufacture

of CANDELABRA and LAMPS of every description, exhibiting a very large amount of that artistic

talent in design for which the French have long since made themselves famous. We are well acquainted with the show-rooms of this firm, and can truly state that we have rarely seen so many beautiful objects, of their kind, brought together as they exhibit; the metals used are principally bronze, brass, and or-molu. The candelabrum engraved below is exceedingly rich in ornament, but by no means overloaded; the tripod forming the base has at each angle a demi-figure of grotesque character; above this, to conceal the plain shaft, are three females standing on an ornamental platform, which figures may be regarded as caryatides or supports to the higher parts of the composition :

these we consider very elegant both in form and decoration. The lamp which forms the subject of the other engraving is intended to be fixed to a wall; the design scarcely belongs to any definite school or period, but is rather of a mixed character, yet so harmoniously put together that no incongruity is apparent in it. The contributions of this class from France are numerous, and, many of them, highly suggestive; it is, however, needless to point attention to this fact; the works sufficiently commend themselves by their variety and excellence.

The ZINC CASTINGS of GEISS of Berlin are very numerous, although his contributions to the Exhibition are limited; they comprise a variety of objects, chiefly for the purpose of the archi- tect,—capitals, cornices, &c. Zinc has been hitherto very little used in England; in Prussia, however, it has been resorted to, more or less, in nearly every structure of modern erection. M. Geiss has devoted his attention chiefly to the produce of statues in zinc; the purity of the casts, the perfection of the chiseling, and dura- bility of the material, combine to recommend it, while the cost of zinc, thus adopted, is about one-eighth of the cost of bronze. We select for engraving the famous "Amazon" of Professor Kiss, of Berlin; the original, in bronze, faces the entrance to the New Museum, at Berlin. The copy exhibited is life-size; one of half life-size has been also produced by M. Geiss. We have no doubt that the exhibition of these statues, so admirably calculated for gardens in England, will be followed by a large importation of similar works. We counted above twenty in the ateliers of M. Geiss; among them Baily's "Eve," "The Boy and Swan" of Kalide, the Stags of Rauch, with several copies after Canova, Thorvaldsen, and the more famous works of the antique.

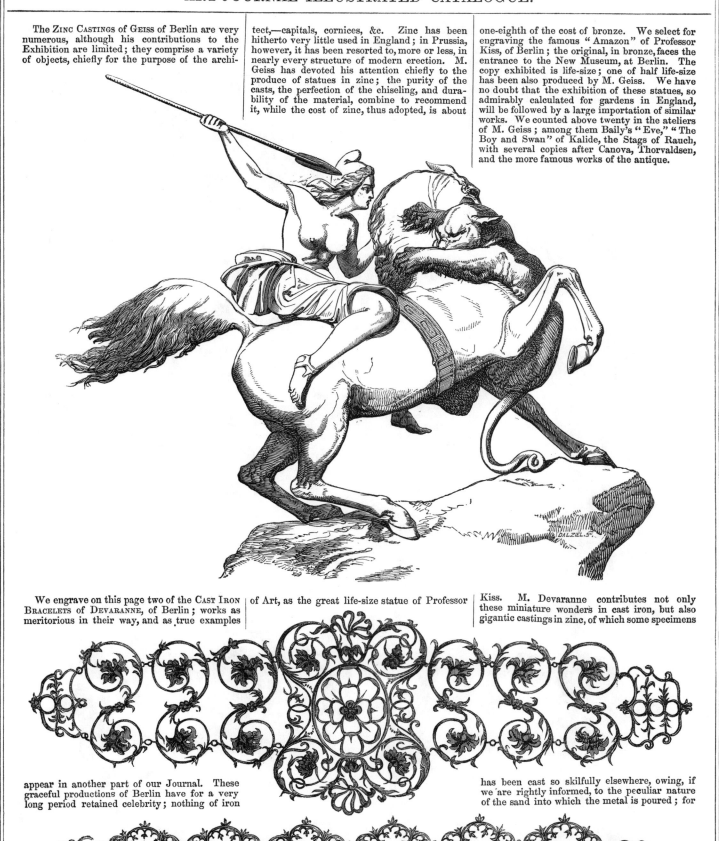

We engrave on this page two of the CAST IRON BRACELETS of DEVARANNE, of Berlin; works as meritorious in their way, and as true examples of Art, as the great life-size statue of Professor Kiss. M. Devaranne contributes not only these miniature wonders in cast iron, but also gigantic castings in zinc, of which some specimens appear in another part of our Journal. These graceful productions of Berlin have for a very long period retained celebrity; nothing of iron has been cast so skilfully elsewhere, owing, if we are rightly informed, to the peculiar nature of the sand into which the metal is poured; for the iron principally used is obtained from English mines. The collection exhibited by M. Devar- anne will attract universal attention; they con- sist of necklaces, brooches, bracelets, pins, and other objects, so skilfully designed and delicately wrought as to be absolute marvels of Fine Art.

The PILLAR, surmounted by a group, and the TABLE which commences the next column, are from the ROYAL IRON FOUNDRY OF BERLIN; they are, of course, made of cast iron. This establishment is under the immediate direction of the Government. The pillar is designed by Professor Strack; the base shows a claw tripod, from which rises a shaft encircled upwards by a triad of graceful figures, terminating with a flat top, whereon is placed a highly-spirited Amazon group, the work of Professor Fischer,

figures, in bas-relief, form a kind of entablateur below its surface, which is supported by four winged demi-figures springing from the shaft.

This is moulded and ornamented with considerable elegance; indeed, the entire object is one of much artistic beauty in its several parts.

The annexed engravings form portions of a BRIDLE, contributed by Mr. PENNY, of London, a metal chaser, who has executed the whole of the ornamental work in electro-plated silver. He calls it the "Prince of Wales's Bridle," having made it with a view to its being adopted by his Royal Highness. The emblems with which it is decorated, therefore, bear reference to the position of the Prince in connection with a great maritime power. The ornamental outer edge of the winker, here engraved, is composed of dolphins, sea-horns, and foliage; the inner edge has an anchor, with foliage entwined; the centre of this part, which is not engraved, shows the

also of iron. The dark tone of this metal is greatly relieved by an inlaid thread of silver, beautifully wrought into one of the most chaste and simple of the antique configurations. The Table is unique in its design; a series of antique

heraldic arms of the Prince, his coronet, &c. The rosettes, which form the centre-piece in the engraving, have a foliage border surrounding the coronet. The buckles, head-stall, face-piece,

loops, &c., are also ornamented. The leather-work is manufactured by Mr. LANGDON, of London. The design of the harness, altogether and in detail, is by Mr. W. Harry Rogers.

The EMBROIDERED ALTAR-CLOTH is by Mr. T. HARRISON, of London: it is a very elaborate specimen of gold embroidery upon a field of rich crimson velvet. In the centre is the monogram I H S surrounded by a "gloria" of twelve principal rays and stars. In the spaces are intro- duced two conventional roses surrounded by stars. A flowing pattern of trefoil and gothic pine-apples forms an elegant border to the cloth, and the whole is edged by a massive fringe of gold four inches in depth. The design for the embroidery is the work of Mr. W. Harry Rogers.

The BIT for a horse, commencing this column, is contributed by Messrs. ASHFORD, of Birmingham, extensive manufacturers of what is termed "saddlers' ironmongery," such as steel-bits, stirrups, whips, and whip-mounts, but all of a superior quality. The example here introduced is intended for the use of a lady: it is of pierced

The BOOK COVER, the back of wh'c'i appears on the opposite column, is exhibited by Messrs. | BONE & SON, of London. They are designed by Mr. W. Harry Rogers, and cannot fail of being

steel, highly polished, is exceedingly light in con- struction, and may be regarded as a novelty.

admired for the lightness and elegance of the composition, which is entirely of a floriated character, an arrangement of the ivy, holly, and other evergreens worked into a pattern with much taste. It is almost as effective in what the trade call "blind-work," as when richly gilt.

THE INDUSTRY OF ALL NATIONS.

A FOWLING-PIECE, contributed by M. SAUER, of Suhl, Saxony, shows some exquisite carved work, emblematical of its uses, on the stock. The gun itself is of peculiar construction in its manufacture, tending to obviate the dangers attending any sudden explosion; we have before us diagrams of its mechanical arrangement, but which we cannot afford space to introduce into our pages.

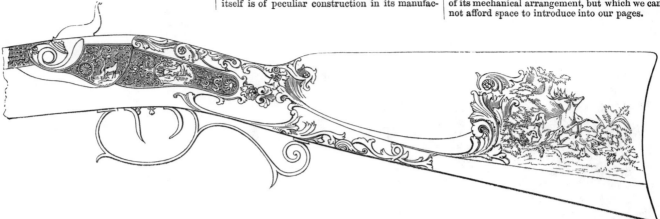

The CHATELAIN-HEAD is exhibited by Mr. THORNHILL, of London; it is entirely produced by hand, in hard steel, chiefly by means of minute files. The principal portions are flat, perforated and engraved, but a slight projection is given to the more important ornaments or emblems introduced. The design, which is by Mr. W. Harry Rogers, is in the Italian style, consisting of foliage surrounding an oval compartment. This has the monogram V.A., and is surmounted by the royal crown; beneath are the Prince of Wales' eathers, and a lable inscribed 1851. Six medallions contain the crests of the illustrious promoter of the Exhibition.

IVORY POKAL, by CHRISTIAN FRANK, Fürth, near Nuremberg. The pokal is of gothic form, and beautifully carved in relief, illustrative of subjects taken from the old German Niebelungen Lied, after the paintings of Jul. Schnorr von Carolsfeld. The relievos are : From the fourth adventure, 'Sigfried with the Saxons;' seventeenth adventure, 'Sigfried mourned and entombed;' twenty-second adventure, 'Briemhild received by the Huns;' thirty-seventh adventure, 'The death of Rudiger.'

The SCISSORS are also by Mr. THORNHILL; the ornamentation is an adaptation of the Italian style. They are highly to be commended as examples of the taste of the designer, whoever he may be.

Messrs. CORK & EDGE, of Burslem, Stafford-shire, manufacturers of earthenware, supply the markets in England and on the Conti-nent with ordinary articles of domestic use, in which they endeavour to combine utility with an amount of ornament that will not prejudice economy. Our first cut represents a TEAPOT of brown glazed ware, of very cheap construction, but not without its peculiar grace in design. A patented branch of their business

is devoted to the ornamentation of similar articles by inlaying clays of various tints, thus producing an indestructible colouring for the leaves and other ornaments, such as appear

upon our second specimen of their works. The WATER-JUG, which completes our selection of articles from this establishment, is a tasteful arrangement of forms; the water-lily being

introduced in the base of the jug with very good effect. It must be borne in mind that all these articles are constructed only for the cheapest market; and we give them as instances of improvement in such branches of our national industry as were but a few years ago, as must be acknowledged, most inartistic in taste.

Messrs. FAUDEL & PHILLIPS, of London, ex-hibit a STATE BEDSTEAD, of needlework, pro-duced principally from British materials worked

entirely by Englishwomen in London; it includes almost every description of ornamental needle-work commonly called "Berlin," and embroi-

dery. A lengthened description of this costly and beautiful piece of furniture would fill half our page; we must therefore be content with speaking of it as a work in every way honourable to the taste and enterprise of the manufacturers, who have long been famous in their trade.

The two specimens of CARPETS on this page are from the factory of Messrs. HENDERSON & Co., Durham, whose establishment produces a large variety of Venetian and damask stair-carpets, as well as of Brussels carpets for all purposes—distinguished by beauty of design, brilliancy of colour, and fineness of quality; while the prices which we understand they command in the market, testify to the high character they hold

among the "trade." For the last seventeen years this house has worked entirely from drawings expressly designed for them, and thus at an early period they materially contributed to give effect to that principle of property in design, the justice of which is now universally admitted. The establishment of a woollen manufacture in Durham, dates back as far as the commencement of the seventeenth century, with funds supplied

out of a charitable trust connected with the city, but the manufacture languished till 1619, and was then abandoned. In 1780, another attempt was made, and was equally unfortunate, two successive parties having failed in working it out; but in 1813, Mr. Gilbert Henderson, the father of the present enterprising proprietors, undertook the task of establishing a manufactory confined to the production of these carpets only.

The CHATELAINE, which, with its various details occupies this page, is the contribution of Mr. DURHAM, of London; it is an excellent example of steel-manufacture, displaying considerable taste and fancy in the entire composition; while the various articles which form the a fine effect. The modern chatelaine is but a reproduction of an article of decorative ornament, worn by ladies in our own country more

than a century and a half ago. The watch, the scissors, *etui*, pincushion, &c., were then ostentatiously appended to the dresses of the ladies,

quite as much for ornament as for use. The elegant and ornamental character of the object may

pendant group are designed with much taste, and worked up with considerable skill. The numerous *facets* upon the ornamental knobs and enrichments which cover the entire surface of the chatelaine, give to it again ensure its favourable reception; and the beauty of such as that we now engrave must recommend it even to the fastidious utilitarian.

THE INDUSTRY OF ALL NATIONS.

The RICHLY-EMBROIDERED MUSLIN DRESS, of which we engrave a part, is one of the many contributions of Messrs. BROWN, SHARPS, & Co., of Paisley. These manufacturers have long been famous; having obtained eminence not only for the excellence of their work, but for the purity and beauty of their designs,—and it is known that they have employed in the production of subjects for their numerous workers, artists whose reputations have not been merely provincial. Our engraving can of course afford but a limited idea of the skill of the designer: in this, as in many others of the articles contributed by the firm, he has aimed at copies of natural flowers, and has avoided those conventional forms which for a long period were considered indispensable to workers in muslin. The dress to which reference is here made, will be found among the richest and most elaborate productions of the needle. It will readily be supposed that patterns of this description unavoidably lose much of their true effect, by the necessity that compels us to have them drawn on a greatly reduced scale, to suit the size of our pages. Hence what seems to possess a redundancy of ornament in the engraving, although delicately and carefully drawn on the wood, takes a far less crowded, and a bolder, form on the manufactured article; this will be understood when we state that the pattern measures, in the original, upwards of three feet in height by four in width.

A LINEN BAND, designed by S. M'CLOY, a pupil of the Belfast School of Design, and produced by Mr. M'CRACKEN, manufacturer of linen ornaments, Belfast, presents a pattern of much elegance. The subject is derived from the hawthorn in its autumnal or ripe state, when the berries assume their deep red colour. The arrangement of this composition is exceedingly well managed; and in the manufactured article

it has a rich and brilliant appearance, the foliage being embossed in gold, with the red berries on a blue ground; the centre shows the hawthorn in bloom, coloured after nature on a white ground. To this design was awarded the first prize of three pounds, offered last year by Lord Dufferin to the Belfast School for the best design for ornamental linen; it is a work uniting simplicity of subject with great skill in adaptation.

We engrave one of three drawings transmitted to us by Professor KAHSZMANN, of Vienna; it exhibits HEBE OFFERING NECTAR TO THE EAGLE OF JOVE. The Professor, we understand, occupies a high position in Austria: his works are generally of a poetical order; but he has been entrusted with some "for the nation" which are in closer proximity to actual life. Happily for the sculptors of the Continent, their governments find them frequent employment; private "commissions" are rare.

how much of grace, dignity, and manly vigour may be sacrificed to render homage to the so-called "jolly god." These examples of his manufacture are highly creditable to Mr. Meigh; they are works of a right good order,

From the contributions in Porcelain and Earthenware of Mr. CHARLES MEIGH, of Shelton, Staffordshire Potteries, we select three objects: the

and exhibit marked improvement in one of the most extensive and best conducted of the factories of Staffordshire. It is only of late that

one, a CLOCK CASE, of very elegant and appropriate design, executed in statuary porcelain; the next, a VASE, also in statuary porcelain—copied, we believe, with some alterations, from a French model; and next, one of those Bacchanalian DRINKING CUPS, ornamented with figures after Poussin—which seem to have been invented for the purpose of showing

Mr. Meigh has paid attention to the Letter class of goods; but for many years he has enjoyed high repute as a producer of admirable works in earthenware; and he is among the largest exporters in the kingdom.

In the production of CAMEI the continental artists have achieved a well-deserved reputation; we engrave three very beautiful works of this class, the productions of M. JULIN, of Liege. The first is a copy after Horace Vernet of his "Chasse au Faucon," very delicately and beautifully rendered.

The same artist's well-known picture of "Mazeppa" has furnished the second subject; the third is a charming group of "Galatea and the Sea-Nymphs." The grades of tint in camei are fortunate aids to the sculptor in producing striking and interesting effects; these advantages were so highly appreciated by the ancients, that they endeavoured

to imitate them in their glass works—of which a well-known instance may be cited in the Portland Vase. The works of the ancients in this department of art were frequently cut upon onyx of large dimensions; one of the most celebrated is preserved at Vienna, and represents the apotheosis of Augustus. The antiques differ from the modern

camei, being cut upon tinted stones, and not on shells (conchylie); the latter being an imitative art in another material, and the result of a comparatively modern era—the taste for camei having been resuscitated by the famous family of the Medici, and perfected, under their auspices, in Florence.

T..e TERRA COTTA works of Mrs. MARSH are situated at Charlottensburg distant about four miles from Berlin; the lady by whom they are conducted is the widow of the manufacturer who formed the very admirable establishment. Here are produced works of the highest artistic merit, works designed by the best artists of Prussia, who do not "shame" to dedicate genius to the improvement of the humblest articles of

daily use. We select for engraving four of the productions of Mrs. Marsh;—the POKAL or

drinking-cup is a copy; the GOTHIC VASE is from the design of Professor Strach. But the most beautiful of the objects contributed by Mrs. Marsh is a FOUNTAIN, which we also engrave. This work was produced expressly for the Exhibition.

The VASE, filled with artificial FLOWERS OF SILVER, is the production of STRUBE AND SON, Jewellers, and Silver and Gold Workers, of Leipsic. The vase is an object of much delicate beauty: the flowers are not made in dies, but are the production of the artist's hand, and are accurately modelled from nature.

We saw at the establishment of Messrs. Strube much that was rare and valuable, but in this particular branch they are unrivalled.

The works of M. FALLOISE, of Liege, in wrought metals, are of the highest order of merit; the cover of a SNUFF-BOX we print on this page; and works of great ability on subsequent pages.

This page, and the two pages which follow, are devoted to a few of the contributions of M. MATIFAT, of Paris, an extensive manufacturer of bronze articles, both useful and ornamental. In our illustrated notice of the Exposition in Paris of 1849, we engraved a number of the objects contributed by this most ingenious artist, being particularly struck with their beauty of design and very superior style of workmanship. We have reason to

lead of all other nations in bronze casting; still it is only within a few years comparatively that she has made any considerable move in advance of the old routine system of manufacture; while among those who have quitted the

beaten track, and have introduced new ideas and new arrangements of the best models of antiquity, M. Matifat may take his stand with the very foremost, throwing into his profession a zeal, energy, and perseverance which, united

with skill and taste, could not fail of success, and to elevate him to a high position in his especial branch of manufacture. Having thus awarded him the praise to which he is justly

entitled for his productions generally, we proceed to remark upon the objects we have engraved from a few of his numerous contributions. The first is a FOUNTAIN, of somewhat

small dimensions, suitable for a conservatory; among the floriated ornaments are birds, a squirrel, and a snake; all of which are introduced with the skill of an artist who desires to

make his design both natural and elegant. The first on this column is a VASE or TAZZA, of the style of Louis XIV., cast in iron, its diameter is eight feet, and its height five feet;

know that in this we conferred a benefit upon more than one of our own manufacturers, to whom our pages introduced M. Matifat, and who have availed themselves of his talent and experience to raise the character of their own productions; for this gentleman, like all men of true genius, is influenced by none of those petty and unworthy feelings which would cause him to "hide his lamp under a bushel," fearing lest others should derive light from it. France has for a long time taken the

the form of this vase is exceedingly elegant, and its ornamentation simple, but of pure taste. Underneath are two smaller engravings, one of a DRAWER-HANDLE, and the other a portion of an ESCUTCHEON. Next follows a JEWEL-CASKET, of embossed steel, the joints are of iron, damascened with gold, the frames are of silver.

Paris, for some years past, has been regarded as the great manufactory for the finest productions in bronze, calling into employ many excellent artists and the most skilful workmen; for it must be borne in mind that the majority of the best works are sculptured by the hand from the model, as it comes rough from the mould.

To resume, however, our notice of M. MATIFAT'S contributions. The present page commences with a TAZZA and COVER, of chased iron; the flowers in the centre are enamelled, the foot and

Then follows a FLOWER-BASKET, which, being of silver, may be used as a centre-piece for a

the interior are inlaid with gold damascene work, imparting to the object a rich and costly effect.

The next object is a TAZZA, of considerable dimensions, and exquisite in form and workman-

dessert service : the numerous figures in this

ship. The body is surrounded with a wreath of snakes, foliage, and flowers ; and other snakes are twisted into the forms of handles : the base and pedestal are decorated in a similar manner.

design are judiciously distributed throughout

the composition. An ITALIAN ARCHITECTURAL ORNAMENT, executed in bronze, concludes the

can celebe, exhibiting on the side we have engraved a combat between a man and a centaur.

enamels. The next is a EWER of very elegant form, and highly embossed in the manner of the

We come next to a VASE, the style of which the artist terms Assyrian; it stands two feet and a half in height, and is beautifully studded with

antique. The last engraving exhibits a CHANDE-LIER of simple but pure character, in which the relative proportions of the different parts are

page; it is distinguished by great beauty of proportion and elaborate chiselling. A GAS PILLAR,

of chaste design, is introduced above; to which succeeds a small VASE, modelled after the Etrus-

evidence that the design has emanated from an artist well instructed in those

principles on which are based the beauty and harmony of curved lines.

A drawing-room CLOCK, made of or-molu, is contributed by Messrs. HOWELL & JAMES, of London. It is designed by Mr. ADAMS, an artist of talent, who has in this produced an elegant work of art, with emblems most appropriate to the subject. Below the dial are four bas-reliefs of children, representing the "Seasons," and on each side are female groups symbolising Childhood, Youth, Womanhood, and Old Age. A basket of flowers crowns the top, from which hangs a wreath encircling the dial. The scroll work at the base is exceedingly bold, while the pedestal exhibits more delicate ornamentation.

We next introduce an engraving from a splendid horizontal grand PIANO-FORTE, one of the specimens which we have selected from the contributions of Messrs. COLLARD & COLLARD, of London. The case and the music-stand are richly carved, and the instrument altogether accords well with

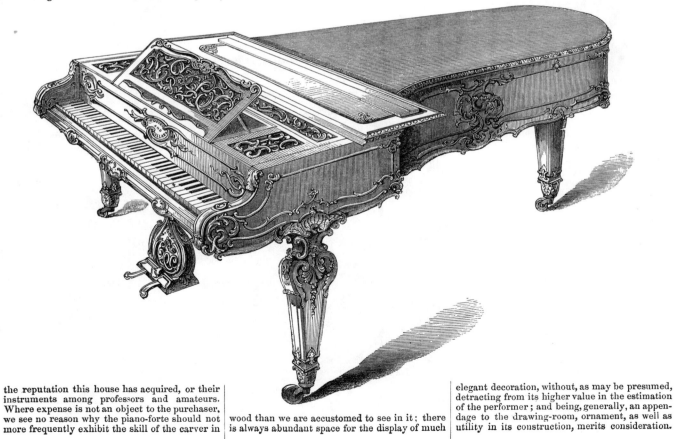

the reputation this house has acquired, or their instruments among professors and amateurs. Where expense is not an object to the purchaser, we see no reason why the piano-forte should not more frequently exhibit the skill of the carver in wood than we are accustomed to see in it: there is always abundant space for the display of much elegant decoration, without, as may be presumed, detracting from its higher value in the estimation of the performer; and being, generally, an appendage to the drawing-room, ornament, as well as utility in its construction, merits consideration.

From the contributions of Messrs. HARCOURT BROTHERS, of Birmingham, we select three—two

BELL-PULLS, and a VASE of bronze. These gentlemen are eminent manufacturers of the several

objects for which the great factory of hardware has been long famou.. Their manufactory o'

"household" metal furniture is very extensive.

We introduce on this page another engraving of one of the PIANOS of Messrs. COLLARD & COLLARD, of London. It is richly decorated, and forms a most elegant work of art-manufacture.

The engraving underneath is from one of the carpets contributed by JAN HEUKENSFELDT, of Delfdt. It is ot a good order of Art, and will do credit to this long established and justly

celebrated manufacturer, who presides over a very extensive factory of the best Dutch carpets.

Among the fine DIAPERS and damask linens received from Dunfermline, are some singularly rich and beautiful TABLE-CLOTHS, manufactured by Mr. BIRRELL, from designs furnished by Mr. Paton—an artist who has for upwards of a quarter of a century aided the manufacturers of that famous and venerable town. We have engraved one of them on this page—bold and elaborate in design, and in all respects worthy of

covering a regal table. In the corners of the border we discern the "St. George," and in the centres of the same part, the badges of the Order, the Thistle, and St. Patrick. In the centre of the cloth is a medallion bust of Her Gracious Majesty. This table-cloth is made from the finest Flemish flax.

We introduce here four copies of the backs of WATCHES,—the watches contributed by Messrs. ROTHERAM & SON, of Coventry. They exhibit marked improvement of style, and do great credit to the extensive establishment from which they emanate. The designs are good, and the workmanship is excellent. They are enamelled, and tastefully set with jewels, so disposed as to give much beauty and agreeable effect to the forms.

THE INDUSTRY OF ALL NATIONS.

While Sheffield contends successfully with the metropolis in the manufacture of steel goods, she unquestionably takes the lead of all other towns for the excellence displayed in her silver and plated articles adapted for ordinary use; and even goes so far as to rival many of her competitors in what is more especially intended for ornamental purposes, and is moreover executed in the most costly metal. In two or three recent numbers of the *Art-Journal*, we made our readers acquainted with a few of the most important manufacturers of this populous and busy town, introducing, at the same time, numerous engravings copied from their productions. The FISH-KNIFE and FORK, inserted below, are manufactured by Messrs. MAPPIN BROTHERS, of Sheffield, and will bear comparison with the best examples of a similar description of metal work.

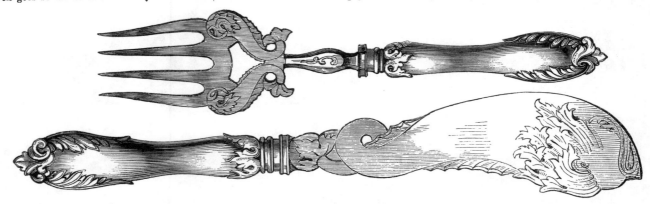

A STATE CHAIR and a STATE BANNER SCREEN, by M. JANCOWSKI, of York, are rich and costly examples of embroidery and decorative furniture. The chair is embroidered on ruby-coloured silk velvet; on the back is the royal coat of arms, the lion raised in gold, the unicorn in silver, with a gold coronet; the crown is worked in gold, silver, silks, and jewels. From the ribbon which shows the motto, a wreath of the rose, shamrock, and thistle, worked in silks, is suspended, and the roses are raised so that every leaf may be lifted up. The seat exhibits the plume of the Prince of Wales, worked in a new style of silk embroidery, having the appearance of silver; the coronet is in gold, silver, and jewels; the motto in gold and silver.

numerous assistants, by whom, we are informed,

The chair is made up in a splendid carved and gilded frame, trimmed with solid gold bullion fringes. The Banner-screen is embroidered on pale blue satin, with gold, silver, and silks trimmed with rich bullion; it represents the York City Arms; the pole, six feet ten inches in height, is surmounted by the Royal arms finely carved; the pedestal is also richly carved. Both these gorgeous objects reflect the highest credit on the taste and judgment of M. Jancowski and his they have been entirely designed and carried out.

A SHAWL, from the manufactory of Messrs. JOHN MORGAN & Co., of Paisley, has a rich and most elaborate pattern, reminding us of some of the best designs that are imported from the East—but greatly improving upon them. Besides shawls, the manufacturers are also producers of printed and tartan fabrics to a large extent, specimens of which are likewise to be found in the Exhibition. In all these cases, the patterns are designed, and the goods are manufactured, dyed, and finished on the premises of Messrs. Morgan.

From the establishment of M. GABAIN, of Berlin, which we visited during our late tour through Germany, have been forwarded a large variety of SILK STUFFS. We engrave on this page one example, of a graceful palm pattern, designed by Professor Bötticher, of Berlin. This pattern is about five feet in height, by twenty-seven inches in breadth, when it is repeated. This weaving is done on a satin ground, and it is produced in various colours, as well as in different tints of the same colour. We may, hereafter, introduce other productions of this house.

We fill up this page with one of the contributions of Messrs. HOOLE & ROBSON, of Sheffield.—A FENDER, remarkable for the grace of its design as well as for the beauty of its execution—qualities for which this eminent firm have obtained much celebrity; deservedly so, as we shall be enabled to show in our engravings from others of their works in subsequent pages. The combination of steel and bronze adapted by them is, in many instances, productive of the happiest effects. Perhaps there is no class of our native manufacturers who have made greater advances in the field of improvement than those connected with the polished steel trade.

A PEDIMENT, designed and modelled by Mr. C. Fox, of Brighton, shows an effective arrangement of the figures introduced into it. The subject is intended to represent the "Arts, Commerce, and Manufactures, promoted by the Great Exhibition." The first group to the left represents Navigation, the next Industry bringing her offerings to Peace. In the centre is the Queen, holding out wreaths of laurel to the various contributors, and to the right the Fine Arts and Science are symbolised in respective groups.

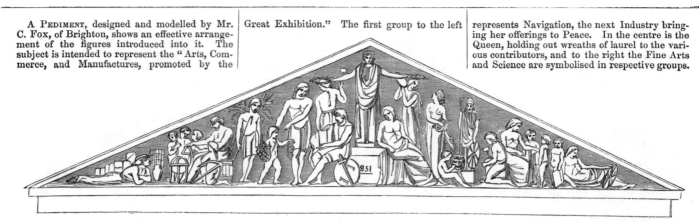

A CARYATIDE, sculptured in oak by M. CRUCHET, of Paris, is a bold and not inelegant conception of an architectural ornament which, of itself, has generally little to recommend it as a decorative object. Used as substitutes for columns, they possess neither the elegance of outline, nor the symmetry of proportion, that render the latter important and interesting features of the edifice with which they are connected. It would seem that the origin of these figures appertains to Egyptian architecture, for they are recorded in all the traces of this style of building that have come down to us; and they were adopted, though sparingly, by the Greeks, from whom we have derived one, now in the British Museum among the Elgin collection,

We engrave here one of the contributions of Professor RIETSCHEL, of Dresden—a dead CHRIST, over whom mourns the VIRGIN MOTHER. The artist holds rank among the most eminent sculptors of Germany: to him has been confided the task of executing the principal national monuments of Saxony; and the sculptured decorations of the Theatre of Dresden are the production of this master-mind of his country. His sculptures will excite in England the admiration so universally accorded to them throughout the rest of Europe. We had—in 1850—the privilege to see this accomplished

which was taken from the Acropolis, at Athens. | artist at work upon this, the latest, and perhaps | the greatest, of his many admirable productions.

Few knowing the vast resources and the long experience of the eminent firm of Messrs. HUNT & ROSKELL, of London, who now conduct the business formerly carried on by Messrs. Storr & Mor-

timer, will be surprised to find them making a display in the Exhibition commensurate with the reputation of an establishment that produces many of the most costly manufactured articles in the precious metals. Without disparagement to any other house in London, in a similar branch of business, it may be said that Messrs. Hunt & Roskell have no rival in the extent of their transactions, and a visit to their show-rooms is like inspecting a museum of Art. We, therefore, feel that we do not pay an unmerited compliment to these manufacturers in gold and silver works of

every kind and description, by devoting two or three pages of our Catalogue to a notice of their contributions. In the remarks we have occasionally made in the *Art-Journal* upon the comparative

merits of foreign and English silver-work, it has been stated that the inferiority of the latter has been in a great measure attributable to the absence of good designs, and to the superior taste and delicacy of finish in the foreign workmen. Recent

political events abroad have, however, brought over a number of the latter to this country, and there cannot be a doubt that we have greatly benefited by this fusion of adventitious aid with English energy, perseverance, and capital. More-over, manufacturers have found it essential to their interests to seek the assistance of other heads than those of the mere artisan, however skilful as a workman, to invent, and suggest, and improve. Hence from these two causes a decided change

for the better has, within the past few years, been perceptible in every branch of this department of Industrial Art; and we may add, without egotism, that the pages of the *Art-Journal* have had some influence in affecting this amelioration,

proceed to the notice of the various subjects selected from Messrs. Hunt and Roskell's contributions. The first page commences with two bronze STATUETTES; the former represents a Hindoo girl plucking the sacred moon-plant (*sarcostema viminalis*), and the latter depositing her lamp in the waters of the Ganges. The originals of these statuettes are, we believe, executed in silver, and formed a part of the Ellenborough

by means we need not now enlarge upon. With

these few brief introductory observations we

testimonial. The group that succeeds form the ORANGE GOODWOOD PLATE, for the year 1846; it represents William of Nassau at the Battle of Nieuport. This is followed by the TESTIMONIAL presented to Mr. B. Lumley, lessee of Her Majesty's Theatre; it is designed and modelled by Mr. A. Brown; the figures, appropriately introduced, are those of the sister muses who preside over dramatic and musical festivals. The column on

the second page commences with a DESSERT STAND, showing a Hindoo flower-setter under a banyan tree; the succeeding objects are two ICE-PAILS, formed by the lotus, supported by other Indian plants; these three objects are from a service presented to the Earl of Ellenborough. The large engraving on the same page is a massive and costly CANDELABRUM in silver, a testimonial presented to the Marquis of Tweeddale. The subject of the group is taken

from Buchanan's "History of Scotland," and illustrates the historical fact connected with the rise of this noble family; a countryman, named Hay—the family name—is, with his two sons,

leading the Scots to the defeat of the Danes, A.D. 980. The composition, which evinces remarkable spirit, is also designed and modelled by M. A. Brown. At the head of the third

page is an elegant CUP, followed by a silver-gilt CASKET, in the style of the cinque-cento period, set with antique gems; and below this is a CUP to correspond. A group in silver, of Mazeppa,

comes next; great spirit is imparted to this work by the animals being "relieved" from the ground, the horse, especially, appears as if flying. The last engraving is from a TESTIMONIAL presented

to Sir Moses Montefiore. It is scarcely necessary to remind our readers that Sir Moses is of the Hebrew persuasion, and that the design, which is by Sir J. Hayter, has reference to certain events connected with the past and present history of the Jews. Thus, the sphinxes indicate the captivity of Israel in Egypt; the figures are Moses,

Ezra, the great deliverer of the people, a Jew of Damascus, loaded with chains, and one released; under them are appropriate texts in Hebrew, with the vine and the fig-tree overshadowing. The group on the summit represents David rescuing the lamb from the jaws of the lion, and the bassi-relievi show the passage of the Red

Sea, and the Destruction of Pharaoh's host; Lawless Violence in the world, typified by wolves

devouring the flocks; the Millennium as spoken of by Isaiah; Sir Moses and Lady Montefiore

landing at Alexandria; Sir Moses obtaining the firman from the Sultan; and two other subjects.

The SILVER CUP, engraved below, is designed, modelled, and embossed by the exhibitor, Mr. SHARP, of London; he terms it the "Justice Cup." It exhibits round the body, in bas-relief, Justice protecting the Innocent, and driving from the earth Violence, Fraud, and Discord.

A PANEL, carved in wood, and *carton-pierre*, by M. CRUCHET, of Paris, will attract attention, not only from its position, but for the artistic arrangement of its various groups, and the bold

execution of the work. The centre is filled with a design modified from Albert Durer's "St. Hubert," and the lower composition shows a group of children engaged in agricultural operations.

The CARPET pattern engraved below is from the manufactory of Messrs. PARDOE & Co., of Kidderminster, one of the largest establishments in that town; it produces an infinite variety of goods, from the costly velvet to the commoner kinds, but all of more than ordinary excellence.

Mr. BIELEFELD, of London, the extensive manufacturer of ornaments in PAPIER-MÂCHÉ, exhibits a large variety of his manufactures, from which we have selected five specimens for engraving, namely, two corbels, one bracket, a

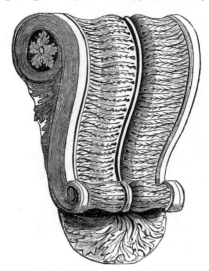

centre-piece, and a cornice or moulding, all of them designed with true artistic taste, and executed with very considerable sharpness and delicacy. Mr. Bielefeld manufactures almost

superseded the use of plaster ornaments, and are not unfrequently used instead of the more costly

designs; the facility with which it may be put together and fixed up; its lightness, and, lastly,

materials of stone and wood. Its hardness, durability, and ready assumption of all forms and

its cheapness, are all qualities highly desirable in a manufacture of the kind, and which recommend

exclusively for the trade; or, in other words, supplies architects, builders, and decorators with the ornaments required for the edifices they may be erecting; and, in the present day, these papier-mâché manufactures have, in a great measure,

it above every other employed in interior decoration. We have, on more than one occasion, visited and reported Mr. Bielefeld's most interest-

ing establishment, and have had opportunities of inspecting the very extensive variety of ornamental productions constantly issuing from it.

Perhaps there are few branches of British Industrial Art in which greater advance has been made during the past few years than our

glass manufactures exhibit: in quality of material, in form, and in design, the works of the present day manifest a decided superiority over

those of a quarter of a century ago. The three GLASSES on this column, manufactured by Mr. CONNE, of London, are in themselves sufficient

evidence of this progress; the ornamental design in the first and second examples is characterised by delicacy, and in the third by boldness, while the form of each respectively is in good taste.

From upwards of one hundred specimens of DAMASK TABLE LINEN and COLOURED TABLE-CLOTHS, manufactured by Mr. BEVERIDGE, of Dunfermline, we have selected six for introduction on this and the two following pages. Mr. Beveridge's manufactory is among the first, if not the most extensive, in the town and its neighbourhood, employing about fifteen hundred

pair of hands out of some five or six thousand engaged in this branch of trade. The varieties of fabric woven in Dunfermline may be stated to consist of damask table-linen, table-covers,

linen floor-cloths, and diapers of all descriptions; more than one half of the goods so manufactured, and these chiefly of the finer sorts, are disposed of in the home market, the remainder being exported, principally to the United States. Table linen has greatly benefited by the introduction of the Jacquard loom, which is used for every description of cloth, from that made expressly for her Majesty's table, to the coarsest "whitey-brown," destined to cover the pine-board of some American backwoodsman. Some idea may be formed of the present advanced state of the manufacture, when it is known that for the design of a table-cloth and napkin, such as some of those represented on our pages, as much as one hundred pounds are frequently paid. Our

A CIMITAR and SCABBARD, by Messrs. WILKINSON and SON, of London, is a most elegant specimen of manufacturing art. It is of silver, chased and gilt, and is ornamented with one hundred and four precious stones, consisting of emeralds,

first engraving is from a TABLE-CLOTH of damask, woven in an arabesque pattern of great boldness. The second is also a damask TABLE-CLOTH, with napkins to correspond; they are of classic design, the centre exhibiting figures of Cupid and Psyche. This page commences with a TABLE-COVER of arabesque pattern, in various colours; it is made of silk, cotton, and wool. This is followed by a

linen damask TABLE-CLOTH, with napkins to correspond; the border is Gothic, having the figures of St. George, St. Andrew, and St. Patrick in the corner niches, with St. George and the Dragon in the centre. This pattern is singularly beautiful. The articles confer honour upon the manufacturer. They are, we understand, principally designed by Mr. Paton, of Dunfermline.

rubies, turquoises, jacynths, carbuncles, &c., &c., inserted in arabesque patterns. The blade is of the finest temper; it combines embossing with engraving, blueing, and gilding, so as to form two elevations of an highly ornamental pattern.

We resume on this page the contributions of Mr. BEVERIDGE, of Dunfermline. The first engraving is from a linen damask TABLE-CLOTH, having napkins and doyleys to correspond. The pattern introduced is borrowed from the vine. The next is a TABLE-COVER, in what the manufacturer terms the French style; it is woven in a variety of rich colours, in wool, silk, and cotton. It seems almost unnecessary to add that the circumscribed space to which we are compelled to limit our engravings, detracts somewhat from the boldness of the designs. There is a curious history attached to the introduction of this art into Dunfermline—from Drumsheugh, near

On this column are engravings from two exquisitely beautiful CASKETS, manufactured by Mr. WERTHEIMER, of London. The engraved work on these objects is of the most elaborate and delicate description; they are adorned with malachite and precious stones, and are, in every way, worthy of finding

a home in the most sumptuous boudoir. The lower one is placed on a superbly gilt stand, the base of which has also malachites inserted. While so many exquisite works—worthy rivals to the best of those which "the great era" produced in Germany and France—are contributed from

Edinburgh, where it was secretly practised at the beginning of the last century. A man, named Blake, feigning to be of weak intellect, found his way into a weaving-shop, and was permitted to amuse himself underneath a loom, where he carefully observed the manner in which the cords and other parts were arranged, and, by the aid of a good memory, and some previous knowledge of the general mechanism of the loom, he brought away the grand secret, and was not long in reducing it to practice. In no branch of Art-Manufacture do we perceive such unequivocal signs of advancement as in the damasks produced of late years in Scotland and in Ireland; of this our

Catalogue supplies sufficient proof; those of Belfast, engraved in subsequent pages, are honourable to Ireland; the great manufacturing capital of the island is, in all respects, worthily represented; while the ancient renown of "gray Dunfermline" is more than sustained by the productions of its looms, which find their way, common or refined, to every country, and almost every district, of the civilised world. In such articles as those under notice, we can have no dread of foreign competition; neither in the material, its fabrication, nor even the decoration to which they have been subjected, shall we be surpassed by the manufacturers of Germany, Belgium, or France.

the Continent, it is with exceeding pleasure we direct attention to those which have been created in England; Mr. Wertheimer is, we understand, a German, but one who is to be regarded as a British subject. We believe the coming of such men among us to be the surest way to benefit ourselves.

The RIBBON patterns occupying this column are from the manufactory of Mr. C. BRAY, of Coventry. The

former of the two designs has a quaint yet elegant

border, and the centre shows two light and graceful patterns. The latter contains a greater variety of beautiful subject, disposed in a highly effective manner.

The manufacture of PAPIER-MÂCHÉ into a great variety of useful articles of large size is the result of the efforts made, within a comparatively recent period, by the various artisans who have devoted their attention to this important branch of the industrial arts.

It is not many years since the limits of the trade were circumscribed to a tea-tray, but now we find articles of furniture, not only of a slight and ornamental character, such as ladies' work-tables or boxes, but of a more substantial kind, in chairs and sofas for the draw-

ing-room, or the entire casings of pianofortes. All such examples of the variety and comprehensive nature of *papier-mâché* works are exhibited by Messrs. JENNENS & BETTRIDGE, of London and Birmingham, and our pages testify to their beauty These manufacturers have earned a reputation by their unceasing endeavours to improve the character of such productions,—a reputation which is certainly well deserved, and which will be increased by their contributions to the Great Exhibition. We commence our series of illustrations with an INKSTAND, designed by H. M'Carthy, a sculptor of great ability, the animals being in oxidised silver; the entire surface of the inkstand is black, and the base upon which the stag stands is ingeniously designed for an envelope-box. We follow with the most novel and beautiful of the series of these manufacturers' works,—the "VICTORIA REGIA" COT, designed by Mr. J. Bell, the eminent sculptor. The body of the cot is nautilus-shaped; it is of a dark tint, upon which is richly emblazoned the rose, nightshade, and poppy. The flowers of the *Victoria regia* decorate the base,

and gracefully curl over the cot as supports for the curtain. The entire fittings are sumptuous in character, but in the best possible taste. Our next example exhibits a very novel and graceful adjunct to the boudoir, in the LOTUS-TABLE, also designed by Mr. J. Bell; it is, perhaps, one of the most original conceptions contributed by the manufacturers whose works we are describing. The floriated decoration which covers its surface is eastern in character, possessing all its elaboration of form, and all its vivid beauty of colour, the effect of the whole being gorgeous in the extreme, but not by any means offensively gaudy, a qualification that is not always duly considered, though it always should be, in works of this class. An improvement is effected by constructing the shaft of the table in the style of a telescope, and allowing each part to be

lifted for use as required. The ELIZABETHAN CHAIR is a favourable specimen of the success

which may attend the manufacturer who fear-

second group comprises a VASE, originally designed for the late Princess Sophia; it is richly

lessly carries out his conceptions in any material, however discouraging it may appear in the outset. The peculiar character of decoration embraced by this style has been effectually preserved, but it has been rendered very light and elegant by the perforated work, and the colouring and gilding, which adorn it. It is remarkably firm and strong, but the ornamentation prevents it from appearing heavy. Of a totally different character is our second CHAIR, in which lightness and gracefulness of contour have been entirely considered, and are well carried out. It is termed the "Légère Chair," and has been provisionally registered by its makers, who seem

to be aware of its claim to popularity. Our

inlaid with mother-of-pearl and gilding on a pink ground. The lady's WORK-TABLE is decorated in the same taste, and is of very novel form. The POMPEIAN FLOWER-STAND is a graceful and elegant ornament to the drawing-room. The WRITING-DESK seen in the foreground is inlaid with imitative gems by the patented process, employed exclusively by this establishment with the happiest effect. The small CROCHET-BOX beside it is ornamented with a classic bas-relief, electro-silvered by Elkington, the subject being the story of Niobe. Our last engraving shows a group of TRAYS, the old staple branch of the trade, which are designed with freedom and decorated with good taste; we give an example of the simplest as well as of the most fanciful, that we may fairly represent these works. The centre one was made for the Duchess of Sutherland; its shape was expressly designed to admit the tea-urn nearer to the dispensers of "the cup which cheers but not inebriates;" the tray to the left is richly inlaid with patent pearl ornaments; the design of the other is plainer.

Mr. G. W. ADAMS, of London, exhibits numerous objects of silver, and silver-gilt plate, of more than ordinary excellence in design. We have selected from his contributions, of which, by the way, he is also the manufacturer, a DESSERT FORK and SPOON, and two DESSERT SUGAR

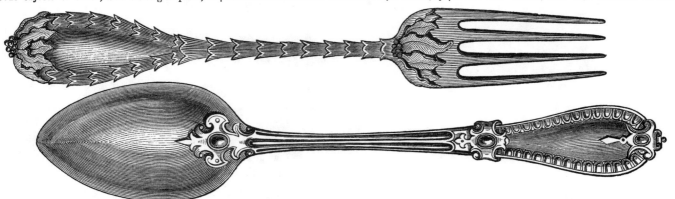

LADLES. The patterns of the former are remarkable for their simple elegance; there is little ornamentation in them, but what there is, shows the best taste. The latter are richer and more elaborate in their design, in which the vine and hop plants, with their respective foliage, are

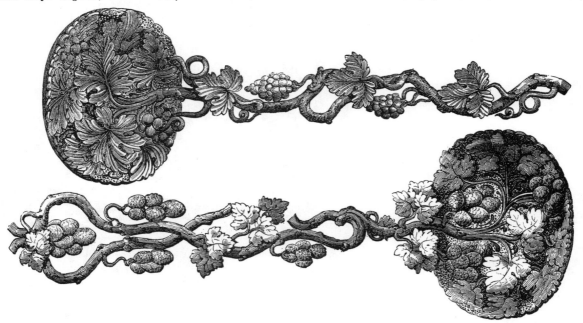

brought in most effectively. The works of our silversmiths undoubtedly exhibit great progress during the last few years; they have certainly kept pace with the increasing taste of the age and the demand for the beautiful, in all matters connected with the chief manufacturing arts.

Liége, for many years famous for its manufactory of fire-arms, shows well in the great Exhibition. We engrave here a most elegantly orna-

mented PISTOL, made by M. MANDAN, of that city; it is certainly as fine a specimen of elaborate engraved work

as we remember to have seen so applied. The design of the decoration is in the Romanesque style, and is displayed with considerable taste.

The three WATCHES, the backs of which we engrave on this column, are manufactured by Mr. W. H. JACKSON, of Clerkenwell; they are

elegantly designed and elaborately engraved.

The internal construction of these watches shows,

we understand, several important improvements.

M. GEERTS, of Louvain, who has been extensively employed by the Belgian government in decorating the town-hall of that city with statuary, and the stalls of the Cathedral of Antwerp with groups of wood-carving, contributes a group of angels, carrying the slaughtered innocents of Herod's massacre heavenward, and comforting an un-

fortunate mother. It is executed in light wood, and expresses a novel and poetic idea embodied in the taste of the mediæval artists who flourished in the Low Countries in the fifteenth and six-

teenth centuries; indeed, the eminent sculptor has been singularly happy in catching the style and spirit exhibited in works of that period, but in a great degree refining upon the school.

Mr. URLING, of London, for many years well known as an extensive manufacturer of lace, contributes a white LACE SCARF, in imitation of Brussels point, ornamented with British plants and flowers in needlework. The date, 1851, is encircled by the rose, thistle, and shamrock. The straight lines of the border are embroidered in gold, and worked upon a fine, clear net, for which Mr. Urling long ago obtained a patent. The design for this scarf was, we believe, made expressly for the manufacturer by Miss Gann, a clever pupil of the Government School of Design.

The CLARET-JUG and TEA-SERVICE are contributed by Mr. DODD, of London, whose taste and knowledge in the art of design are, if we mistake not, the results of considerable artistic experience, which is abundantly manifested in the objects before us. These are manufactured of silver, richly chased; a series of medallions, illustrative of different subjects, occupies the body of each, and the spaces between them are filled in with enrichments, elaborately executed. When we compare such forms and ornaments as these with the works of half a century back, there can be but one opinion as to the progress made.

Some rich and elaborate carving will be seen in the SIDEBOARD, manufactured by Messrs. TROLLOPE & SONS, of London. There is considerable novelty of design in the pillars that form the framework of the glass, while the whole of the carving shows great elegance of design united with exceeding delicacy in the manipulation; it has been executed at a very large cost.

From numerous specimens of engraved and cut GLASS, contributed by Mr. W. NAYLOR, of London, we have selected several and formed them into a group, which will exhibit their

various forms and ornaments to great advantage. The patterns are cut with extreme minuteness.

This column is devoted to a series of VASES, executed in white terra-cotta, by Messrs. DOUL-

TON & WATT, of Lambeth, whose attention has only recently been directed to objects of an

artistic character; those we have engraved may be regarded as a prelude to further success,

which increased experience must insure. The use of terra-cotta, or of artificial stone, as applied

to objects of art and of decoration, is by no means new in this country, although such application has been of late very limited. Half a century since, it was carried on to a great extent by Messrs. Coade, of Lambeth.

The Serpentine Marble Works, established at Penzance, in Cornwall, contribute many examples of this beautiful material. We select a few specimens, more illustrative of form than of colour,

Two of the richly-decorated and admirably constructed Fire-grates of Messrs. Hoole & Robson, of Sheffield, are introduced on this page; other of their productions will appear elsewhere.

These gentlemen are foremost among the best manufacturers of the kingdom; their establishment has been long celebrated, not only for its large extent, but for the admirable skill of its

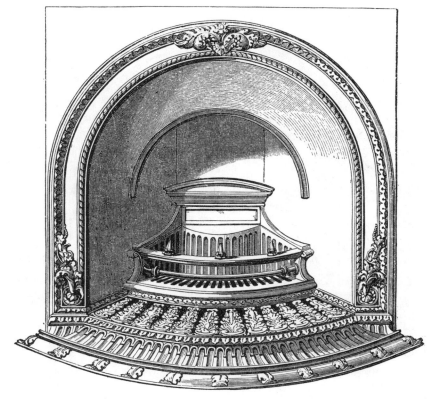

the latter being the most striking recommendation these works possess. The slender Vase at the head of our page, the Font in the centre,

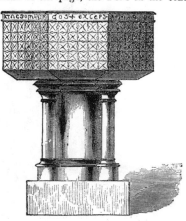

and the Vase at the base, are all beautiful, and are considerably enhanced by the variegated colours which pervade the marble. The geolo-

productions, and their contributions cannot fail to attract very general attention. They were among the first to introduce that happy mingling of brass and or-molu with iron, which, under judicious management, is so effective in giving

grace and elegance to the fire-side; and they have taken especial care to obtain all the advantages which can be derived from the proper application of art to their purposes, employing thoroughly educated artists in the superintend-

gical riches of our own land are, in very many instances, well displayed throughout the British departments of the Exhibition, and strongly testify to their value and beauty.

ence of their works. In this class of manufacture England stands pre-eminent; regard being had, however, to the fact that the English fire-

grate is comparatively unknown upon the continent, and that consequently none of its fabricants have attempted to enter into competition with us.

The art of glass-painting is carried on in England principally at Birmingham and at New-

A group of the VIRGIN and CHILD, by M. VANDER HAGEN, a Belgian sculptor settled in London, will remind those who have studied ecclesiastical sculptures of some of these classical

castle-upon-Tyne; each of these towns boasts of possessing extensive establishments for these beautiful productions, and each is a formidable rival to the other. The ILLUMINATED WINDOW is from the manufactory of Mr. GIBSON, of Newcastle-upon-Tyne; its ornamentation is derived from the early Norman style; fillets of ruby and green, interlacing on a stone-coloured ground, form geometrical compartments; in the top one is the cross, and in the centre of the others are bosses composed of rich colours; the whole design resulting in tracery filled with elaborate ornament, is worked in black outline relieved by shadow; the border is in enamel on a blue ground. This window will be much admired for its gorgeous, yet simple and unpretending effect.

and well-modelled compositions. It is very symmetrical in its proportions, and the drapery is arranged in an easy flowing style, that gives grace and firmness to the principal figure.

The desire to possess decorated weapons of offence and defence belongs not to our age; in the days of chivalry, the knight and the warrior were accustomed to encase themselves in steel and iron "curiously wrought," and felt almost as much pride in the ornaments as in the temper of their good swords. The armourers and sword-cutlers of Brabant competed then with those of Madrid, Toledo, and Damascus, to produce the most elegant examples of their workmanship, many of which are still preserved. Even the introduction of gunpowder only changed the application of their art from armour and swords to guns of every size and description. The GUN-STOCK here engraved is by M. TOUREY, of Liége. It is very elaborately carved, and inlaid with gold, silver, and platina, in the enriched style of the time of Louis the Fourteenth.

A very beautiful example of wood carving is exhibited in a BENETIER by M. KNECHT, of Paris. Its character is well adapted to the style usually followed in ecclesiastical structures, being an arrangement of the vine in Gothic forms; the centre shows the "Virgin and Child," the former treading on the serpent.

The group—the FORTUNE-TELLER—is contributed by Professor WICKMANN, of Berlin, a sculptor of eminent rank in Germany. He is an artist who especially studies grace; his works exhibit exceeding refinement, yet in combination with rigid adherence to truth. This work he has executed in marble; it was designed expressly for the Exhibition. The intention of the sculptor is to tell the story of a young girl "spaeing" the fortune of another.

The work is happily conceived, and wrought with the highest finish. During our visit to Germany in 1850, in the atelier of M. Wickmann, we had the pleasure to examine many other fine examples of the admirable artist's genius, and it will be our privilege to engrave some of them hereafter for the *Art-Journal*. With that view we have received copies from the sculptor, whom we shall hope thus to make better known than he is in England.

A FRIEZE, sculptured in wood by M. LIENARD, of Paris, represents a boar-hunt in the olden time; the party have just come on the lair of the wild animal, and are preparing to attack him. The design is very spirited, the figures are grouped with much pictorial effect, and the work

is boldly yet delicately carved in alto-relievo. M. Lienard is, we believe, a young artist who has acquired very considerable reputation in Paris as a designer, and, judging from the specimens he has sent to the Exhibition, of his own handywork, he can execute with as much skill as he invents. We understand that not a few of the leading Parisian manufacturers of ornamental articles are indebted to him for some of their best designs.

The FLORAL ORNAMENTS, executed in leather, and contributed by Messrs. ESQUILANT & Co., of London, are excellent specimens of this description of manufacture. They are made of the stoutest material, and may be readily mistaken for wood-carvings; hence their peculiar applicability for the internal decoration of houses, and for the saloons of steam-ships, for which it is perhaps more especially adapted, as less liable to split or break off than wood; in fact, where cheapness, durability, and ornament are required, these leather productions are valuable.

An EMBROIDERED CHEMISETTE, designed by J. WAUGH, pupil of the Belfast School of Design,

An example of CARVED WOOD, also by M. LIENARD, of Paris, shows it to be the work of an artist. It is sculptured in alto-relievo; the design has reference to field sports, the three compartments and manufactured in muslin by Mr. J. HOLDEN, of Belfast, is in good taste; it gained the first prize

exhibiting respectively foxes, deer, and partridges; the sides of the centre-frame, birds and hunting implements; while the base supports two or three dogs. Festoons of leaves encircling the frames enrich the composition, and impart to it much elegance by their graceful arrangement. of five pounds, offered by Lord Dufferin last year to the Belfast School, for the best drawing suited to this elegant portion of a lady's dress.

The Ironworks of M. ANDRÉ, of Paris, are of great magnitude, furnishing every kind of ornamental objects which the manufacture of this metal supplies, principally of an importance commensurate with the large resources of the establishment. We have selected, as examples of their productions, a cast-iron group intended for a FOUNTAIN, which is very original in design; all the materials of the composition are drawn from objects associated with water, amphibious

There is a class of manufacturers in France whose artistic talents are more frequently called into requisition than in England,—the makers of window fastenings and long window bolts; we have seen in Paris a large variety of these objects, on which taste and talent of no ordinary kind have been expended. We engrave here a

animals, and aquatic plants. Among the former the chief is a crocodile holding a fish in his mouth, beneath this is an otter to the right, a tortoise to the left, and a large frog at the third angle: from the mouths of these animals the jets of water are intended to rise, and they are surrounded by the water-lily, floating reeds, and bending rushes. The other example is from a

WINDOW-BOLT, by M. COUDRUE, of Paris, as an excellent example of this kind of manufacture; it affords, in its various details, suggestions of which other producers may profitably avail themselves.

The WORK-TABLE which concludes this page is manufactured by Mr. C. F. GRUBB, of Banbury, Oxfordshire. As the production of a self-educated artizan, it shows considerable taste in design, and ingenuity of execution. A wreath of flowers is

cast-iron CHIMNEY-PIECE, in what is called the Louis Quatorze style, a style still much in vogue among the French: such an object so manufactured is a novelty in this country, so far as our observation has extended, and it is one from

which our own manufacturers may, we should think, borrow an idea with no little advantage, though it may be doubted whether iron would ever be extensively used as a substitute for marble in the decoration of first-rate domestic edifices.

carried round the top, from which are suspended sprigs of ivy reaching to the pedestal; this is formed of dock leaves, and at the end of these are seen rabbits, that constitute the feet of the table—a novelty in ornament worthy of notice.

We select from the works of Messrs. GRAINGER, of Worcester, a series of articles which exhibit a

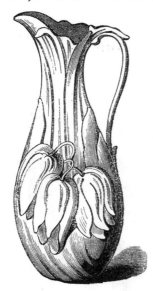

peculiar fancy in design, combined with much

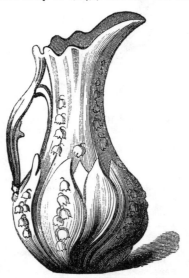

simplicity of decoration. The JUGS are covered

with leaves and flowers, or appear as if constructed with interlaced leaves, a style of ornamentation for which Messrs. Grainger have a peculiar reputation. The difficulty, however, of adapting this mode of decoration to the forms and uses of the articles is considerable: it has been combated with judgment, but not always

simplicity; the few water-leaves which decorate it being applicable and unobtrusive, and the general contour graceful. The COFFEE-SERVICE is a quaint and curious group, designed after the style of the old continental china, but possessing

handles are formed of wheat-ears, with their stalks and leaves. The same decoration forms the boundary line of the tray, also made in china. As a light and elegant service for the boudoir, it possesses attraction; and though with success. We consider some of the objects we engrave as among the curiosities of earthenware manufacture, but are not prepared to enforce their claim to unqualified approval. The EWER and BASON is agreeable from its entire some originalities of its own in the form of its outlines. It is covered with an open honeycomb pattern, which shows the rich blue ground through its perforations—a style of decoration in great vogue more than a century ago. The presenting the appearance of its costly prototype, it is manufactured at a comparatively small cost; indeed, this remark will apply to the generality of works issued from the extensive manufactory of Messrs. Grainger.

The great improvements made of late in all the appointments of "an Englishman's fireside," are visible to the least observant. Stoves of all kinds and forms, fenders of the most fanciful designs, and enrichments of the most classical description, have been freely used in their decoration. We here present a specimen of good taste in FIRE-IRONS, the originals of our group

We present two groups of the works of Messrs. BROADHEAD & ATKIN, manufacturers of silver and plated goods, of Sheffield; they embrace some very good examples of Decorative Art applied to objects of ordinary use, or to those which form the ornamental adjuncts to the

dinner-table. The tea and coffee-pots, with the cream-jug and sugar-basin *en suite*, exhibit a happy rendering of forms with which we are in some degree familiar, but with ornaments presenting the charm of novelty. In the series of illustrations which occupy our Catalogue, a large

number of designs will appear, that have been executed both in clay and metal, to give variety to the breakfast service, and most of them prove

an anxiety to leave a beaten track. Our larger group contains flower-stands, a cake-basket, a claret-jug, and a bottle-stand, all of good design.

being the work of Messrs. H. & W. TURNER, of Sheffield, who have adopted a style of decoration which gives a sufficient amount of ornament, without detracting from the rigid utilitarian principle, so necessary in producing works of this class, and which ought ever to be borne strictly in remembrance by the designer.

We fill this page with a FENDER, to which the manufacturers have given the name of the "snake fender," made by Messrs. JOBSON & Co., Sheffield,

for Mr. W. S. Burton, of London. Other works of Messrs. Jobson, for which we could not arrange in this division, will appear in subsequent pages.

We commence this page with an engraving from the back of a very elegant WATCH, manufactured by MR. JONES, of London. It is ornamented in a rich, elaborate, and tasteful style.

The BAROMETER is manufactured by MR. DOBBIE, of Falkirk; it claims merit as being made on a plan by which the least possible rise or fall

MR. A. PELLATT, of London, exhibits a TEA-SERVICE with its TRAY, designed by Mr. Binns, which he designates the "Bridal Breakfast Ser-

vice," and especially intended for a bridal present. It is painted with emblems, adapted to such an auspicious event, in the language of flowers.

A piece of TAPESTRY, for a screen, worked in heraldic patterns by MISS BIFIELD, of Islington, aided by a large number of her pupils, is a very ingenious and clever specimen of needlework. It is unnecessary to explain the armorial bearings, which are sufficiently well known, except perhaps the two lowest; these

of the mercury is ascertained with the greatest precision. The case is richly and carefully carved.

are the arms of the Duke of Wellington and of the late Sir Robert Peel, significant of the great military and political leaders of the present age. Each quartering is worked on a separate portion of velvet, and afterwards carefully united so as to form an entire piece.

We may presume to say that there is no class of manufacturers whose talents seem to have been brought out with more success than those engaged in the various branches of cabinet-work; and there is, perhaps, no description of manufacture in which taste, ingenuity, and artistic skill may be more effectively exercised. Furniture, whether useful or merely ornamental, at once reveals its own story of the degree of talent and the length of time devoted to its execution; all connected with it, to use a homely phrase, is plain and aboveboard, and the eye cannot be deceived by false appearances, nor lured to admire by the display of glittering colours, as is the case in many other operative arts. The SIDEBOARD introduced here is manufactured and exhibited by Messrs. HOWARD & SON, of London; the back and front are inlaid with fine plate glass, enriched by carved floriated ornaments of "cunning workmanship" in the Italian style.

Our next subject is a CARPET contributed by WATSON, BELL, & Co., of London; the ground-work of this carpet is simple but in good taste: the centre, however, and the border are rich and massive in design, and most effective in the arrangement of their well-selected colours.

This page contains specimens of JEWELLERY, produced by Messrs. WATHERSTON & BROGDEN, of London; eminent manu-

facturers, who have studied to combine richness of material with beauty of design and skill in arrangement. The

contributions exhibited are of great value, but they will attract attention less from their actual worth than from the ability they manifest; they will be worthy competitors with those continental pro-

ductions which have established the fame of so many fabricants, especially of France, to whom, until very re-

cently, we appeared willing to yield the palm without dispute. The bracelet which heads the page was suggested by one of the Nineveh monuments; the brooches, or more properly, breast ornaments which follow, several of which are deduced from

flowers and leaves, are chiefly composed of enamels united with precious stones.

The STATUE of Cupid is the work of Mr. P. MAC DOWELL, R.A., whose well-earned reputation as a sculptor of high merit it is unnecessary to dilate upon. He here represents the winged boy in the act of drawing a shaft from his quiver.

Few of our readers who may not have seen the original of the annexed engraving will have any idea from what it has been copied; it is, in fact, a CAKE, from the celebrated establishment of Mr. GUNTER, of London, who has employed a clever Italian artist, M. Conté, to design it for him, and to model the elegant little figures which ornament the base. The work reflects credit to all parties concerned in producing it, and is worthy of being perpetuated in more enduring material.

The CHIMNEY-PIECE is exhibited by Messrs. BRINE, BROTHERS, of London, and manufactured after a design by Mr. T. Sharp. It is elaborately carved in statuary marble, with cast metal ornaments, electro-gilt, mounted on the pilasters, frieze, and spandrils. In the last are the initials

of the Queen and Prince Albert, formed with the stems of the rose, shamrock, and thistle, which entwine them. The work is nine feet high.

The beautiful decorative IRON CUP here intro- | duced is by M. FALLOISE, of Liége. The upper

shows the interior, with its varied enrich- | ments. The ornamentation is of the time of

Francis I., a period when the arts of all kinds | had reached a high point of civilisation.

The Jewellery of M. LEVY PRINS, of Brussels, has achieved celebrity in the capital of Belgium; and will not be without many admirers in our own. There is much of novelty in the arrange-

ment of the leading lines, which give the contour to each of his bijoux; and there is also con- siderable fancy in the combination of flowers, leaves, and jewels, that make up the composition.

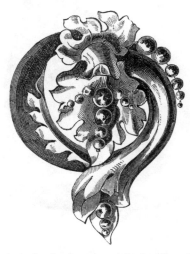

The taste for floral ornament in jewellery has been very prevalent of late; and it is a good and a happy taste, inasmuch as the brilliant colouring of an enamelled leaf or floret is an

excellent foil to a sparkling stone; and we have scarcely seen the designs for jewellery at any period more tasteful, elegant, and appropriate, than they are at the present day. There is a wholesome novelty about these designs, which tends to strengthen the well-grounded belief that the manufacturer in brooches is about to leave the beaten track, and to study for himself,

and give the result to the world in a free untrammelled spirit. The demand for novelty in such articles as these is incessant, and we are sure that the workman who can best supply that

demand in a really original as well as tasteful manner, will surely meet his reward. The continental manufacturer has hitherto had the largest share of merit awarded to him for design, but for

execution and sterling goodness of material, we believe our own workmen to be as unrivalled in this as in other branches of Industrial Art. There cannot, however, be a doubt that he may still learn the other qualifications from his continental neighbour, which, when he has achieved, may make him regardless of dangerous rivalry.

This Cup, by M. FALLOISE, of Liége, is of iron; the ornament

upon it is of the most delicate and fanciful kind, and is produced by

cutting the surface away into the various forms | required, and inlaying it with gold and silver;

the variety of tint obtained by this means is very | pleasing; the SHIELD is also similarly enriched.

The china-works of Messrs. CHAMBERLAIN, of Worcester, will uphold the reputation of the long-established "Royal Porcelain Works,"—an industrial foundation which belongs to the his-

tory of English ceramic manufactures, and which has flourished for more than a century in "the faithful city" of its location. It would be difficult, in the present day, for new manufacturers

to obtain the same amount of *éclat* which attached itself to some of "the old houses" in by-gone times; a fact which may be accounted for in the quality of the competition everywhere

around them. Achieving a celebrity so long since, the Messrs. Chamberlain have retained it in the specimens they now contribute to our Industrial Congress in Hyde Park, inasmuch as

they are elegant in form, and beautiful in decoration. Our cuts will give faithful ideas of their *contours*, although they can but hint at the

at the head of our page are of antique simplicity, appropriately decorated with scriptural scenes, their general surface being entirely covered with

ing another of our groups, the SCENT-BOTTLE being an exceedingly graceful and elegant adjunct to the boudoir. The honeycomb pattern is, we

will not fail to note the excellence of the painting in many of the articles contributed by this firm.

the praise of substantial excellence to the productions of Messrs. Chamberlain, and are glad to

colours which enrich them. The VASES are generally of good form, and present much variety. The COMMUNION-CUPS and WINE-FLAGON an open honeycomb pattern, giving them great delicacy and richness. The same style of enrichment has been adopted in the articles form- believe, peculiar to this establishment; we are not aware that examples of its peculiar character have been produced elsewhere. The observer They have, indeed, always aimed at superiority in this department. Altogether, we can award see our elder fabricants still vigorous in the field, and still upholding the honour of our native trade.

MR. WOODRUFF, of Bakewell in Derbyshire, contributes some TABLES constructed of the

We engrave underneath the centre of a COUNTERPANE, which exhibits considerable improvement over the ordinary style adopted with so

monotonous an effect in articles of the kind. It is the work of a hand-loom weaver, JOSIAH LUDWORTH, of Bolton. The peculiar description

of bed-cover, called counterpane (from *countre-point*) is not now made extensively, except of a very low quality; it is of the most durable kind, but has been supplanted by *quilts*, on which the pattern is produced by the Jacquard loom. The knots or loops which form the pattern engraved

are pulled up by the hand with a small steel instrument, similar to a shoemaker's awl. This operation has been performed on this counterpane no fewer than 844,800 times. The article is creditable to the industry of an ingenious workman; and as such we have engraved it.

spars of the county, in Mosaic. We engrave a Vase of black marble, and the border of a CHESS-

TABLE, both remarkable for simplicity and taste.

A TABLE-TOP executed in glass mosaic by Mr. H. STEVENS, of Pimlico, is an example of the artist's ingenuity in adapting his materials to the composition of a good design, and of his patient industry in perfecting his work. Mr. Stevens exhibits several objects of a similar character, heraldic designs, pedestals, &c., all of

which have a brilliant effect in the variously coloured glass of which they are made. This glass mosaic is coming into fashion for ornamenting fire-places in drawing-rooms, and for decorative objects in large halls, for which it seems to be adapted, and where the colours are introduced with judgment, the work is very beautiful.

The two pages which follow, contain the contributions in PORCELAIN and EARTHENWARE of Mr. JOHN RIDGWAY, of Cauldron Place, Staffordshire Potteries. They exhibit examples of the useful rather than the ornamental; Mr. Ridgway's attention having been more especially

and discharge pipes attached, and to be screwed down to the floor." But it will be perceived that although the usefulness of these articles has been the primary consideration, their elegance has also been properly cared for, and they are really graceful additions to the dressing-room, free of the trouble attendant on the use of the ordinary ewer and basin. Another novelty

they generally are, at prices which confine them exclusively to the rich. We have always fully appreciated the value of decorative Art, and, sometimes, had to deplore the want of a judicious acquaintance therewith in our manufactories; yet, while we are willing to bestow

directed to improvements in the forms and decoration of objects which are the wants of every day. The establishment of Mr. Ridgway is one of the largest, and among the best conducted, of the many factories of Staffordshire; and there is no manufacturer who has obtained higher reputation for the excellence of the materials employed. The works exhibited by him will demand consideration on this ground. We first engrave two of several "Fountain Hand-basins"—objects which Mr. Ridgway devised in order to meet a suggestion of the Board of Health, for a frequent and easy supply of pure water, and facilities for the rapid disposal of water that has been used. "These vessels may

appears on our page, a STAIR-RAIL, also made in earthenware, and susceptible of much that is ornamental in painting and gilding; there is a lightness and an elegance in this object, not without a peculiar value, when used appropriately, for terraces, &c. The large group delineates a graceful TEA-SERVICE, remarkable for its simplicity. The amount of decoration is but small, but it is good of its kind, and as symmetry of contour has been chiefly considered, as well as that recommendable quality, economy, we cannot but think it has claims to attention on these heads. We must be understood, in some instances, to be doing what we trust the public may also do, when we award due merit to all manufacturers who endeavour to improve ordinary articles of domestic use, while they do not, at

commendation, when deserved, on the ornamental articles which now meet the eye at every turn, and testify to the enlarged acquaintance of our mechanical designers with the leading principles of elegance, we are not the less prepared to give the meed of praise to the simple, the tasteful, and the economic works, which are to render pleasure as well as service to the humbler classes. We also frequently see, with satisfaction, a simple treatment adopted even for expensive works; it is not elaboration of ornament which makes elegance, or gives dignity to design, a fact with

be fixed by any plumber conversant with such work. They require neither wood nor brick-work about them, but simply to have the supply

the same time, too greatly tax the buyer. There is as great a merit in this as in the production of articles of higher elaboration, produced, as

which all who have studied Classic Art are sufficiently familiar. The principal pieces of a DINNER-SERVICE, which fill another of our columns, are equally remarkable for the simplicity with which they are designed. The ornament upon them is of the most unpretending kind, and all the better for its unobtrusiveness. It consists entirely of a few simple scrolls and fanciful leaves,

which form the handles or encircle the bases of the various articles upon which they are introduced. The general form of each article is well preserved, and its elegance enhanced by the contrast afforded in the ornament thus sparingly in-

troduced; and the result is exceedingly satisfactory. The FOUNTAINS are of a more ambitious character, and they may also be considered as novelties. The purity of well-glazed pottery gives it a peculiar applicability for such a purpose, and

the happy manner in which its surface might be rendered agreeable to the eye, by the decoration so readily placed on it, should give it a claim to the attention of persons of taste. Flowers and foliage, or tints of varied hue, might give variety

and beauty to such decorative adjuncts to the garden, of which none of the generally-used materials are equally susceptible; and the "coolness" of their appearance, a particularly acceptable quality in those seasons when gardens and fountains are especially agreeable, is also considerably enhanced, when formed of porcelain. The upper fountain of the two which we engrave, is designed in the taste of the seventeenth century, and is, therefore, to be considered as a type of a peculiar style, which was sometimes introduced

with good effect on old Delft ware, and occasionally appeared as a centre for the dinner-table. It is susceptible of bright masses of colour, the boldness of its surfaces, as well as their occasional angularity, affording full scope for this. Our second example is more classic in its outline, and elegant in its proportion; floral ornament is sparingly

introduced on its surface, and its general effect is that of chaste simplicity. It will at once be apparent that there is a decided "opening" for such a branch of pottery-manufacture; one that will much add to the reputation of the Staffordshire manufacturer if taste be properly directed; and one that will be welcomed in the present day, when so much is required and patronised by persons of refinement; we trust

the "fitness" of articles for the localities to which they are to be devoted may be more carefully studied than has been our wont in years gone by; this object, which should be scrupulously considered and provided for by the manufacturer, would achieve entire success. Mr. Ridgway is an extensive as well as a valuable contributor to the Exhibition, as they who know his establishment might have expected.

A BOOK-COVER, manufactured by Mr. LEIGHTON, of London, from a drawing by his son, is worthy of commendation. It was designed for an edition of Thomson's "Seasons;" the four great divisions of the year are, there-

fore, stamped upon it round a circle, on which appear the twelve signs of the zodiac; in the centre, a floral group, comprises the crocus of spring, the rose of summer, the ripe corn of autumn, and the holly of Christmas.

THE GIRL WITH A HOOP is a charming little figure, sculptured in marble, by Mr. WEEKS, of London. The statue stands about four feet high, and is the portrait of a young lady; but the composition is

purely ideal, and intended to show that portrait-sculpture may be so treated as to contain as much fancy as works that are entirely inventive. Mr. Weeks holds high and deserved rank among British sculptors.

We introduce on this page one of the RIBBONS contributed by Messrs. Cox & Co., of London and Coventry; the design is graceful and effective, and may be accepted as one of the proofs of our progress in competition with our more advanced neighbours of the continent.

The two subjects which occupy this page are from a TABLE-COVER and a CARPET, manufactured by Messrs. TEMPLETON & Co., of Glasgow. They are termed by the makers, "Patent Axminster," from their close resemblance to the costly and well-known carpets first made at Axminster; the

difference being that the latter are composed of separate "tufts" tied in by the hand, while Messrs. Templeton's manufactures are entirely woven, a process which originated in their establishment. We need scarcely remark that the softness, beauty, and richness of these fabrics

are all that the most luxurious can desire. The first of our engravings exhibits a most elaborate pattern of floriated ornament; that of the other consists of flowers and scroll-work, in Louis Quatorze style. About four hundred pairs of hands are employed in this establishment.

Mr. J. SPARKES HALL, of London, exhibits many improvements in modern BOOTS and SHOES, together with a curious series of well executed

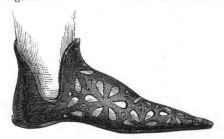

fac-similes of ancient ones. The first and second of our cuts are copied from originals of the

fourteenth century; the third is a fac-simile of the late Duchess of York's shoe, which was re-

markable for its smallness. His modern improvements exhibit an ingenious adaptation of

Honiton lace to ladies' shoes; we engrave a slipper of blue satin thus decorated for the Queen;

also the front of a shoe in vulcanised india-rubber, upon which a rich pattern is imprinted in gold;

and a model slipper of perforated leather, showing blue silk beneath the ornament decorated with tambour stitching and lace rosettes.

The bronze manufactory of M. VITTOZ, of Paris, supplies the GROUP OF VASES and the CLOCK engraved below. The former are modelled after the best antiques, presenting great beauty of outline, and are embellished with some exqui-

sitely wrought classical designs. The latter forms the centre-piece to a candelabrum; the figures are of bronze, the ornaments and dial of plain gold, the hands and indices of burnished gold. The boldness and breadth of the compo-

sition are strikingly apparent; there is an entire absence of everything approaching to *petitesse* in its details, the introduction of which would have marred the noble simplicity of the design. The

base of the clock serves as a pedestal to a well-modelled figure of Michel Angelo. The whole is placed on a stand of black marble, of sexagonal form. At the establishment of M. Vittoz

are produced some of the largest bronze works made in Paris, as well as the more delicate and elaborate objects for merely ornamental pur-

poses. Among these, we saw a few months since a large number of fine statuettes, and a life-size figure of a dead Christ, from the model of Priault.

The engraving that commences this page is a portion of a TABLE-COVER, designed by Mr. Gruner, (of high reputation as a designer,) and executed by MRS. PURCELL and her assistants, in silks and wools. The pattern, in all its varied compartments, is very beautiful, full of subject, yet clear, distinct, and carried out with a definite purpose; there is no portion of it which may not be made suggestive to a variety of manufactures. The execution of the tapestry by Mrs. Purcell is most perfect; this, however, might be looked for in one who, we believe, was trained in the school of the late Miss Linwood, whose exhibition of needlework was, it will be remembered, for many years, among the popular sights of the metropolis.

The group below consists of GLASS objects, contributed by MR. J. G. GREEN, of London; they are of the purest crystal, engraved in the most elaborate and artistic style; the forms are borrowed from the best antiques. The large Jug to the left is termed the "Neptune Jug," a representation of that deity being depicted upon it: next to this is a Cream-jug, ornamented with a kind of arabesque pattern. The two large Jugs

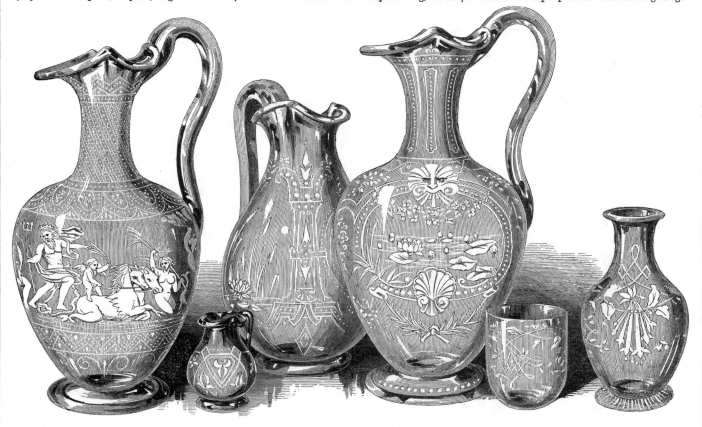

that succeed are beautifully decorated with various devices, in which the water-lily takes a prominent place. The other objects are a Water-caraft and Tumbler, adorned with the fuschia-plant. We scarcely ever remember to have seen glass more exquisitely engraved than in these specimens.

The group of CUPID and the NYMPH is by Mr. THRUPP, of London, one of the most rising sculptors of the English school; the subject is treated with considerable originality as well as with much artistic feeling. The Nymph seems to be persuading the boy to direct his shaft towards a certain object, which Cupid appears averse to do; it is evidently a matter for consideration.

The designs for BERLIN WOOL-WORK which fill the present column are exhibited by Mr. ANDREW HALL, of Manchester, and are constructed on an improved plan, which places the outline on the canvas or foundation to be worked, together with many of the colours indicated in their

places; only leaving it to the worker to increase the number of shades by which the requisite softness will be produced. By this means the constant necessity for counting the threads is obviated, errors in counting are avoided, and the

sight is less taxed. The interlaced patterns we select are simple and good in design; the slipper is decorated with ivy leaves and berries, and is novel and effective. The taste for embroidery has ranked high amongst the elegant arts of

The three DECANTERS which are next introduced are from Mr. SUMMERFIELD, of London, whose manufactory is at Birmingham, and is carried on under the name of Lloyd & Summerfield. These

objects are of the purest cut crystal, ornamented with much novelty of design, the forms whereof being in very bold relief, bring out the colour of the glass in an exceedingly brilliant style.

refined life in past ages, and modern experience teaches us that it still maintains its position; it well becomes the manufacturer therefore to devote his attention to this widely-spread taste, and endeavour to obviate any tendency to common-place imbecility of design in its pursuit.

To the contributions of Messrs. FEETHAM, of London, we shall endeavour to do justice in other pages of our catalogue. They consist of hardware, and comprise the ordinary productions

of the trade,—of excellent design and manufacture. We occupy part of the first column of this page with a few of the minor articles of this

firm : an IRON KNOCKER, the heads of FIRE IRONS, and three metal BELL-PULLS. It is scarcely necessary to say that if our selections were not thus

limited, we should be able to afford a far more adequate idea of their works; they add considerably to the exhibition of British Industrial Art.

SHEFFIELD has been long famous for its manufacture of cutlery, and the improvement exhibited in all its various branches of the trade we have already had occasion to note. Mr. G. WILKINSON, one of its best SCISSORS-MAKERS, has contributed some specimens of his own peculiar art which

formed of the lily of the valley and its leaves, are very tasteful. There is quaintness, as well as elegance, in the other designs. In fact, restricted as design may appear to be when applied to so simple

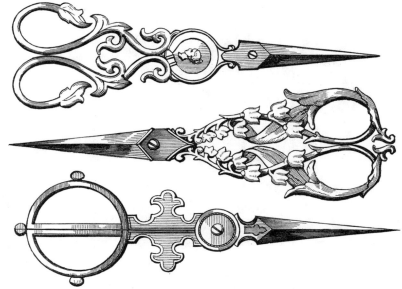

as a coat-of-arms to this purpose. The arms, supporters, crest, and motto of the Cavendish family are made to do duty in this way without any disagreeable result. We conclude our series

fully bear out the deserved reputation of that enterprising town. The first on our page has been manufactured by him for the "Indian Steel Company," and is of much delicacy and elegance of design. The group which follows presents great novelty of form; the flowing curves of the handle,

a thing as the handle of a pair of scissors, it is surprising how varied it may be made through the aid of a clever designer. We present an ingenious adaptation of so unpromising a subject

with a large pair of scissors, which also have "the charm of novelty." Sheffield, in this branch of Industrial Art, has maintained its supremacy, and defied the world, for more than

a century. We have no fear of its losing the rank it has obtained. During a recent visit, we were offered, by one manufacturer of scissors, the means to examine no fewer than 7000 executed designs. Mr. Wilkinson has not only studied to improve the forms of objects of a comparatively costly character; he has very essentially improved the commonest articles of

his produce, so as to make them more convenient as well as more elegant. This advance is especially shown by comparing the tailor's shears of his manufacture with those in ordinary use, and especially the scissors constructed with a very simple spring, so as to open and close with facility.

From a variety of fine SCULPTURES exhibited by Mr. THOMAS, of London, we have selected five examples, to show his diversified talent and taste in those objects to which this branch of the fine arts is most generally applied. Mr. Thomas has for a series of years been engaged under Mr. Barry, in

unwearied, and his success has kept pace with his exertions. Many of the

modelling the ornamental details of the New Palace of Westminster, and in sculpturing several of the figures with which it is already decorated, and others which are destined hereafter to find a place in that magnificent edifice. His labours in this important and arduous undertaking have been

aristocratic mansions throughout this country can also testify to the varied

character of his natural and acquired endowments as an architect, sculptor, decorator, and designer, in all of which professions he seems equally at home. The first group we have here engraved is entitled CHARITY, it is intended for part of a monumental group; the treatment of the subject is most artistic, and the sentiment conveyed is perfectly in unison with the title. By the side of this is an engraving of a bronze figure from Shakespeare's "Tempest," ARIEL DIRECTING THE STORM; Mr. Thomas's conception of the character is very spirited. Below these figures is a CHIMNEY-PIECE for Preston Hall, the new mansion of Mr. E. L. BETTS; the subjects on it are Dorigene and Griselda, from Chaucer, with a medallion of the poet in the centre, and on either side of the principal figures a bas-relief carrying out the incidents of each: the stove and fender which are to be placed here, we purpose engraving elsewhere. The statue of FAIR ROSAMOND follows on this page, a work of goodly proportions, telling its own pathetic tale: and lastly a FOUNTAIN, of which the subject is "Acis and Galatea" surrounded by Tritons; this, like the chimney-piece, has been executed for Mr. Betts's mansion.

ROSOMONDA.

A PIANO-FORTE, by Messrs. BROADWOOD, of London, the eminent makers, is an elegant example of the taste they frequently display in the manufacture of their instruments. The legs, and such portions of the case as admit of decoration, have been judiciously supplied with it in the rich

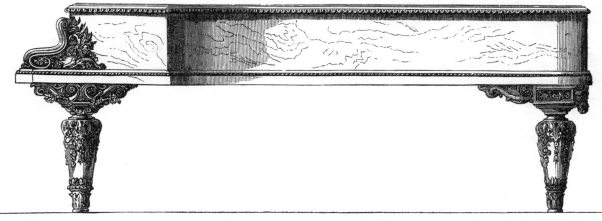

style of Italian ornament. The case of this instrument, which is made of the beautiful Amboyna wood, was manufactured by Mr. Morant, of London.

This page commences with a PORTFOLIO-TABLE, carved and inlaid; and an EBONY TRIPOD, both manufactured by Mr. WILLIAM JONES, of Maescalad, Dolgelly, N. Wales, from designs furnished by a gentleman of that neighbourhood, Mr. H. Reveley: these contributions, from a place so far removed from the great marts of operative industry, are highly creditable to the parties who have brought them forward. The table is

intended for displaying a portfolio or book of large prints; the top of it lifts up like a reading-desk, as seen in the engraving, and its great recommendation is that it avoids the necessity of stooping. By removing the ledges in the front and sides, it is converted into a table for the purposes of writing, drawing, &c. Mr. Jones is, we understand, a person who has raised himself from the condition of an ordinary carpenter to one of considerable provincial eminence as an ornamental carver in wood.

Among the numerous contributions from Germany is a SECRETAIRE, by M. VON HAGEN, of Erfurt. It is made of walnut-wood, the design is in

Our next subject is a HOT-AIR STOVE, made by Messrs. LEARNED & THATCHER, Albany, United States; it is intended for a drawing-room or parlour, and consequently is manufactured with a considerable amount of tasteful ornament to render it suitable for its destination. There is doubtless some peculiarity in its internal construction with which we are unacquainted, for the drawing supplied to us from America speaks of the

stove being patented. The basin at the top holds, we presume, water, as we have seen in similar articles in our own country; and in this basin is placed a small vase of coloured glass, probably for the same purpose: the latter gives a judicious finish to the entire object, which is one highly creditable to the manufacturers as both useful and ornamental.

the Renaissance style, and it is beautifully ornamented with inlaid ivory, ebony, and brass, forming altogether a good example of manufacturing art.

This engraving is from an improved ventilating STOVE GRATE, manufactured by Mr JEAKES, of London: we introduce it chiefly on account of its excellent ornamental character, but it possesses recommendations that entitle it to extensive use; the principle of these is that, when heated, it emits no unhealthy effluvium.

A musical instrument called a GUITARPA occupies this column: it is invented and constructed by DON JOSE GALLEGOS, of Malaga. The tone of this ingenious piece of mechanism comprises that of the harp, guitar, and violoncello; it has thirty-five strings, twenty-six of which and twenty-one pegs act upon the harp,

We introduce here a REVOLVING TABLE, for the use of sculptors and modellers, manufactured by PALMER & CO., Brighton, after a model by San Giovanni, the

sculptor. It is to enable sculptors to turn round with facility any object upon which they may be at work. It is equally applicable for showing busts or statues.

producing in their full extent the diatonic and chromatic scales: six strings belong to the part of the Spanish guitar, while the violoncello part has three silver strings and eighteen pegs. The pedestal by which it is supported is so constructed that the instrument may be either elevated or depressed at pleasure.

MESSRS. RANSOME & PARSONS, of Ipswich, exhibit, among other articles, the VASES, in artificial stone, which we have selected for engraving:

we do this, however, rather with reference to the material than to the forms, which, though

good, are not new. The material differs from all other artificial productions for similar pur-

poses, flint forming its basis; it may be made to imitate any description of stone, from the finest marble to the coarsest and commonest sandstone.

The town of Wolverhampton is a formidable rival to Birmingham in the extent of its manufactures in papier-mâché, and its light iron-ware productions of every kind. It is almost impossible to enumerate the variety of articles included in this category; but we may in particular, allude to tea-trays of every description, coal-vases, candlesticks, bread-baskets, ornamental baskets,

&c., &c. The business transactions in these and similar manufactures, are most extensive, both for the home market and for exportation. Messrs. WALTON & Co., of Wolverhampton, are among its chief manufacturers, and, consequently, their contributions to the Great Exhibition are on a proportionate scale of magnitude and importance, including a large variety of trays, sundry

vases, tazzi, coal-scoops, dish-covers, &c. On this and the following columns we engrave six subjects —a Tazza, a Coal-vase, and four Trays, all, excepting the second, made of papier-mâché. The TAZZA is decorated with Roman ornaments in gold and colours; the COAL-VASE is also ornamented with the same materials. The Trays show the several styles of the Byzan-

tine, the German Gothic, the Renaissance, the Alhambresque, and the Elizabethan, worked in gold, pearls, and colours. Many of the manufactures contributed by Messrs. Walton are painted with much taste and elegance, as representations of landscapes, and historical and fancy scenes. The perfect adhesion of an opaque glass fused by heat on the surface of wrought iron, so

has long been considered a great desideratum by all manufacturers of hardware; this object

two kinds of enamel; that intended for better purposes is of a pure white colour, that ıpon

expensive, and is equally effective and durable:

as to produce a smooth and even enamel, capable of withstanding the effects of the atmosphere, Messrs. Walton & Co. seem to have successfully attained. The articles shown are covered with more common goods is black, and is applied to coat the articles both inside and out. It is less the contributions of this firm are very attractive.

A FLOWER-HOLDER, manufactured by Mr. BALLENY, of Birmingham, is well and appropriately designed; the cup exhibits grapes and leaves of the vine, the stem of which is twisted into a handle.

A CARRIAGE-LAMP, contributed by Messrs. HALLMARKE, ALDEBERT, & Co., of London, forms the subject of the annexed engraving. It is made of the finest and most massive glass, beau-

tifully cut and set in silver; it is, altogether, one of the richest and most creditable specimens of such articles we remember to have seen.

A piece of SILK. contributed by the Committee of the SPITALFIELDS SCHOOL of DESIGN, shows much beauty of pattern, which is composed of groups of flowers, with fern leaves and trails of ivy; it is designed by the present assistant-master, Mr. Brown, who was a pupil of the school.

A BEEHIVE, designed by Mr. W. WILSON, of Berwick-upon-Tweed, exhibits a novel and good form, applied to a

We introduce here a HALL STOVE, manufactured by M. H. C. GRAAMANS, of Rotterdam; it possesses nothing new in its shape, but the ornamentation is in good taste, and stands out in bold relief from the flat. The Dutch have long been celebrated for

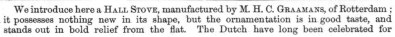

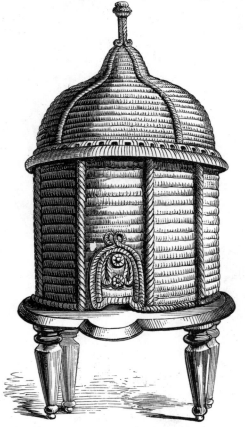

common object; one that might be made an ornament to the garden. It is the work of a highly ingenious artisan.

their decorative furniture of every description; much of their carved work finds its way to England, and several contributions in this style will be found in the Exhibition.

The VASE beneath, and the FAN-LIGHT, or, as the French term it, the *Oeil de Bœuf*, commencing the next column, are made of white terra-cotta, by M. GARNAUD, Jun., of Paris. The former is of considerable size, presenting an agreeable adaptation of somewhat novel ornament to an antique form. The fan-light is, of course, intended to surmount a doorway; it is about five feet in width, by three feet and a half in height. The material is very durable, and possesses the advantage of being far cheaper than stone, to which it bears a strong resemblance; it is much used in Paris for all kinds of architectural decoration.

The engraving that follows is a portion of a very elegant CARPET, contributed by Messrs. WHITE, SON, & Co., of London. The pattern of the ground consists of a few well-arranged sprigs, and is, accordingly, very simple; but the centre, the corners, and the border present features of great boldness and beauty. The wreaths of flowers on the last portion, and the shells and scroll-work on the corners, exhibit taste in the

designer of no common kind; nor will the pattern of the inner border fail to attract the attention of all who estimate purity of character in ornamental work. This design emanates from Messrs. White & Co., who are, consequently, its proprietors; they exhibit several other excellent productions.

A fine damask linen TABLE-CLOTH, manufactured by Messrs. HUNT and SON, of Dunfermline, is here introduced. It was made expressly for the use of Her Majesty when sojourning at her home in the Highlands, and is, therefore, most appropriately adorned in the centre with a view of the Castle of Balmoral. The borders present illustrations applicable to the healthy and manly amusements pursued by Prince Albert and the visitors to the Royal residence, especially that of deer-stalking, and the spaces are filled with some of the natural productions of the mountain and the glen.

' On this page we exhibit another of the RIBBONS manufactured by Messrs. Cox, of London and Coventry. Those who are acquainted with the ancient and venerable city are well aware of the immense advances they have made of late years, not only in design, to which we believe the Government school has very largely contributed, but in the study and application of colours, and especially in the process of dyeing.

Mr. BLAKELY, of Norwich, contributes some splendid SHAWLS, woven expressly for the Exhibition. Our space does not permit us to enlarge upon the beauty and merits of those we have here engraved; it must suffice to say they are of the very best order of design, material, and

workmanship. Norwich has long been famous | for this description of manufacture; it will lose | none of its credit in the Great Exhibition.

Messrs. PAYNE & SONS, of Bath, contribute a VASE, in silver, after a marble antique in the Capitoline Museum. It is enriched with bold and highly relieved foliage and interlacing flower scrolls, the handles springing from Silenus' heads. The work is a very elegant specimen of art, and highly creditable to a provincial manufacturer.

We follow with a VASE formed of very different material : it is of terra-cotta, designed by the distinguished sculptor, and architect, Mr. John Thomas, and is contributed by EDWARD BETTS, Esq., who, having discovered a valuable vein of rich clay on his estate, at Aylesford, in Kent, has established a pottery there in order to make it serviceable to Art as well as for purposes

of utility in agriculture and in manufactures. We shall heartily rejoice if this project succeed : at present, it is notorious that in England with "all appliances and means," we have, of late years, almost entirely neglected this branch of Art.

M. FRAIKIN, the eminent sculptor of Brussels, has contributed some of the poetical works for which he is so justly famed. Among others, he has sent to the Exhibition the kneeling figure here engraved ; it represents a damsel, quaintly habited in the taste of the fifteenth century, in an attitude of devotion ; the figure is remarkable for its purity of treatment and delicacy of expression.

The musical instrument is manufactured by Messrs. LUFF & Co., of London. It is termed an HARMONIUM. We, of course, have had no opportunity of testing its merits as a musical instrument, but, knowing that this long-established firm bears good repute in the profession,

there is no doubt of its possessing excellencies in this respect, which we must leave to others more competent than ourselves to decide. We can testify to the elegance of its external appearance.

Throughout the task we have undertaken, to prepare this "Illustrated Catalogue," we have scrupulously avoided instituting a comparison between the works of any one manufacturer and those of another, whether of our own country or from foreign lands. Our object is to select, according to our best judgment, whatever is most beautiful and most worthy of being singled

out from the great mass of contributions for especial notice, let who may be its producer.

On this occasion the critic's pen is used only to describe and to eulogise; were it desirable to

use it as generally applied, we might sometimes be tempted to enter upon the comparative merits of many of those works we have had the opportunity of inspecting, both in the Exhibition and in the ateliers of the fabricators. It will, however, be thought by all who are fortunate enough to get a sight of the most ex-

quisite Tea and Coffee Service, manufactured by M. Durand, of Paris, that any work of a similar character brought into competition with it will be put to a severe test, so pure is the taste that has designed, and so skilful are the hands that have been engaged in working it out. The whole service is of massive silver, modelled, chased, and engraved in the very first style of

placed; the body of the tripod forms a tea-urn, and on the plateau at its base stand the coffee-pot and the tea-pot; the tea-cups and coffee-cups are ranged round the bottom. It may readily be imagined, when the whole are "placed in position," how superb an appearance is presented by such a combination of truly rich and costly

art. It is valued at forty thousand francs. The centre-piece stands about four feet high; the figures introduced into it are of bronze, which affords a striking and effective contrast to the white metal. Midway in the centre-piece are four baskets for cakes, &c.; the angles of the tripod support each a small vase, on which the cream-jug, sugar-basin, and water-basin are

objects. Besides the centre-piece, we have engraved the cream-jug, the sugar-basin, and the tea-pot; it will, of course, be seen that neither of these is engraved to its proper scale of size, but drawn to suit our column. The coffee-pot and water-basin are *en suite*. We regret we could not arrange for their introduction also.

The next engraving is from a piece of WOOD-CARVING, exhibited by Mr. RINGHAM, of Ipswich. It is composed of wheat and wild flowers, and is executed with considerable spirit and freedom.

A GLOBE, manufactured by Messrs. JOHNSTON, of Edinburgh, is a beautiful work of manufactured art, showing some fine carved work, the principal features of which apply to the subject.

The corner of this page is occupied by an engraving of a HALL or OFFICE STOVE, manufactured by Messrs. ROBERTSON, CARR & STEEL, of the

This engraving is from a group, the work of a true artist, SAN GIOVANNI, of Brighton; whose models from nature are of the purest and best order of Art. It is the only object he has sent.

Chantrey Works, Sheffield. Other of their excellent and useful productions, on a larger scale will be found in subsequent pages of this catalogue

The CARPETS here engraved are from the manufactory of Messrs. HENDERSON & WIDNELL, of Lasswade, near Edinburgh, successors to the well-known firm of Whytock & Co. This establishment is celebrated for its make of the finer sorts of carpet, those termed "tapestry" and "velvet-pile," and also of carpets similar to the Axminster, Persian, and Tournay fabrics, woven in one piece. We have seen carpets produced by this firm equal in texture, richness of colour, and beauty of pattern, to any foreign fabric of a similar description; engravings from some of these, with a lengthened notice of the extensive manufactory, were introduced into the *Art-Journal* about four or five years since. The

improvements introduced by Mr. Whytock and his successors into the process of weaving and printing these carpets have been the result of much study and long experience; we may adduce as one instance as regards the weaving, the new method of applying the shuttle. Those who have seen the workmen at the Gobelins, in Paris, employed on similar carpets, must have observed how the shuttle is thrown from hand to hand; instead of which Mr. Henderson uses the cross-bow, to draw it at once across the largest carpets, thereby saving a considerable portion of the

workman's time. Again, the necessity for expensive block-cutting and engraving has been superseded, and the process greatly simplified by the plans adopted by the present proprietors of this establishment. Among the other advantages arising from their new method, not the least important is that there is scarcely any limitation to the number of colours that may be used in line without increasing the expense; more than twenty are not unfrequently thus introduced, while a good opportunity is afforded to the considerate artist to vary his colours or shades.

A TABLE-COVER, of which we introduce the half, is worked in tapestry by MDLLE. HUNSON and her assistants, of Paris. The design is in the Arabesque style, and was furnished by M. Clerget, a most elegant designer and skilful draughtsman, especially for textile manufactures; he carries on an extensive business, in conjunction with Mdlle. Hunson, in the production of tapestries. In the centre of this table-cover is the well-known Arabic inscription, "God is great;" the pattern is executed in the finest silks and wools.

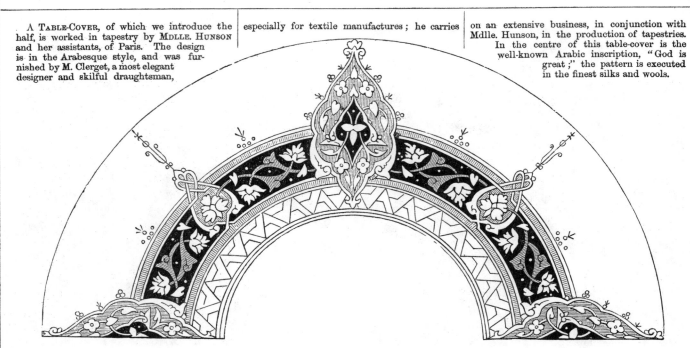

A STATUE of Saher de Quincy, Earl of Winchester, to be executed in bronze, is by MR. J. S. WESTMACOTT; it is intended to be placed in the House of Lords.

MADAME GRUEL, who conducts one of the most *récherché* book-binding establishments in Paris, exhibits several specimens of the Art which has made her house celebrated among the bibliopolists of the French metropolis. We engrave on this page an Ivory BOOK-COVER.

A damask TABLE-CLOTH, manufactured and exhibited by Mr. JOHN HENNING, of Waringstown, near Belfast, shows a clever floriated pattern. The design is by Hugh Blain, of the Belfast School of Design, to whom was awarded Lord Dufferin's first prize for a table-cloth.

An ALBUM-COVER, by Mr. BUDDEN, of Cambridge, is highly creditable

Messrs. S. R. & T. BROWN, of Glasgow, extensive manufacturers of embroidered muslins, exhibit several truly beautiful designs, principally

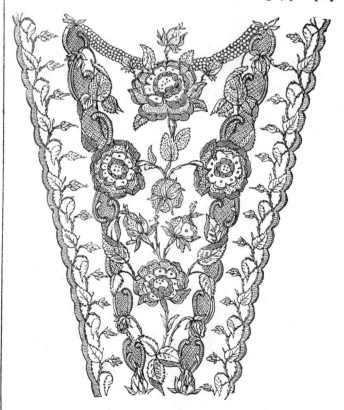

to the taste of a provincial binder; it is executed in gold and colours.

adapted to ladies' dresses. We engrave from their various contributions a CHEMISETTE of a simple but very elegant pattern of roses and leaves.

The four engravings which occupy these two columns represent COAL-BOXES, to use the only term that seems applicable to their purpose, although it is inappropriate, when the form of these objects is regarded; they are manufactured in japanned iron by Mr. H. FEARNCOMBE, of Wolverhampton. The first, the shape of which assimilates to that of a tureen, is ornamented in the Italian style, and is worthy of being imitated in silver. The two following are of the form of vases;

both are very elegantly designed, especially in their pedestals. The last represents a nautilus shell set on a piece of coral rock; the handle of the lid represents a sea-horse. The novelty and beauty of this design must challenge approbation; indeed, the entire set quite merits being

devoted to a more honourable, though not more useful, purpose than that for which each is intended. They are designed and modelled by Mr. F. Wright. Wolverhampton has long been cele-

brated for its japanned iron-ware: such works as these must tend to increase its reputation.

In conformity with our plan of representing every meritorious producer of articles which exhibit improvements derived from the influence

of art, we introduce upon this and the succeeding column four examples of the EMBROIDERED WAISTCOATS contributed by Mr. J. W. GABRIEL,

of London. The first two are worked in gold on rich silk, and are designed mainly for court dresses; the other two are wrought in silk upon black cloth: the ornamentation is derived principally from natural flowers. The style of modern male attire affords little opportunity

for the embroiderer and ornamentist to display their skill; the only garment which admits of the least approach to elegance being the vest;

and even this is generally discarded by persons of good taste. In the patterns here engraved, however, we see much that is truly graceful.

Mr. TOMLINSON, of Ashford, Derbyshire, one of the many ingenious manufacturers of the native spars and marbles of the county, contributes, among other articles, the TABLE here

An INKSTAND, or to designate it more correctly according to its varied contents, a com-

engraved. The stem as well as the top is made of black marble; a wreath of flowers and leaves in their natural colours encircles the top; the table is entirely formed of the spars of Derbyshire.

pendium for the writing-table, made and contributed by Mr. COLE, of Clerkenwell, is a most

useful and elegant work of manufacturing art; novel in character when the variety and arrange-

ment of its "fittings" is considered, and most elaborately engraved and richly ornamented.

In the notices which have appeared from time to time in the *Art-Journal*, descriptive of the progress of manufacturing design, we have found occasion to notice those productions of foreign houses remarkable for ability and taste, and among the rest that of M. MOREL, who has, however, for the last few years become a resident in London. His works are equally deserving of high praise, as well for design as for execution, and display great and varied fancy combined with the highest artistic finish. We furnish three

elaborate ornamental taste of the East, the quatrefoils containing views of the principal buildings in Constantinople; it is a very brilliant

production. Not less so is our second example, an AGATE CUP, the mountings richly chased in gold, and their effect heightened by the most

examples from his contributions to the Crystal Palace. The first is an ENAMELLED CUP, executed for the Sultan; it is richly decorated in the

vivid enamels. Our third engraving is from a rich COFFER, jewelled, chased, and enamelled, and intended to contain the original manuscript

of M. Guizot's "Life of Washington." We shall engrave elsewhere other of the productions of M. Morel, which are all of the highest merit.

We continue on this page engravings from the contributions of M. MOREL. The first is a VASE, in the style of the sixteenth century; the bowl is made of agate, and the setting of gold enamelled; the handle is composed of drapery attached to a single figure at the top; a group of a Triton and a Nereid form the stem. The beauty of the foot is enhanced by the

the top, bowl, and stem are made of separate pieces of rock crystal, richly mounted in enamelled gold. The CUP in the

centre is a truly elegant piece of workmanship; the dragon which forms the handle is one of the most perfect

introduction of pearls. The next is a TOILETTE-GLASS, of massive silver, with six branches for lights; the style is that of

specimens of modern enamelling in gold; some of the colours are exceedingly difficult to produce. The shell-like bowl is one entire piece of lapis-lazuli; the stem is formed

is a statue of Queen Elizabeth on horse-

Louis. the Fifteenth, with flowers, birds, and squirrels introduced. The CUP and COVER to the left at the bottom of the page is in the style of the sixteenth century;

of struggling sea-nymphs, with their tails entangled, and resting on a bed of coral; the foot is enamelled in the best Italian taste of the Cellini school. The last subject is a FLAGON of gold and silver, enamelled; the body is of rock crystal. There

back, by M. Morel, which is a fine example of silver embossed with the hammer.

The Porcelain manufactory of Messrs. HERBERT MINTON, & Co., is at Stoke-upon-Trent, the principal town of the famous district known as the "Staffordshire Potteries." The establishment has long been eminent for the production of admirable works. The head of the firm is a gentleman of accomplished mind, and of refined taste, and his large resources have been made available to obtain good models, and valuable assistance, wherever they could be found, in all parts of Europe. His collection at the Exhibition consists,

of an extensive variety of objects, all of which are of the highest merit; it is not too much to say, that the corner of the gallery in which they are placed has

been a point of attraction to visitors, and that here, at all events, foreigners have been enlightened as to the capabilities of British producers to encounter competition with the whole world. We engrave several of Messrs. Minton

& Co's. productions, commencing with the DESSERT-SERVICE, purchased by Her Majesty. The series (which is entirely original in the models, arrangement, and decoration,) is one of exceeding beauty, designed with pure artistic skill, and exhibiting, in manipulation and finish, a degree of refinement that has rarely, if ever, been surpassed in modern art. The subjects have been elaborately treated; it would seem as if the utmost

very novel combination. Our first cut is of a JELLY or CREAM-STAND; the companion to which is an "ASSIETTE MONTÉE;" between them is a FLOWER-

amount of labour had been expended upon them,—yet nowhere do they seem crowded or overladen; a result which arises, no doubt, mainly from the delicacy of the material, the figures and ornamentation being of "Parian," slightly gilt, and the baskets of richly decorated porcelain,—a

BASKET, supported by four figures, representing the seasons. A TRIANGULAR FRUIT-BASKET, and an OVAL FRUIT-BASKET, follow, and fill this page. The second page devoted to the works of Messrs. Minton & Co. commences with the SALT-CELLAR and small FRUIT-DISH,

or compotier, and terminates with the SUGAR or CREAM-BOWL,—parts of the beautiful dessert-

service, of which the leading objects are pictured

on the preceding page. The two groups of chil-

dren sporting with goats are in Parian,—that exquisite material in which England remains unrivalled,

and which is only second to marble. They are original designs, executed in the style and spirit

of the last century, and it is not too much to say that the delicacy of the modelling, and the grace and truthfulness of the attitudes have been seldom equalled. The two small FIGURES are elegantly formed; they are in gilt Parian, with

the stands in porcelain tastefully decorated, and serve as candlesticks. They are original designs in the style and costume of Louis Quinze. On the third page are pictured, first, a VASE

FOR PLANTS, of terra cotta, designed expressly for Messrs. Minton & Co. by the Baron Marochetti; it is of very large size. The second is likewise for plants, and also of terra cotta; a fine com-

position, executed with exceeding care. The third cut is from a WINE-COOLER, which forms the centre-piece of the dessert-service, and is, on the whole, the most meritorious object of the collection; our limited space does not permit us to describe it; and our fourth is from one of the numerous admirable STATUETTES, in Parian, ex-

the whole collection, we find abundant evidence of that matured judgment, and refined taste, by

which the manufacturers of Great Britain have been, of late years, elevated; and which, in the

hibited by this house. Of these Messrs. Minton & Co. have produced many, from original sources;

some after eminent foreign sculptors, but chiefly from the leading artists of our own school. In

present Exhibition, have so largely contributed to uphold, and will extend, our national repute.

The silver manufactures of Mr. M. EMANUEL, of London, evince great taste in design, and some very excellent workmanship. He exhibits a variety of objects besides those we have here engraved, such as gilt candelabra, gilt plateau,

flower stems, and the pedestal is composed of groups of figures and horses. The two objects commencing the other columns are silver DESSERT STANDS. The vine forms their stems, at the

most important contribution of this manufacturer is a large silver CLOCK, designed by Mr. Woodington, the well-known sculptor: it is, truly, a fine work of art. Between four figures,

base of which children are at play with animals; the dishes are supported by a sort of trellis-work of the leaves and fruit of the vine. But the

indicating the "Seasons," is one of "Time," in the attitude of repose; above the dial is a bas-relief, representing the winds and their various

with china racks and medallions, processes of gold manufacture. The first we introduce is one of a pair of rock crystal CANDLESTICKS,

silver, and gilt, with figures of children, sea-horses, and marine objects, composing the base. The next is a FLOWER-VASE, of richly coloured glass, mounted in silver; the handles are made to represent boys climbing upwards to the

attributes; and, surmounting the top, is Phœbus driving the chariot of the sun; the composition of this group is full of spirit, and the whole of

the figures are exceedingly well modelled. Mr. Emanuel has done wisely in securing the services of an artist of acknowledged talent and repute.

The appended engraving of a SIDEBOARD is from one manufactured and contributed by Mr. T. W. CALDECOTT, of London. The material of which it is made is old English oak, and it is carved, in the Renaissance style, with much taste and spirit; this style, when freed from the affectation with which designers are too apt to deform it, is well adapted for displaying a bold and effective ornamentation, such as we find in the work before us. There is here no breaking up of the general character of the ornament into unmeaning details, for the sake of gaining an apparent richness. The great merit of the decoration is its close adherence to the style adopted.

The CARPET is manufactured and exhibited by Mr. HARRIS, of Stourport. It is termed a "Brussels velvet pile," and is one of several, equally excellent, which this extensive manufacturer contributes. The design is a cordon of leaves of the *Clitoria arborescens*, enclosed by a trellis work of flowers, among which the *Lilium tigrinum* is conspicuous. This is among the best productions of British manufactured art.

The contributions of our fellow-subjects in Canada are not without a considerable portion of interest, but they are chiefly of a character which does not come within the scope of our plan of illustration; indeed, are not of a description to admit of it, even with less limitation. The wealth of Canada lies in her agricultural and mineral productions, of which she contributes to the Exhibition a large variety of examples. Among her textile fabrics are several specimens highly creditable to her manufacturers, and there are some engineering objects worthy of notice, especially a powerful and most elegant fire-

engine. We have selected, from the few productions that we deem would make effective engravings, a SLEIGH, of elegant proportions, manufactured by

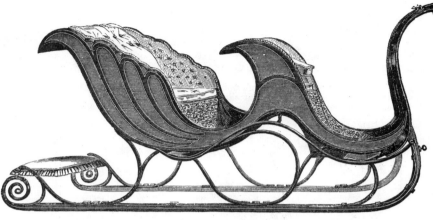

community exhibit no little taste, and spare no expense. to put their carriage and all its appointments, into suitable condition. The to exclude as much as possible the severity of the cold, are often very costly. There are

which are worthy of minute inspection. The rides and drives round about Quebec, Montreal,

harness of the horses is generally very gay, and beautifully ornamented; while the fur robes in which the riders envelope themselves some choice specimens of all these objects in the Canadian department of the Exhibition,

Toronto, &c., are, during the winter months, quite lively with the showy equipages, and

Mr. J. J. SAURIN, of Quebec. "Sleighing," as it is termed, forms one of the principal amusements of the Canadians of all ranks, who can afford to keep one of any description, and the wealthier part of the

musical with the bells suspended from the heads of the horses. The FURNITURE, also engraved on this page, is manufactured by

Messrs. J. & W. HILTON, of Montreal. They are made of black walnut, boldly carved, the chairs are covered with crimson and gold damask.

We introduce here the pediment of a FIRE-PLACE, manufactured of Derbyshire black marble, by Messrs. JOHN LOMAS & SONS, of Bakewell. The caps and bases of the columns are of Sienna marble; the frieze is inlaid with an elegant scroll, executed in marbles of various beautiful colours.

The three ancient KNIFE-HANDLES are from the collection of the GRAND DUKE OF SAXE WEIMAR, who possesses several thousands, ranging from the thirteenth to the eighteenth centuries. Many of these are both curious and very costly.

The CHANDELIER is manufactured by Mr J. FARADAY, of London. It is constructed upon a principle for which a patent has been obtained, whereby all noxious vapours arising from the gas are carried off, by means of the descending draught; the lights

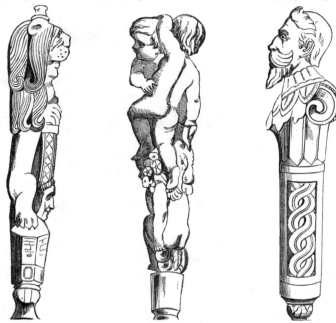

Messrs. B. R. & J. MOORE, of Clerkenwell, exhibit an eight-day CLOCK, with lever escapement, striking the quarters and hours on fine cathedral-tone bells. The plate upon which the clock stands is steel, highly polished and enamelled.

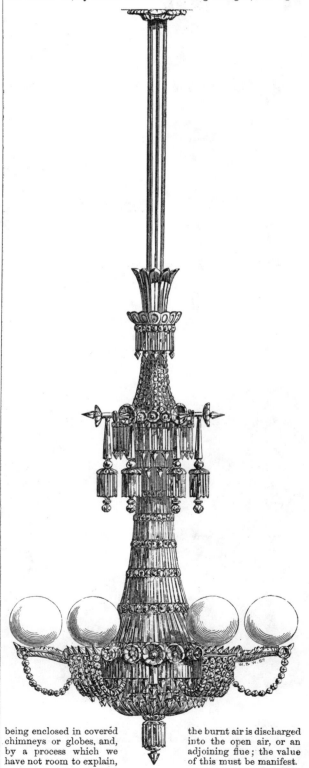

being enclosed in covered chimneys or globes, and, by a process which we have not room to explain, the burnt air is discharged into the open air, or an adjoining flue; the value of this must be manifest.

The ALTO-RELIEVO, by Mr. NELSON, of London, is a portion of a monument proposed to be erected to the memory of the officers and men of the fiftieth regiment of the line, who fell on the banks of the Sutlej, in 1845-6.

We insert on this column another KNIFE and SHEATH, from the collection of the GRAND DUKE OF SAXE WEIMAR.

A BOOK-COVER, carved in box-wood, by Mr. Rogers, forms one side of a magnificent Bible, exhibited by Mr. NISBET, of London. The subject of the beautiful design in the centre, is "The Brazen Serpent in the Wilderness."

The handle exhibits busts of Gustavus Adolphus, and Christina, king and queen of Sweden.

We fill this page with engravings from the productions of Messrs. T. WILKINSON & Co., of Birmingham,—works which entitle these manufacturers to much praise. A scene from Paul and Virginia, "that

gentle story of the Indian isle," furnishes the theme for the first of our examples; the incident chosen from the tale is Paul's expostulation previous to Virginia's departure for France, the flowers of the Indian

plant which overshadows them forming a graceful receptacle for lights. The centre-piece, with tritons and sea-nymphs under a canopy of real coral, is an attractive work. The second CANDELABRUM at the foot of our

page is a poetic conception admirably adapted to its uses; the subject, Prometheus endeavouring to regain the fire taken by Jupiter. The TEA-URN,—a vase of Etruscan form resting on a rock, has the novelty of a

basement decorated by figures of children playing musical instruments. These works are very creditable to the establishment from which they

emanate, and are satisfactory testimonials of the zeal with which the manufacturers of our large and celebrated industrial marts are determined to uphold the character they have so long enjoyed, and desire to maintain.

The first engraving on this page is from a carved BOOK-COVER, by Madame GRUEL, of Paris. It is a beautiful example of the taste which this celebrated house displays in all matters of art.

A state CARRIAGE-LAMP, by Mr. B. BLACK, of London, is richly ornamented in chased silver.

One of the most costly and admirable works of its class in the Exhibition is the BUFFET, designed and manufactured by Messrs. COOKES & SONS, of Warwick. Any attempt to describe this elaborately carved piece of workmanship would, in our limited space, be out of the question. All we can do is to explain that the designs are chiefly suggested by Scott's "Kenilworth."

It is, altogether, a work of manufacturing art, that reflects the highest credit on the producers.

The two engravings which commence this page are from the iron-foundry of M. DUCEL, of Paris. The first is a FOUNTAIN, of large dimensions, exhibiting dolphins supporting a shell, in which stands a figure, springing from aquatic plants. The other is an iron VASE, to be placed in a garden; it stands four feet and a half high, and is richly decorated. At each end of the three angles, above the pedestal, is a winged figure.

The subject underneath is from a CLOCK-CASE, executed in terra-cotta by Messrs. PRATT, of Burslem. It is of large size, and intended for the exterior of a building, for which its truly excellent design peculiarly adapts it. The figures, which have an antique character, and are elegantly posed, are well modelled, and the entire composition is conceived in an artistic spirit. We should be pleased to see greater attention paid to this branch of manufacturing art, for which there is, indeed, ample room.

A brocaded SILK, designed and exhibited by Messrs. LEWIS & ALLENBY, of London, and manufactured for them by Messrs. Campbell, Harrison, & Lloyd, of Spitalfields. The elaborate nature of the pattern, and the unusual number of colours (fifteen) with which the silk is brocaded, require for its production nearly thirty thousand cards, and ninety-six shuttles. As a specimen of weaving, it is of the best order.

This page is completed by the introduction of an engraving of a piece of RIBBON, manufactured by Mr. J. C. RATCLIFF, of Coventry. The pattern is suggested by the convolvulus plant, and shows a good adaptation of its graceful forms. The ribbon is termed by the manufacturer a "bro

caded damask-figured lutestring." It is made in a nine hundred Jacquard machine, employing fifteen hundred cards, and it has in it three thousand eight hundred and sixty-eight threads of warp silk. We engrave it as much for the "curiosity" of its manufacture, as for its design.

The productions of Mr. ASPREY, of London, are among the most remarkable for good taste, beauty of design, and excellence of execution. We think they

need fear no comparison that may be instituted with other works of their class in the Exhibition. Our selection comprises a TOILET-GLASS, with an

open framework and handle of a highly ornamental character, in flat chased work, richly gilt. The MINIATURE GLASS beneath it is provided with a prop,

and is constructed in the lightest manner,—so as at once to be elegant and useful; the framework is fanciful in design, but it will be seen that its general character is

good and useful, and convenient for the boudoir table. The TAPER-STAND is an equally elegant article; the entire bowl is cut from cornelian;

cabinet, is equally sumptuous in its fittings; it is richly chased and gilt, a large malachite

stone beneath. The INKSTAND is a fanciful composition; the large slab upon the top is a

which the richly-gilt open-work mountings have a singularly good effect, the arrangement of tints being further aided by the introduction

the receptacle for the taper, the little figures, and the ornamental handle and foot, are chased and gilt. A JEWEL-CASKET, in the form of a

decorates the lid; the doors beneath are in gilt open work, displaying slabs of the same costly

rare bloodstone. The CASKET is, perhaps, the best of the series; it is formed of ebony, upon

of coral cameos. The groups of entwined serpents which cover the lid, and form the feet, are happily conceived and well executed.

We consider the ORNAMENTAL JEWELLERY of Messrs. C. ROWLANDS & SON, of London, suffi-

Hence we have now imitations of flowers, either

taste, are essential to work out such designs. The jewellers of Paris have long been without

ciently important and beautiful to devote a page to the illustration of a few of their contributions. The business of the manufacturing jeweller has undergone a great change during the last few years, for there is a fashion in the works of his hands, which, perpetually changing, compels him to seek new methods of exhibiting his taste and skill. We may instance, as an example, the manufacture of watch-seals, a branch of their art

singly or in groups, in which not only their forms are closely followed, but oftentimes successful attempts are made to produce natural colours

rivals in this description of art-manufacture, and, it must be admitted, have taught our fellow-countrymen many lessons, which they have profitably turned to account. The first subject we introduce of Messrs. Rowlands' contributions is a BRACELET, set with rubies, in gold, of exquisite workmanship. The next three subjects are from BROOCHES; the first of these is in a style which, we believe, the French jewellers originated; the setting of this is of gold, the large stone between

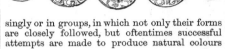

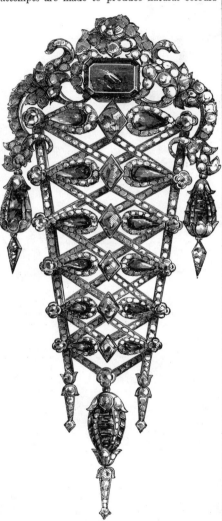

that is now rarely called into exercise; a few years since, a gentleman was seldom seen without two or three of these appendages glittering on his person. And again, in such objects as ladies' ear-rings, which are almost wholly out of date, except as worn on what may be termed "state occasions." These alterations in the style of ornamental dress have compelled the manufacturer to devote his attention chiefly to bracelets, ornaments for the head, and brooches. The

by the introduction of precious stones; it will, therefore, be easily conceived that great

the figures is a carbuncle, and brilliants decorate the drops; it is a very rich and elegant ornament. The second brooch is composed of rubies and brilliants in a costly setting; while the third is little else than a mass of diamonds, strung together in the most graceful form, in imitation of a bouquet of flowers. The last subject is a BRACELET. This bracelet is made up of diamonds and enamels; the large stone in the centre is a carbuncle. All of these jewelled ornaments are not only of a most costly description, but they

last-mentioned objects, though of distant origin, have assumed a totally varied form and feature from even their more immediate predecessors.

delicacy of workmanship, as well as considerable

exhibit taste on the part of the designer, combined with ingenuity and skill on that of the artistic workman of a more than ordinary character.

The two subjects commencing this page are contributed by M. PAILLARD, a bronze manufacturer of Paris. The first is a CLOCK of massive design, which, however, from its being pierced or open towards the bottom, loses much of the heaviness it would otherwise present. The dial is surmounted by a group of children playing with birds; they form a most pleasing picture. The other object is a GIRANDOLE, corresponding in style with the clock, but the child is at the base, and the birds are perched among the branches.

America, among her consignments of manufactured objects, contributes several worthy of being introduced into our pages. The United States present a wide field for the operations of skilful artisans in ornamental articles; as their wealth increases, so do also their taste for the elegant and the beautiful, and their desire to possess what will minister to the refinements of life. This is ever the case with nations, as they advance in intellectual power, and in the just appreciation of what confers real dignity on a people; and their moral strength keeps pace with their pro-

gress in intelligence. The PIANO-FORTE here introduced is designed and manufactured by Messrs. NUNN & CLARK, of New York. It is richly carved in rosewood, and the execution of the work is creditable to the skill and ingenuity of the workmen who have produced it.

Messrs. WOOLLAMS, of London, exhibit a great variety of new and beautiful designs in paper-hangings, a branch of the industrial arts which has received much improvement during the last quarter of a century in England; perhaps we may safely assert that there is scarcely any one trade in which greater progress is visible. The

and very deservedly, inasmuch as the character of each style, and the taste of each age, have been studied, and its most characteristic features

applied with success to the adornment of our walls. The series upon the present page are good examples of this fact, and exhibit much

variety of style; the elongated panel, is a free translation of the best Italian period, when a Raffaelle did not disdain to devote his transcendant genius to the walls of a Loggia, and produce a style which has never been surpassed,

amid all the changes of fashion. The gorgeous taste of Persia has furnished the theme of the second of our series, the fanciful and brilliant hues of which are, of course, but to be guessed at without the aid of colour; the same remark

reputation for good design and tasteful colouring which the continental houses almost monopolised, is now abundantly shared by the home producer;

must apply to our third example, in which the style of the decoration adopted in that far-famed building—the Alhambra—has been chosen, and

re-produced with great success, and at a cost which enables the moderately-wealthy to rival the dearly-purchased luxuries of the East.

The visitor to the Great Exhibition may search in vain through the whole length and breadth of the vast edifice for works more truly beautiful of their class, than those contributed

by M. FROMENT-MEURICE, the eminent goldsmith and jeweller of Paris. There is a certain point

at which the productions of the industrial artisan, as we are accustomed to call every one engaged

in handicraft, cease to be manufactures, and are entitled to be classed, absolutely, among works of Art; but we are too apt to draw the line of distinction between the artisan and the artist, where none, in truth, should exist. Thus, for instance, if one man sculptures a large figure

have performed. This is an injustice of comparatively modern date; it was not practised centuries ago, when the respect due to art of all kinds was greater than it is now. It was not so much the "Perseus" of Cellini, that won that

or ornament in marble he is ranked with the latter; while, if another does a similar work on a diminutive scale, in some metal or in wood, he most frequently finds himself placed in no higher grade than the former, without any regard to the real excellence of the work that either may

accomplished sculptor his rank, as his salvers, and his cups, his dagger-hilts and sword-handles, —these it was that made the artist. Wherever mind is brought to bear upon matter, so as to leave upon it the impress of genius, not mere

mechanical ingenuity, the result becomes entitled to the highest award that can be accorded to it. We would, therefore, in accordance with these preliminary remarks, claim for M. Fremont-Meurice, as also for many others whom we

could name, both British and foreign producers, that position which, in our judgment, they merit, and we feel assured that all who are able to appreciate art, must see in this and the following page, which contain engravings from

his contributions, that we are not arguing upon false premises. The first subject is an exquisitely wrought TOILET TABLE in silver, inlaid in parts with a kind of niello-work : it is intended as a present from the Legitimists of France to

the Duchess of Parma. The whole design of this object is singularly rich and beautiful; any description would be superfluous, as it sufficiently tells its own tale of the taste and well-directed study bestowed upon it. The engraving across the

page at the bottom is from a BRACELET, of the early mediæval style ; in a rich gothic frame-work are three compartments, containing, we

first page, the upper is an elegant little LOOKING GLASS, in an elegant silver frame, and the lower a CLASP of novel design. On this page the first two subjects are BROOCHES, with jewels in their centres, and the frame-work supported by

presume, representations of scenes in the life of St. Louis ; the centre or chief one, seems to represent his death. Of the other two subjects in the

winged figures : below these is another CLASP, in a similar style to the preceding. The JUG and SALVER, are the same, on an enlarged scale, as those seen on the table in the former page ; they are full of elaborate workmanship of the highest

order. The CASKET is also to be found on the table ; this, perhaps, is the finest of the works this eminent goldsmith exhibits ; it would do

honour to his renowned Florentine prototype, and France may well plume herself on her artistic skill when she sends forth such productions.

THE INDUSTRY OF ALL NATIONS.

The following DESIGN, is intended to ornament the top of a box of sewed muslins or cambrics. It was designed by S. M'CLOY, of the Belfast School of Design, for Mr. M'Cracken, an extensive manufacturer in that town, and it obtained the first prize of two pounds given by Lord Dufferin at the recent exhibition of the works executed by the pupils of the above School. The convolvulus plant has suggested this very graceful pattern.

The BRACKET and SCREEN are among the contributions of the PATENT WOOD CARVING COMPANY, of London, whose operations are chiefly conducted by the aid of machinery. We have engraved, either here or elsewhere, for the original of the screen stands about sixteen feet high, occupying a conspicuous place near the transept, while the bracket measures about as many inches.

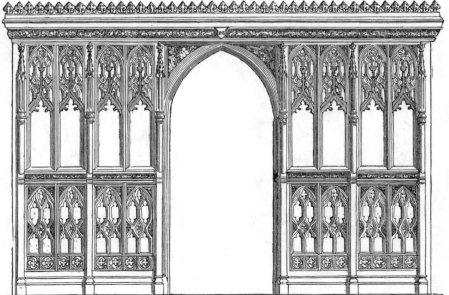

The works of Messrs. ELLIS & SON, of Exeter, to which we devote this page, exhibit a great amount of taste, combined with much sensible utility, particularly in brooches, where the "patent safety chains" enable the wearer to use them without fear of their becoming unfastened when once properly secured; the simplicity with which this desirable end is attained is one great merit of the invention: the point of the pin is received into a sheath to which a chain is attached, and this chain being drawn tight and passed through a notch, cannot by any possibility slip. We engrave three specimens of these BROOCHES, the two upper ones in plain silver, the third a more expensive combination of gold and jewels, especially remarkable for the beauty of its setting, which is quite worthy of the best days of artistic jewellers-work. It is not only in productions of this kind that Messrs. Ellis command attention; the JEWEL-BOX, which forms the third of our series is very richly deco-

rated, particularly with filligree work, which we have it not in our power to exhibit in a woodcut. The FISH-KNIFE at the bottom of our page is remarkable for the applicability of the figures and ornament which enrich its surface, and adds another to the many proofs of well-directed study exhibited in all branches of modern British manufacture, and which was never so well developed as now.

THE INDUSTRY OF ALL NATIONS.

We occupy this page with examples of the ability of a London house, in a branch of manufacture that has given high reputation to Sheffield, Rotherham, Birmingham, &c., and to which places we generally look for the supply of such articles. London is scarcely acknowledged as a manufacturing city, except for objects of furniture or luxury; for metallic works we expect to look elsewhere. Yet London contains

in its streets many establishments of much extent, skill, and power, scarcely known to the busy throng which pass their doors,—some of whom, using the articles there made, imagine they have been fabricated in provincial towns. Mr. PIERCE, of Jermyn-street, has contributed STOVES, FENDERS, and the appurtenances of the fire-place, of a very tasteful and yet sumptuous kind. The latter term may especially apply to the STOVE we have

selected for engraving. The chimney-piece is in marble of various delicate hues; the fender, fire-irons, and ornamental adjuncts to the grate, are formed of massive silver. This costly work is of large proportions, and has been executed for the Earl of Ellesmere. The FENDER at the head of the page is a graceful design, comprising figures and ornaments equally well disposed. The same remark will apply to the one

beneath, in which dogs and deer bound forth from enriched scroll-work of elaborate convolution. The brilliancy and beauty of these works entitle them to high praise. The combinations of polished steel, gilding, and marble, are altogether in the happiest style, and will uphold the reputation which the manufacturer has enjoyed for many years: there is no question that England stands unrivalled in this branch of art.

The engravings on this page are from CARPETS contributed by Messrs. TURBERVILLE SMITH, & Co., of London. It is very difficult to form anything like a correct notion of the richness and beauty of these fabrics, when the colours are represented only by graduated shades of black, but the patterns, however delineated, speak for themselves. In the first, we have only the fern-plant, one of the most graceful productions of

the woods and hedgerows, and, as seen, worked out in this carpet in shades of the liveliest green, nothing can be more ornamental. For the second pattern, the flower-garden seems to have been rifled of its gayest and choicest flowers, to furnish the designer with materials for his work, so much that it almost requires one well instructed in botany to make out a list of its contents; and yet there is nothing overdone, nor any absence

of the most elegant harmony. Therein lies the skill of the designer in bringing all his selections into one mass of beautiful colouring without offending the purest taste. We think it will be generally conceded that our best carpet-manu-facturers have not come into the field of com-petition without being fully prepared for the contest. The carpets engraved on this page were designed for Messrs. Smith by Mr. E. T. Parris.

Messrs. H. WILKINSON & Co., of Sheffield, exhibit the CENTRE-PIECE we here engrave; it is a clever combination of figures and foliage, standing on a pedestal of enriched character. The branches

We have, ere this, found occasion, in our pages, to recommend to favourable notice the beautiful

for candles bend forward from the main stem

with an easy lightness, and the glass dish in the

"ILLUMINATED GLASS" of Mr. KIDD; that term has not been inaptly used by him as its designa-

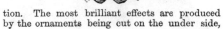

tion. The most brilliant effects are produced by the ornaments being cut on the under side,

centre is of good form. "The IONIC INKSTAND," in the Elizabethan style, is a simple but graceful

necessary for the library table. The manufacturers uphold the high reputation they have acquired.

and filled with silvering, giving them the effect of embossing. Many of the forms are good.

CHINA—"the central flowery Nation"—is

represented through the contributions of various

persons, chiefly European. By far the most

important portions of the collection are sent by Messrs. HEWETT & Co., of Fenchurch Street, and comprise a large quantity of articles remarkable for their value and beauty. The IVORY BASKET which we engrave is an elegant example of taste,

and action predominates. With a little more ease in the flow of its lines it might be made an elegant and desirable addition to the boudoir of the European belle, reflecting the fair face as

stand of ebony; it is used as a medicine-cup. The entire design has much freedom and fancy, combined with the peculiar taste of the fabricant and the nature of the foliage. Beneath is a Japanese sweetmeat box on wheels; it is con-

combined with the patience and care for which the Chinese workmen are celebrated. The LOOK-ING GLASS, on its carved stand, has more freedom of design than we find in works coming from China, where mathematical precision in thought

pleasantly as it now reflects the Crystal Palace.

The other articles on our page are contributed by Mrs. CHRISTOPHER RAWSON: the upper one is an elegant CUP cut in soap-stone, upon a foliated

structed of a red lacquered ware; the boxes being formed to fit into each other in a variety of shapes. The archaic taste of a peculiar nation, schooled into a certain precise tone of mind, is strikingly visible in all these works.

The manufactory of Messrs. RICHARDSON, at Stourbridge, is chiefly famous for its productions in CRYSTAL GLASS, which they have carried to the utmost extent of brilliancy and purity. An examination of their contributions in decanters, wine-glasses, goblets, cream-bowls, butter-coolers, &c., will at once carry conviction that in this branch of the art England excels every other country of the world. Bohemia asserts, and probably maintains, its supremacy in the manufacture of coloured glass, but it cannot enter into competition with us as regards that which is colourless.

them in these most essential matters. There is one point which, in justice to Messrs. Richardson, we must not omit to notice : all the articles they have sent to the Exhibition are produced

by British workmen ; so that whatever merit they possess, and it is unquestionably great, is

their establishment is Mr. W. J. Muckley. Among the objects emanating from this factory

seen in the Exhibition, and forming portions of

the contributions of other manufacturers, are the glass pillars and domes to the bronze and

We are rapidly gaining upon them on their own ground, and it will be seen, by comparison, that,

of late years, we have so far studied forms and ornamentation as to have already far surpassed

due to the taste and talent of our own countrymen : the principal designer and engraver in

other candle-lamps exhibited by Messrs. Blews & Son, of Birmingham, which are exceedingly novel in style and rich in colour; of these we shall

engrave specimens. The two DECANTERS with which we commence our illustrations, are of the purest crystal; the lozenge-shape cuttings bring out the prismatic colours with exceeding brilliancy: the GOBLET at the head of the second column is elegant in form, and the introduction of the vine upon the cup,

of the cutting, while it retains all its boldness. The next subject is a BUTTER DISH of crystal,

designed after the style of the antique. The VASE that follows is very elegant; it is manu-

enamel colours. The DECANTER completing

that page is most lustrous, and the lozenge-shaped cutting exceedingly bold. All the objects introduced in this page are of crystal of the purest kind; the beauty and variety of the cutting in the

though not a novelty, is appropriate. The FRUIT DISH and STAND that follows is of ruby glass covered on flint, and then cut through, showing the two colours to great advantage. The WINE GLASS is very elaborately ornamented, and the stem, which looks a little heavy in the engraving, loses this appearance in the original object, by the style

factured in opal; the scroll and band at top and bottom are gilt; the flowers and fruit painted with vitrified

whole of these works cannot fail to secure to them unqualified admiration. The large group at the bottom consists of one of each articles in a set of glass for dessert purposes, consequently they are all of a similar pattern, except the CLARET JUG, which is cut in a similar style, but is somewhat varied in its decoration.

Messrs. LAMBERT & RAWLINGS, of London, exhibit a variety of objects in the precious metals, adapted for useful and decorative pur

poses; such as soup tureens and stands, ruby glass cups with silver mountings, designed after the antique, all characterised by a taste ac-

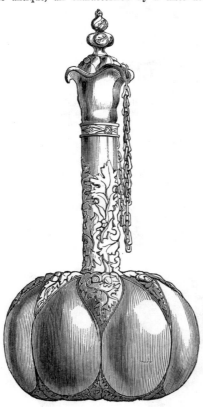

quired by long years of experience. We have selected from their contributions a pair of massive WINE FLAGONS, each standing twenty-two inches high, and holding eleven quarts:

they are richly chased and partly gilt, their style is antique, and they are hammered out of the

winged horse; and this is followed by an elaborately chased silver twelve-light CANDELABRUM

ounces; the design is appropriate to the Great Exhibition—Britannia, with the olive-branch of

plate. The next illustration is from a SALT CELLAR, the model of which is a Pegasus, or

and DESSERT CENTRE combined; its height is four feet, and its weight nearly twelve hundred

peace, is welcoming the representatives of the four quarters of the earth, heralded by Tritons.

The ornamental FRINGE for a window is the manufacture of Mr. R. BURGH, of London, who conducts an extensive business of this description; one of considerable importance, as connected with domestic furniture, and in which he finds ample room for the display of good taste.

The annexed engraving is from a COUTEAU DE CHASSE, by M. DEVISME, of Paris; it is a beautifully decorated piece of workmanship. The handle is of carved ivory, the hilt of polished

A CLOCK, manufactured by Mr. J. WALKER, of London, merits high commendation, from the truly elegant and artistic character of the design. The case is electro-gilt; the pedestal, of turquoise-blue glass, is surmounted by a group of figures, representing Britannia, in the robes of peace, directing attention to the progress made by Time and Science in the civilisation and

steel, chased, and the scabbard of dark steel ornaments on a grey ground. There are many elegant objects of this description by the French exhibitors, equally meritorious in character.

happiness of the people of Great Britain; this is illustrated by a series of seven subjects, revolving, by the aid of machinery, in the base of the clock. The several parts of this work might be described at length; altogether, there are few more meritorious productions in the Exhibition.

Birmingham has recently made great progress in the production of the better sort of plated and silver manufactures, so much so, indeed, as to have become a formidable rival to Sheffield, a town whose supremacy in this department of business was, till now, indisputable; however,

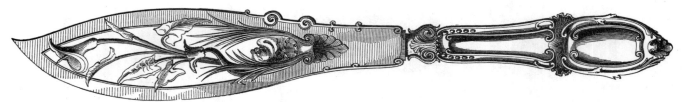

there is ample room for the manufacturers of both these important places to display their ingenuity and skill to the best advantage, and so contend for the palm of excellence. We engrave on this page some of the works contributed by the establishment of Messrs. PRIME & SON, of Birmingham. The first subject represents a BUTTER-KNIFE; the handle is in the Italian

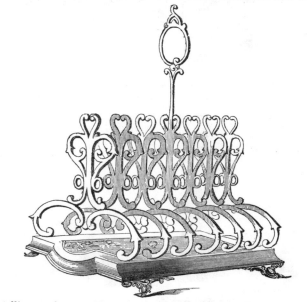

the industrial arts, are in nothing more manifest than when seen in

metallic manufactures. The various processes of electrotyping, magneto-

style, and the blade is ornamented with an open floriated pattern. The LIQUOR STAND that follows offers considerable novelty in its design, which shows the utmost harmony in the ornamentation of its several component parts. To this succeeds a CAKE BASKET, the form of which is decidedly good, and the chasing in excellent taste. The TOAST RACK shows also a

very meritorious design; and the TRAY underneath it is equally entitled to commendation. Lastly, the ASPARAGUS TONGS, which complete the page, are sufficiently enriched with ornament to render them an elegant appendage to the dinner-table. We believe that all these manufactures are executed in magneto-plated silver. The results of scientific research, when applied to

plating, and others, have greatly tended to produce this satisfactory result.

Messrs. Horne, Allen, & Co., of London, among other examples of Paper-hanging, exhibit the panelling, a portion of which we engrave. A richly-composed group of flowers and foliage runs round the entire design, which is executed with much care and precision, and exhibits considerable taste in the arrangement of colours. Floral decoration is exceedingly well applied to works

In our report of the recent exhibition of the works from the Government Schools of Design, at Marlborough House, published in the April number of the *Art-Journal*, we noticed the important fact of the utility of such schools for artistic education, which rendered it unnecessary

for the British manufacturer to call in foreign aid. This was vividly exemplified in the instance of Mrs. Treadwin, of Exeter, an eminent lace-manufacturer, who had prepared for a continental

of this class, and when carefully studied, and truthfully rendered, is more gratifying to the eye than any other style of border ornament.

journey to procure designs. Fortunately, she first visited Somerset House, when the design for a Lace Flounce was made the subject of a competition among the students. The successful design was by Mr. C. P. Slocombe, which has since been worked out, and is here engraved.

The two BAROMETERS occupying this column are manufactured by Messrs. GRAY & KEEN, of Liverpool. The cases are made of English

walnut-wood. The first is of Gothic form, and has an elaborated dial plate, in which the architecture of the florid style is represented. The

second was designed for the "Sailors' Home," in Liverpool; it is a fac-simile of a patent anchor, the flukes of which support the ornamental disc.

The two IRON BEDSTEADS, introduced on this page, are from the establishment of Messrs. PEYTON & HARLOW, of Birmingham and London,

houses where we would, possibly, least expect to find them. The great points which should be aimed at in the manufacture of these bedsteads are lightness and elegance, in almost direct

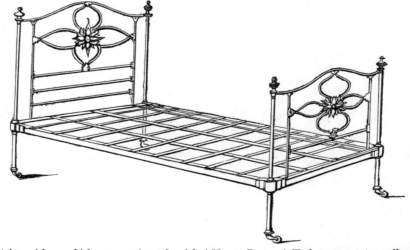

curtains, with us, which our continental neighbours seldom or never use. The productions of

very extensive manufacturers of these articles of domestic furniture, the use of which has, within the last few years, become very general, even in

opposition to those of French make, where solidity is chiefly required. This variation arises from the difference of construction in the two styles, and the adoption of hangings, or

Messrs. Peyton & Harlow are most excellent of their kind, and excellent examples of metal work.

In the course of our continental tour last year, undertaken for the purpose of ascertaining what preparations were making there for this

year's Great Exhibition, we visited the extensive establishment of M. CAPPELLMANS, at Brussels, and, in the course of our report, made an inci-

dental mention of his varied and important manufactory, which is devoted not only to com-

mon earthenware and pottery, but to porcelain of a better kind, and to glass work, in plain

sheets, or in "*verres filigraines*," rivalling in beauty the ancient Venetian works. Among the

common pottery we discovered imitations of popular English forms, and, among the plates,

filled with examples of the CHINA and EARTHEN-WARE contributed by M. Cappellmans. The large

characterised the pottery of the Low Countries two centuries since. The FRUIT-BASKET at the

our old friend, the much-patronised and much-abused "willow pattern." The present page is

VASE is of very fanciful design, exhibiting much of the peculiar and somewhat whimsical taste which

foot of the page, with its supporting angels, is a very graceful and elegant work of its class.

The CHIMNEY-POTS, in the Tudor style, are manufactured

by Messrs. H. DOULTON & Co.

of Lambeth, who also con-

tributed the terra cotta vases engraved on a former page.

The model of a group of a Scottish deer-hunter and his dogs, is by H. M'CARTHY, of London. It is a spirited performance, well composed, and does credit to the designer. It is executed in silver for ornamental purposes.

The CARPET is engraved from a portion of one manufactured by Messrs. A. LAPWORTH & Co., of London, for the state drawing-room of Buckingham Palace; it is a costly and elegant work of textile manufacturing art.

The two FIRE-PLACES are excellent examples of the manufactures of Messrs. ROBERTSON, CARR, & STEEL, of Sheffield, a firm conducting a most extensive business in that town. The latter of the two must attract attention from the novel construction of the fire-basket, which seems of a form calculated to hold a large body of com-

The engraving on this column is from a portion of a SUMMER-HOUSE, made of zinc; it is from the manufactory of M. DEY-DIER, of Vaugirard, near Paris.

bustibles, as well as to throw out very considerable heat; the fire-basket of the other is of a more familiar form. The ornamental parts of both are unexceptionable in design and of highly enriched patterns; the whole seems to combine the double purpose of chimney-piece and stove. On looking at such works of manufacturing

Art as these, we are sometimes induced to institute a comparison between them and the famous "Dutch tiled fire-places," the glory of our forefathers; we scarcely need add our opinion as to which are the most esteemed. Although our examples are somewhat similar, the productions of Messrs. Robertson & Co. are very varied.

His establishment is on a very extensive scale, producing a large variety of articles, of a similar description to those we generally find wrought in other ordinary metals.

We may certainly compliment Messrs. SILK & BROWN, of London, on their very elegant park PHAETON, engraved on this page. It is suspended upon a "swan-necked" carriage, on C and under springs, the whole exhibiting a study of graceful lines and curves. The body panels are painted a rich emerald-green colour, of a dark shade; the carriage and wheels a pale primrose, delicately picked out with green and red. The inside of the phaeton is trimmed in a rich but chaste manner, with green and white velvet lace: the mountings are all of silver.

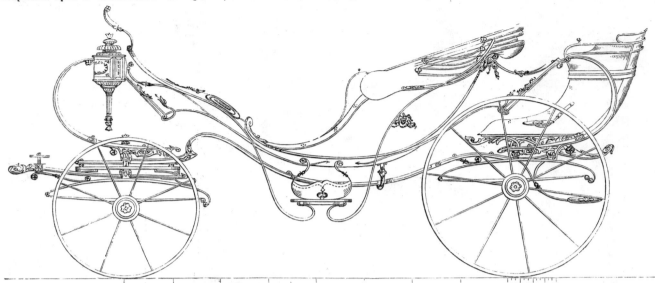

Messrs. HOOPER & Co., of Boston, America, exhibit the elegant EPERGNE, which is here engraved. It is of very tasteful design, and possesses much brilliancy of effect. The amount of decoration which is included in the general design, is neither too sparing in its character, nor too profuse; the vine and its fruit are clustered around the base, or depend gracefully from the

The Baron MAROCHETTI exhibits an emblematic figure of the ANGEL OF SLEEP, with bat-like wings, and gesture expressive of silence. It is

branches, and the infant bacchanals below give life to the composition. The works of Messrs. Hooper are among the most attractive of those exhibited by their fellow-countrymen, both as regards their position in the building, and their general excellence. They deserve the approbation they obtain, and do the manufacturers much credit for the skill manifested in their production.

designed to be placed above the doors of a mausoleum, for which it is a suitable emblem.

A VASE, or fruit-cup, manufactured and exhibited by Messrs. J. WAGNER & SON, distinguished artists of Berlin, is an exquisite example of metallic sculpture. The various figures are admirably modelled, and the ornamentation is altogether in the best taste. It is executed in oxidised silver.

The piece of SILK represented in the annexed engraving is manufactured and exhibited by Messrs. STONE & KEMP, of Spitalfields, who are noted for associating art with their productions. There is evidence of this in the design before us, which, we believe, emanated from the School of Design in the locality referred to. It is satisfactory to find manufacturers avail themselves of the assistance of such institutions.

The circular engraving which appears underneath is from a TABLE-TOP, forming a portion of

From among the variety of objects manufac- 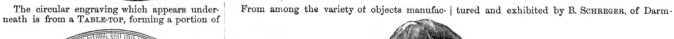 tured and exhibited by B. SCHREGER, of Darm-

the costly and attractive contributions from the Austrian dominions. The table is manufactured by M. KARL LEISTLER, of Vienna; it is inlaid with various woods, arranged in a novel pattern.

stadt, we have selected a PAPER-WEIGHT, which represents a boar-hunt, placed not very appro- priately, but yet ornamentally, upon a base de- signed like a foot-stool in a scroll frame-work.

The English carriage-builder still maintains, in his various contributions to the Exhibition, the high position universally acceded to him in this branch of industrial art. We engrave here a most elegant PARK PHÆTON, manufactured by Messrs. HALLMARKE, ALDEBERT, & HALLMARKE, of London. The body of the carriage has a form similar to that of the nautilus shell; and the vehicle, altogether, is remarkable for its lightness.

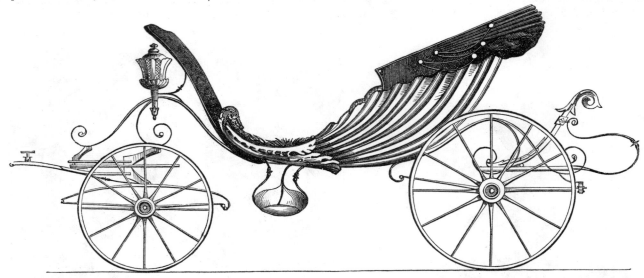

The two SWORDS on this column are the manufacture of Messrs. REEVES, GREAVES, & Co., of Birmingham. The longer one is an officer's FIELD-

The BOOK-COVERS of Madame GRUEL, of Paris, are so truly artistic in design and execution, that we feel no apology need be offered for introducing another of them into our pages. This, like

SWORD; the hilt and mounting of the scabbard are richly chased and gilt. The other is a Highland CLAYMORE, of good, yet elaborate, workmanship.

the preceding, is carved either in ivory or box-wood. The centre of the design shows the Virgin, crowned; the surrounding ornamentation exhibits a kind of trellis-work, partially covered.

Messrs. Towler, Campin, & Co., of Norwich, exhibit some of the exquisite textile fabrics which have given character and reputation to that ancient city. A magnificent fillover scarf with a silk ground, is one of their contributions. It measures four yards in length, and two in width. The sobriety of colour which prevails in these elaborate productions is a proof of the good taste of the manufacturers. We engrave

the centre of one of the SHAWLS, which is but a small portion of the whole, the entire pattern being of the most intricate design, which it would be utterly impossible, adequately, to represent in our pages; it is like exhibiting a leaf from a tree,—but, as that is enough for a botanist to determine its character, so our cut may be received as an assurance of the taste which characterises these beautiful articles of female dress.

The group, in marble, of VENUS AND CUPID, life-size, is by Mr. E. DAVIS, of London. The subject is one that has engaged the sculptor and painter of almost every age, so that it seems impossible to invest it with any sentiment or action approaching to novelty. Mr. Davis has represented Cupid interceding with his mother for his bow, which Venus appears unwilling to place in his hands. The two figures are exceedingly well modelled, and arranged with much grace.

The CANDELABRUM, to hold nine lights, is exhibited by Mr. G. BROWN, of London, an extensive manufacturer of composition articles. It stands eight feet high, and is manufactured in wood and *carton-pierre*, gilded to imitate or-molu.

America has long been noted for the luxurious easiness of its chairs, which combine in themselves all the means of gratification a Sybarite could wish. The AMERICAN CHAIR COMPANY, of New York, exhibit some novelties, which even

increase the luxury and convenience of this necessary article of furniture; instead of the ordinary legs conjoined to each angle of the seat, they combine to support a stem, as in ordinary

music-stools, between which and the seat the SPRING is inserted; this we exhibit in our first cut. It will allow of the greatest weight and freest motion on all sides; the seat is also made

to revolve on its axis. The design and fittings of these chairs are equally good and elegant, and certainly we have never tested a more easy and commodious article of household furniture.

The TABLE-COVER engraved below is exhibited by Mdlle. HUNSON & Co., of Paris, from a design by M. Clerget. It is worked in wools and silks of various rich colours and shades, well selected.

M. DETOUCHE, of Paris, a most extensive manufacturer of clocks and watches, exhibits a superb CLOCK, which is the subject of the annexed engraving; it is manufactured of bronze, gilded. The design of the base is exceedingly bold, and the figures introduced have a purpose

beyond mere ornament, they are pointing upwards to indicate the flight of time. The upper part of the clock shows much elegant and elaborate decoration arranged in unquestionable taste.

The first engraving on this page is from the COVER OF A BIBLE, bound and exhibited by Mr. A. TARRANT, of London. It is an elaborate specimen of the art of book-binding; the ornament is beautiful in design, skilfully worked out, and is highly suggestive for other purposes.

The CARPET is from the manufactory of Messrs. TEMPLETON & Co., of Glasgow, of whose contributions we have given examples in a former page of our Catalogue. We have never seen any fabric of this description richer and more elegant than this : the pattern is full of "subject," displayed with exceeding taste and judgment,—groups and wreaths of flowers, scrolls, and border-ornaments, presenting a combination of beautiful forms.

Messrs. SIMCOX & PEMBERTON, of Birmingham, contribute many admirable specimens of the variety of useful articles which go towards the

fittings of a house, and which, until of late years, were considered beneath the thought of the artistic designer. The CURTAIN-BAND is an excellent sample of the applicability of floral nature

to ornamental art; the BELL-PULL, which succeeds, may be also traced to the same fertile source of decoration, as modified by the particular taste of the architect. An Elizabethan CURTAIN-BAND succeeds, and shows how well the character of

internal decoration of any period may now be carried out in all minor accessories. The DOOR-HANDLE is of much lightness and elegance; and

the CORNICE and CURTAIN ORNAMENTS present an attractive novelty of form. They are all

highly favourable examples of manufacturing art, applied to the exigencies of every-day life.

M. GILLE, of Paris, contributes the porcelain works engraved in our present column, which

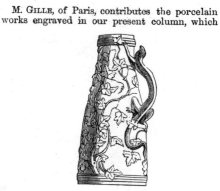

are remarkable for novelty and taste. The handle

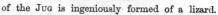

of the JUG is ingeniously formed of a lizard.

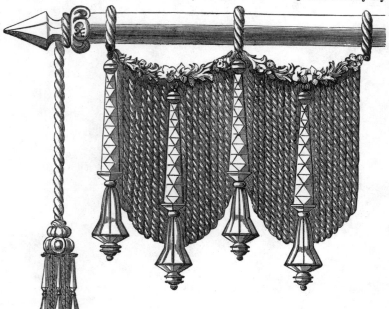

The TOILET-BOTTLE is in the elegant taste of the East. The VASE is that of the old Venetians.

The two objects which occupy this column are from the contributions of M. LA HOCHE, of Paris, who is eminent for the taste he invariably displays in the manufacture of porcelain clocks, and what are termed articles of *virtu*. Indeed, it may be said that his reputation in these departments of manufacturing art is second to none in the French metropolis. The first of

our selections is a very elegant CLOCK, which appears in a vase-like form. The figures are designed with much grace and playfulness of action; the pediment is tastefully decorated with flowers, and the vase, of dark blue porcelain, equals the finest Dresden. The WINE-

COOLER, of light blue porcelain, is another work of great artistic beauty. We cannot speak too highly of the productions of this manufacturer. We are well acquainted with his establishment in Paris, which is full of admirable works, arranged for show in the most attractive manner.

The National Manufactory established at Beauvais is represented by a series of works in tapestry for chairs, sofas, screens, and carpets. The extreme beauty of these productions is worthy of attention, particularly the skilful arrangement of colour they present, which,

though vivid, is so exquisitely toned as to be most grateful to the eye. The woodwork of the furniture is by M. DUVAL, one of the most famed of the Paris upholsterers, and who is specially appointed to mount all the tapestries issued from the National Manufactory, as well as to

superintend other government work. The ornamentation he has executed with much perfection of finish, combining boldness of form with delicacy of handling, the whole being characterised by good taste. We select a CHAIR and a SCREEN as examples of these national works.

The manufactures in PAPIER-MÂCHÉ, of Messrs.

M'CULLUM & HODGSON, of Birmingham, deservedly

stand in high repute. Their productions in this

light and elegant material are characterised by excellent design and great richness in the variety

which it is unnecessary to particularise, as they sufficiently explain their own application. The

turers seem determined to maintain their

of colours introduced. We engrave on this page a number of these useful and ornamental objects,

TABLE is especially unique in its ornament, and the CABINET is most elaborately decorated. There

is no question that England stands unrivalled in this branch of industrial art, and her manufac-

supremacy, if energy and perseverance can effect it.

The white terra-cotta productions introduced on this column are by Mr. BLANCHARD, of Lambeth. The first is a VASE and PILLAR, highly ornamented,

and executed with a sharpness and clearness equal to the sculptured stone. The second is a VASE, less decorated than the preceding, but equally

deserving of favourable notice. We should be glad to see this beautiful material brought into more general application, for which it is well adapted.

A most successful attempt to imitate the style and effect of the real Cashmere shawls may be seen in the subjoined engraving from a

most elaborate character, and aims at producing, on the lighter fabrics, suitable for summer wear, the qualities which have hitherto been

SHAWL, designed by Messrs. LEWIS & ALLENBY, of London, and printed for them by Messrs. Swaisland, of Crayford. The design is of the

found only in the more weighty and costly manufactures of the Asiatic producer. The shawl exhibits much rich harmony of colour.

If we desired to convince a foreigner of the immense wealth which this country possesses in the shape of manufactured articles, we would

invite him to accompany us for a day's stroll through the leading thoroughfares of our vast metropolis, to inspect the contents of the nume-

rous establishments for the manufacture and sale of works in the precious metals; or, what would be as effectual, and cost less time and labour, we would take him to the south-west gallery of the Great Exhibition edifice, to point out to him the profusion of wealth congregated there in glittering heaps, almost, if not quite, realising the dreams of eastern fable. But it is not so much the value of the mere metal to which importance should be attached, as indi-

cating the riches that England contains within

her, as it is the amount of skill and labour

which are brought to bear on the production of

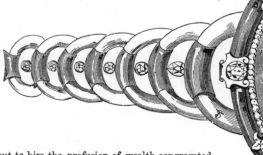

articles of luxury alone, and which must necessarily increase their value tenfold. Thus, the stranger would be led to reflect that, where so

much capital is expended on the production, there must be still larger means at the disposal of the buyers, to call for such an outlay; consequently, his ideas of our wealth receive a two-

fold impression. Among the mass of contributions that make up the costly piles to which allusion has been made, the silver ornaments and the jewellery manufactured by Messrs. S. H. & D. GASS, of London, must, from their magnitude and beauty, attract observation. The most important of these is a SILVER DESSERT SERVICE, of novel character and design, modelled from plants growing in the Royal Gardens at Kew; of this service, five of the objects are engraved on the preceding page, and two on this column. It is quite needless to expatiate upon the taste displayed in the adaptation of these natural forms to manufacturing art. On the second column of the preceding page we have also introduced a jewelled BROOCH, in the style of the *cinque-cento* period; this object requires

close examination ere one can appreciate the beauty of its design. At the bottom of the same page is a BRACELET, set with diamonds and carbuncles, with portraits of the Queen and the Prince of Wales, after Thorburn, A.R.A., and executed in *niello*, engraved by J. J. Crew. A

CHRISTENING CUP, embellished with angels keeping watch over a kneeling child, designed by R. Redgrave, R.A., completes our illustrations of the contributions of Messrs. Gass; but we may hereafter find occasion to pay their stand another visit, as we observed among their pro-

ductions several objects deserving of notice; a silver gauntlet niello bracelet, designed by D. Maclise, R.A.; a silvered and jewelled dessert set, in the Elizabethan style; numerous articles of jewellery, of various kinds, and in diversified style; and a large vase, most ingeniously composed of human hair, executed by J. Woolley.

Messrs. COWLEY & JAMES, of Walsall, exhibit the brass CHANDELIER here engraved, and which consists of floral ornament, of a light and graceful character, well calculated to relieve from weighty monotony, an article which, in the

or even weightiness of appearance, a very objectionable quality, whenever exhibited. In some instances, the style or character of the apartment for which they are intended may demand a certain "weight," but the prevailing idea to guide the

remarkable degree, the design and ornamentation being of the simplest kind; and, we must say, we prefer it to much of the overwrought and highly-elaborated articles, which we are not unfrequently called upon to notice. We are

hands of a tasteful designer, may be made an elegant adjunct to the drawing-room. However elaborate or beautiful the design and execution of such articles of modern furniture may be, we must confess that we think heaviness of construction,

artisan should be the construction of a receptacle for light, which, like that element, should be ethereal, and graceful, and ponderosity be especially eschewed. The BEDSTEAD, by the same manufacturers, has the quality of lightness in a

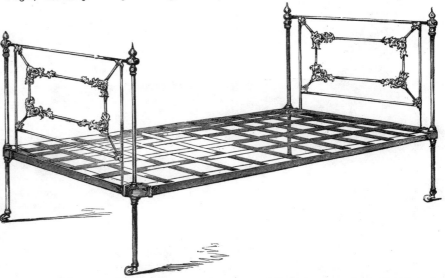

convinced, from long experience, that it is far easier to produce such works, than to confine decoration to that which is simple and appropriate; the former may be done by the ornamentist, the latter only by the artist of taste.

The two CHAIRS and the large SIDEBOARD which appear on this page are the work of Messrs. HUNTER, of London. The chairs are of very elegant design, and are beautifully carved; they are, however, as remarkable for their comfort as for their elegance, and present all that is requisite for the beauty or the ease of the drawing-

wood for decorative purposes. The embellishments of this large and important work are all indicative of its use; the laden branches of the vine encircle it, from between which peep the

The VASE in the centre is a foreign contribution; it is one of the valuable productions of Russia. It is entirely constructed of Jasper, and though good in form, its great recommendation is its large value. The wealth of the Russian mines and quarries has long been a celebrated feature of the country; and the contributions it

room. The sideboard is carved in a bold and massive style, entirely from the wood of the walnut tree, which has been chosen by the manufacturer to show the capability of English

heads of bacchanals; and the cornucopiæ, filled to overflowing with the plentiful fruits of the earth, give large promise of abundance. It is, altogether, a well-conceived production.

has sent us testify abundantly to the truth of "travellers' tales" connected therewith. We purpose engraving, in a future number, other subjects worthy of notice from this vast empire.

It is rather surprising that the English manufacturer of carpets should, till within the last few years, be so far behind his foreign competitor as, it must be acknowledged, he has been, seeing that the use of these fabrics is so much more general here than elsewhere; and it is an axiom among the trading community, that not only the supply of an article should keep pace with the demand, but also that a stimulus should be given to the demand by every kind of improvement of which the object in question is capable. Now there is scarcely an article of ordinary

domestic use better calculated to develope the artistic resources of the manufacturer's mind than those to which we are now referring, whether they are intended for the dwellings of the middle classes, or the mansions of the wealthy, and, in consequence, we have latterly noticed they exhibit a far greater degree of refinement and taste than we were wont to see shown in them. Among the contributors of carpets of various degrees of quality, some rich, and others suited to more common purposes, are Messrs. A. LAPWORTH & Co., of London,

from whose contributions we have made some selections. The first engraving represents an elegant HEARTH-RUG, designed for Messrs. Lapworth by Miss Gann, a clever pupil of the School of Design at Somerset House. The design is simple, but very elegant, being nothing more than wreaths of white and red roses, upon a dark, claret-coloured ground; in the border, a white ribbon is entwined with them. The other subject is from a rich Axminster CARPET; the borders, corners, and centre of this are exceedingly fanciful, but they manifest much beauty.

The palm of excellence in gold and silver ornamental works has hitherto, almost universally, been conceded to the manufacturers of France; but those who have attentively examined British works of this class, and, among others, the productions of Mr. J. ANGELL, of London, will be inclined to qualify their admiration of the contributions of foreign rivals; this, too, with-

out any disparagement of their merits. If we had no other examples in the Exhibition whereby to prove the immense progress made in this department of industrial art we could confidently appeal to these works as evidences of our advance. The present is unquestionably the age of improvement as well as of invention, and every object of ornamental or useful application, from the toy with which childhood amuses itself, to the gigantic steam-

engine that either multiplies the labours of man's ingenuity, or disperses them throughout the world, is a witness to the fact. Capital, taste, and skill have been liberally expended to bring about such improvement. The application of the Fine Arts to manufactures has made rapid strides within the last few years; science has kept pace with them, developing new

the appreciation of the public: hence have arisen renewed efforts on the part of the former to carry still further his improvements, and to invite the patronage of the latter. But we must not exhaust our space with preliminary remarks, to the exclusion of a description of Mr. Angell's beautiful productions. Among the objects for which we could not find room are several groups,

resources of colour and material to realise every new artistic conception of beauty and elegance. The manufacturers have bestirred themselves manfully; in earthenware, porcelain, glass, iron, and metal work generally, and in the textile fabrics, the progress has been marked and rapid; and what is of still greater importance, the labours of the producer have been met by

and salvers in silver and silver-gilt, richly wrought, and finely designed; the subjects we have especially noticed as worthy of being recorded are—"The Battle of Alexander and Darius," on a chased shield; "The Labours of Hercules," on a salver; groups of "Sir Roger de Coverley and the Gipsies," and "Arab Merchants Halting in the Desert." Our selection has been chiefly from works of less magnitude, but not of less value as works of high art. The first is a SILVER CUP, excellent in form, and richly embellished with floriated patterns; the base exhibits an elegant novelty. By the side of this is a CAKE-BASKET, of silver-gilt; the border is enamelled work, as are also the orna-

ments between the indented parts. The GROUP

at the bottom of the page is composed of some

very splendid objects; the large cup to the left

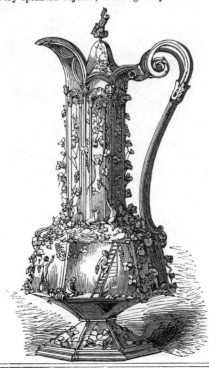

is in gold and enamels; it stands a considerable height, and is most exquisite in its elaborate and delicate workmanship; the centre-piece is

it is a truly beautiful example of the chaser's skill. The smaller objects in the process are scarcely less worthy of favourable remark. On this page we first introduce a SILVER JUG, of a

called the "VINTAGE JUG," is of gold, with the ornaments in silver; the combination of the two metals, one burnished and the other "matted," produces a brilliant effect. The first

one of a set of four table ornaments, intended by their designs to represent the four seasons. The large VASE to the right is of silver enamelled;

fluted pattern, graceful in its proportions: this is followed by another in gold, of Etruscan form, a present to Dr. Elliotson from one of his patients; and the third in the same column,

TEA AND COFFEE SERVICE is of silver-gilt and enamelled in the richest style; the GROUP underneath it is composed of various objects in silver, glass and silver, and silver enamelled;

and the last TEA AND COFFEE SERVICE is of silver, set with enamels. While adverting to the taste which has produced the whole of the objects we have engraved, we are bound to

notice especially the beauty of the enamelling, which we scarcely remember to have seen equalled. The difficulty of enamelling upon silver is, we are assured, not easily surmounted.

We introduce on this column the CAPITAL OF A PILLAR, and a PINNACLE, manufactured by Mr. BLANCHARD, of Lambeth. They are executed in white terra cotta. The former, though ex-

hibiting no originality in design, is wrought with a sharpness and delicacy, as if cut from the solid stone. The latter is one of the largest architectural ornaments hitherto made in this material.

Messrs. SMEE & SON, of London, exhibit the CANOPY BEDSTEAD, of which an engraving appears below. It is manufactured of mahogany,

boldly carved, and the hangings are of rich crimson Spitalfields silk. There is sufficient ornament in this object to constitute it an ele-

gant article of domestic furniture, but the manufacturers have not aimed at producing an elaborate work of industrial art. The CABINET that succeeds is also from the same establishment. It is inlaid with very beautiful marquetrie; the sides have plate-glass inserted.

The CANOE is one of the contributions from Canada. It is made of the bark of a tree, and is exceedingly light in its construction. There is, likewise, in this department of the Exhibition another canoe, much larger in size, capable of holding twenty men. It was brought through lakes and rivers, twelve hundred miles, to be shipped for England. As we observed in a former page, with reference to the contributions from Canada, there are few having any pretensions to ornamental works; utility, rather than display, being the object of the colonial manufacturer. The canoe is an example of native ingenuity.

This engraving represents the centre of a DAMASK TABLE-CLOTH, designed by Joseph Blain, pupil of the Government School of Design in Belfast; and manufactured by Messrs. CORRY, BLAIN, & Co., of the same town, on the new system of steam-loom weaving, which is, we believe, the first successful effort made to manufacture linen damask by steam power. There is also a novelty in the purpose of the design here introduced, which admits of some explanation; each group being figurative and expressive of an object according to the language of flowers. Our space will not permit us to go into the details of the matter, which we must leave to the reader's ingenuity to decipher.

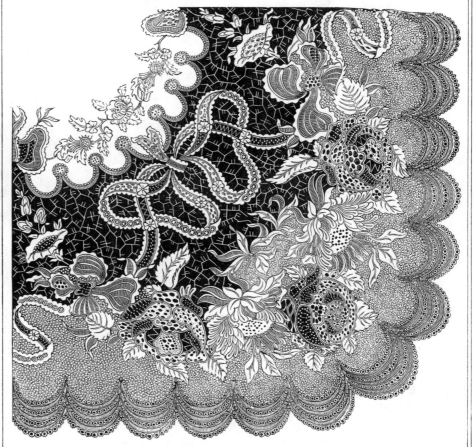

The two subjects occupying the latter half of this page are exhibited by Messrs. B. SALOMONS & SONS, of London; the first is a CANZOU, or LADY'S CAPE, of embroidered needle-work, most beautiful and elaborate in its pattern, and worked with great delicacy and finish. The other engraving is from a French cambric HANDKER-CHIEF that exhibits an equal amount of taste in its design, and of superior execution; it also displays every known description of stitch in this kind of embroidery. It would almost seem that ingenuity and patient industry could go no farther in such matters than have been expended on these textile fabrics, which must have occupied

no inconsiderable time in their production. Hitherto the foreign manufacturer has held almost the entire command of the English markets; but the contents of the south-eastern gallery of the Exhibition shows much in no way inferior to the best fabrics of the continent.

The VASE OF FLOWERS is a well-executed specimen of wood-carving, by Mr. PERRY, of Taunton. The contents of the vase, so to speak, is a bunch of roses only, but the vase itself is ornamented with an allegorical composition, in which the artist's idea has been to show the probable effects of the Great Exhibition upon the whole world. In this Mr. Perry has evinced considerable ingenuity, but it would far exceed the limits of our space to enter upon any lengthened descriptive explanation. The design

upon the stand is a circle of flowers and plants, emblematical of various countries of the globe. We think the artist's intention in his allegorical design would have told better, if done on a larger scale; it is too full of subject for its size.

On this and the two succeeding pages we engrave some beautiful specimens of DAMASK TABLE LINEN, from the extensive and far-famed manufactory of Mr. M. ANDREWS, Ardoyne,

ment of the Growth of Flax in Ireland. Both the NAPKIN and TABLE-CLOTH bear appropriate designs and ornaments; the former contains the arms of the Lord Lieutenant, encircled by a

Belfast. The first two examples are styled the "Clarendon Pattern," having been made for presentation to the Earl of Clarendon by the Royal Society for the Promotion and Improve-

wreath and inscription, with an elegant floriated border; the centre of the latter shows the star of the Order of the Garter, in a garland of the rose, shamrock, and thistle, with other devices.

That our American friends, with all their apparent dislike of pomp and parade, are not insensible to the luxuries and conveniences of life, is evident from the elegant CARRIAGES they exhibit. The one engraved is manufactured and exhibited by Messrs. CLAPP & SON, of Boston.

We introduce on this column another of the contributions from Canada, an elegantly-built and tastefully ornamented single SLEIGH, built by Messrs. M'LEAN & WRIGHT, of Montreal.

On this column are STATUETTES, executed in statuary porcelain, at the works of Mr. COPELAND.

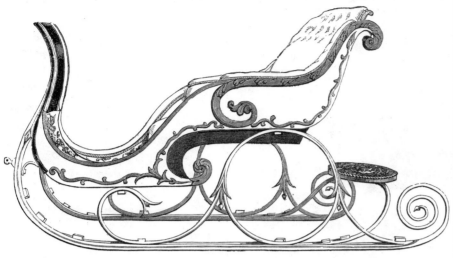

The engraving underneath is from the "Clarendon" DAMASK TABLE-CLOTH, by Mr. ANDREWS, described on the preceding page. It is an admirable specimen of his art-manufacture.

from models by Cumberworth, of Paris; the sub-

jects are the Indian Fruit-girl, and Water-bearer. The attitudes of these figures are very graceful.

THE INDUSTRY OF ALL NATIONS.

Another description of American carriages is copied from a single horse phaeton, manufactured by Mr. WATSON, of Philadelphia. One peculiarity we notice in it, is the unusual size of the fore-wheels compared with the hinder, so contrary to the practice of our carriage-builders, but there is no doubt this causes it to run easily. The body of the vehicle seems very light in its construction.

A wicker GARDEN-CHAIR, contributed by Mr. TOPF, of New York, possesses much novelty, and no little taste, in its ornamental design.

The TABLE-CLOTH called the "Ardoyne Exhibition Pattern," is another of the beautiful fabrics of Mr. M. ANDREWS, of Belfast. It was designed, in competition, by J. Mackenzie, of the Belfast School of Design, who richly merited the prize he obtained for a composition so excellent.

On this and the three following pages, our readers are introduced to illustrations from far-famed establishment, which has now been in existence for more than a century, stands about

seven miles from Paris, and its extensive museum and show-rooms have long been points of attraction to every visitor to the French Metropolis. The number of workmen employed in the manufactory is about one hundred and

some of the PORCELAIN WORKS exhibited by the Government Manufactory at SÈVRES. This fifty, and the artists engaged in the ornamental department are of the first merit, as those who are acquainted with

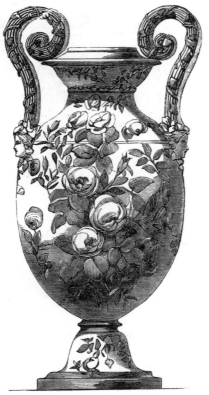

the Sèvres porcelain must readily acknowledge; while the general

direction of the affairs of the establishment is undertaken by

a body of some of the most able artists and scientific men in the country. The present administrator-general is M. Ebelmen. M.

Dieterle, to whom we are indebted for the drawings supplied to us, has charge of the artistic department, under the council; and

M. Vital Roux superintends the ateliers. Our space precludes us from giving a list of the

numerous staff of artists, male and female, by whom these gentlemen are assisted; it is

sufficient to say they are, in every way, qualified for the important duties devolving upon them. Our first engraving represents a LAMP, designed and executed by M. Klagmann;

TAZZA, of elegant proportions, with a light, floriated border under the rim; and this is followed by a VASE of Etruscan form, ornamented with flowers. A covered VASE succeeds this,

on the shade are figures emblematical of Evening, Morning, Silence, and Sleep; on the body are little genii of various kinds. The second column commences with a small, flat-shaped

with Alhambresque borders, exceedingly graceful in shape, and covered with elaborate painting; and the column is completed by a CUP, in the Cellini style, ornamented with designs of

Raffaellesque character. The second page opens with a VASE of ancient form, embellished with

bold and rich groups of flowers; by its side stands another VASE, entitled the "Agricultural

Vase;" on the side seen in the engraving is a labourer conducting his plough, attended by the four Seasons; the opposite side shows a horse, with its characteristic qualities of strength, beauty, courage,

and swiftness; this vase is designed by M. Klagmann. Underneath these is a large VASE, called the "Vase of Labour," symbolised by an elegantly-designed frieze, in which Agriculture, Industry, Study, and Religious Education are represented; the medallions indicate Ceres, Vulcan, and Minerva; the figures on the plinth are the Fates. On the third page is a VASE of Chinese form, decorated with birds and flowers; and, by its side, a TABLE, the top of which has flowers painted by M. Schiltz; the bronze stand is by M. Matifat.

description, to do it justice, would far exceed our limits. The GROUP on the fourth

page is composed of a number of very beautiful objects. The covered VASE that

follows is designed in the best taste; the ornaments are in the style of Raffaelle.

The three objects filling the last column are in the highest degree meritorious.

Messrs. POUSSIELGUE & RUSAND, are extensive manufacturers, in Paris, of every kind of furniture for ecclesiastical purposes, such as chandeliers,

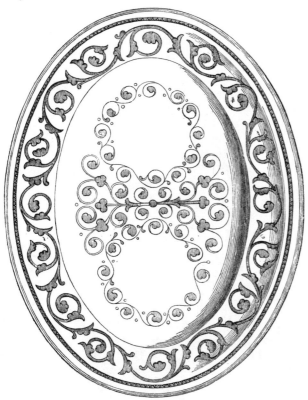

shrines, monstrances, lamps, cups, &c.: this page is devoted to a few of

the ornament is in keeping with the use to which they are applied. The OSTENSOIR, or confessional screen, is an elaborate and rich piece of work-

manship of very elegant
scarcely necessary for us

and novel design. It seems
to remark that, in every-

their contributions, commencing with a communion SALVER and CHALICE of silver, with gilt ornaments. The two EWERS are more decorated, but

thing connected with the forms and ceremonies of the Roman Catholic worship, there is more external magnificence than in any other church.

On this and the following page will be found engravings from a large variety of objects, manufactured by Messrs. APSLEY PELLATT & Co., of the Falcon Glass-Works, London. The first is

a VASE for flowers, forming part of a dessert-service; the cutting is peculiar; fine splits cross each other at right angles, and these, being set into sunken pannels, leave raised flat squares, or

diamonds; the shadows produced by them alternating with the brightness of the splits, produce a beautifully-varied and prismatic effect; the whole of this dessert-service is a fine

specimen of modern glass and glass-cutting. A CLARET-JUG, to be mounted in silver, follows; it affords an excellent contrast between the bright ground and the dead engraving. A WATER-JUG

of pure form and cutting, succeeds; the material of which it is made is exquisitely transparent.

chandeliers composed of white glass, the one prominent object in their manufacture should

produce the splendid natural prismatic colours. Great attention seems to have been paid to this

The whole construction of the next object, a CHANDELIER, is novel, and very effective: in all

be, by the form and cutting of the parts, to break and refract the rays of light, and thus to

essential matter in this chandelier, the whole body appearing one entire mass of glass, cut into large diamond-shape pieces. Underneath this is a GROUP, the centre object of which is the ETAGERER of the dessert-service already referred to; the others are CLARET-JUGS of elegant work-

manship, and SALT-CELLARS, broad and massive in design. This page commences with a CLARET-JUG of antique form, and richly ornamented

with florid engraving. Of the engraving on the first WINE-DECANTER we cannot speak too highly, the deep intaglio of the fruit presenting a roundness of form and delicacy of outline

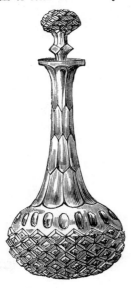

quite unique. The other DECANTER exhibits a style of cutting calculated to bring out the brilliancy of the glass. A CHANDELIER of colossal dimensions is one of the most effective

we have seen for a long time; the drops are very large, although their magnitude is lost in the vast size of the chandelier itself; the fan ornaments, formed of independent drops of different lengths set together, are novel;

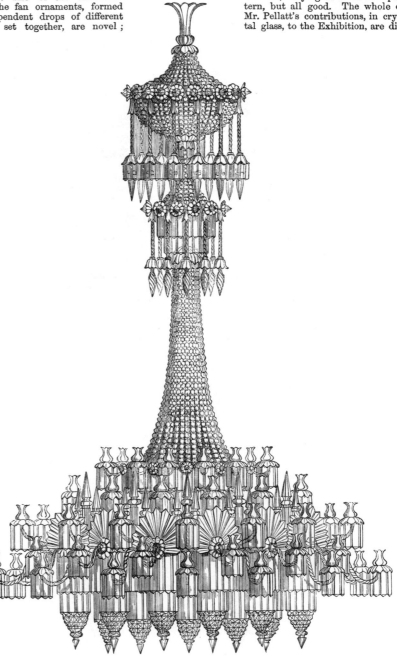

indeed, the entire object is one of great beauty. The last illustration is a GROUP OF WINE-GLASSES, varying in form and pattern, but all good. The whole of Mr. Pellatt's contributions, in crystal glass, to the Exhibition, are dis-

tinguished by sound and pure taste, and by material and workmanship of a most superior character. To this gentleman the art is largely indebted, and to his exertions we may, in a

great degree, attribute the prominent position it has held, of late years, in Great Britain, defying the competition of the world, and excelling, in most particulars, the works of the old Venetians.

THE INDUSTRY OF ALL NATIONS.

Among the contributions in silver and electroplate, exhibited by Messrs. SMITH & NICHOLSON, of London, are the objects from which engravings appear on this page. Our space permits only a very brief description of them. A SALVER, supported by two figures, carrying baskets, repre-

senting Spring and Autumn; these are intended for FRUIT-DISHES. A CENTRE-PIECE, with the story of Narcissus at its base, the object itself

being modelled from the leaves and flower of the plant; and the SHAKSPEARE TESTIMONIAL, presented to Mr. Macready, which is designed in a manner highly complimentary to that great master of the histrionic art. In front of the salver is a FRUIT-BASKET of a very simple form.

The Austrian department has, since the opening of the Great Exhibition, been one of its principal points of attraction. Indeed, for a considerable period before that time, the announcements made as to the various articles intended to be sent had excited much interest. The furniture for a suite of palatial rooms by Mr. CARL LEISTLER, of Vienna, favourably known from the works he had executed for Prince Leichtenstein, was spoken of as a *point d'appui*. Expectation has been gratified, and the originality and beauty of his productions have obtained for him due applause. We have selected for engraving the principal objects of the series; and commence with two CHAIRS, both carved from the beautifully-veined and richly-tinted wood of the locust tree. The execution of the carved work upon these chairs merits high praise; it is exceedingly sharp and well-defined; the

designs are bold and massive. The PIANO is constructed of dark rosewood, inlaid in buhl-work, of gold, silver, and copper tints, producing an exceedingly gorgeous effect; which is further heightened by the figures on each side; the sockets for candles, and the consoles being richly gilt.

The TABLE which follows is also of dark rose-wood; the stem is of a singularly original and beautiful character. The great work of the series, however, is the STATE BEDSTEAD, most elaborately carved in locust-tree wood; it is decorated with a series of statuettes and bas-reliefs in the same material, typical of man's career. commencing with figures of Adam and Eve, on the foot-board, and ending with scenes of his regeneration, at the head. An abundance of carved work of a fanciful kind is

spread over its surface; the hangings are constructed of crimson damask and velvet of various depths of tint, fringed with gold lace, and the work altogether is as sumptuous as it is thoroughly artistic.

The glass manufacture of Bohemia has obtained high celebrity for the taste of its form and the beauty of its colour; and the manufacturers of that country have in no wise done their European celebrity any discredit by their contributions. We select a few examples from the contributions of M. WILHELM HOFFMANN, of Prague.

They occupy a prominent position in the transept—a place of honour their intrinsic excellence deserves. They comprise a great variety of articles, as well for the every-day use of life as for the more luxurious ornament of the boudoir, or its needful elegancies.

There is a delicate appreciation of tender hues of colour in these productions well worthy of attentive study; this elevates the simplest of them far above the gaudy vulgarities occasionally fabricated, and termed "Bohemian glass," and which are chiefly remarkable for the strong contrasts of deep colour, and abundant display of gilding upon their surface. M. Hoffmann's works have no such defects. The large vase and its pedestal is nearly four feet in height, and is entirely of pure white, except where the leaves bend over, and they are tinted with pale green. Altogether M. Hoffmann's display is as satisfactory as that of any manufacturer in the Exhibition.

The TABLE is another of the works of M. Leistler, it is carved from the locust-tree wood

there is much fancy displayed in the arrangement of the ornament upon the central support, which is of a quaint and original character. The design and execution are both alike excellent.

The elegant marble CHIMNEY-PIECE—and GLASS, the frame of which is constructed of the same material—is the work of GUISEPPE BOTTINELLI, of Milan, the figures being executed by DEMOCRITE GANDOLFI, a brother artist of the same city. The design is of much elegance, and highly suggestive.

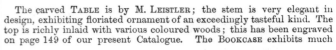

This CHAIR is the production of M. AUGUST KITSCHELT, of Vienna; it is of free and fanciful design, more remarkable for the taste of the upholsterer than the wood-carver. It is covered with velvets of delicate hues, pink and blue predominating; the arrangement of the colours is very tasteful; the trimmings are of a pale golden hue. There is a lightness and fancy in its construction which bespeaks the best taste.

The carved TABLE is by M. LEISTLER; the stem is very elegant in design, exhibiting floriated ornament of an exceedingly tasteful kind. The top is richly inlaid with various coloured woods; this has been engraved on page 149 of our present Catalogue. The BOOKCASE exhibits much

novelty of design; it is constructed of white lime-tree wood, relieved by panels, &c., of satinwood. The group of children which surround the canopy are very beautifully carved, and the entire portion of the ornamental work is executed with force and elegance. It is as beautiful an example of manipulative skill, as of general ability in design. The Italian taste of the renaissance is the predominating character of style

chosen; it has been successfully adapted, in the present instance to a portion of furniture, which "coarse or unskilful hands" have generally made square and unsightly, but which, in the hands of a skilful manufacturer, may be converted into an elegant piece of ornamental furniture.

From the ROYAL PORCELAIN MANUFACTORY of Copenhagen is exhibited a large variety of works of a useful and ornamental character; among the latter, some beautiful figures, busts, &c., in biscuit china, after Thorwaldsen's models. We introduce here his famous group of GANYMEDE.

We have already described and engraved some of the works produced at the Royal Porcelain Manufactory at Dresden, and must refer to former pages of the Catalogue for a description of this establishment. We now add two more

A very tasteful radiating HALL-STOVE is exhibited by Mr. J. HAYWOOD, of Derby, sufficiently rich in its ornamental work to grace the most aristocratic mansion in the land. As it is very

specimens of their works, both of which are remarkable for vigour of conception, in styles the most opposite to each other—the one partaking of the fancy of the east, the other charac-

probable some critical eye may discover a little inaccuracy of perspective in the drawing of the hearth-plate, it is necessary to state that it has been so placed the better to show the design.

teristic of the period when Dresden china first became celebrated throughout Europe for its beauty of form and fabric,—characteristics which appear upon the works we have selected.

On this and the subsequent page we introduce engravings from some of the numerous contributions of Messrs. RICE HARRIS & SON, of the Islington Glass Works, Birmingham. Some estimate may be formed of the extent and importance of this establishment, when we enumerate among its contributions articles in flint-glass, cut and engraved; pressed and moulded glass tumblers, goblets, wine-glasses, sugar-basins, butter-coolers, door-knobs, &c. ; orna-

is a VASE, black coated, with white enamel, richly cut, and ornamented with gold and silver. The

mental glass, of various colours, gilt and enamelled, cut and engraved, consisting of tazzas, compotiers, liqueur-services, toilet-bottles, claret-jugs, vases; specimens of colours combined by casing or coating; specimens of threaded or Venetian glass; in short, examples of almost every kind of object into which this beautiful material is capable of being manufactured. The

small VASE at the head of the succeeding

column is ruby-coloured, with cut gilt lines,

space we have, therefore, devoted to illustrating a portion of them, is not greater than their excellence demands, and we regret our inability to find room for a more lengthened description than we are able to give of what are introduced. The first group consists of VASES and GOBLETS, elaborately engraved and cut; in the centre of the second group of VASES, GOBLETS, and a JUG,

and the next is an opaque yellow VASE, cut and

scalloped with chased gilt flowers; the VASE

that follows is deeply cut in a novel style of

ornament. In the upper group on this page, to

the left, is a VASE of ruby glass, with cut plates.

and gilt chased ornaments; and by its side a large GOBLET and COVER, of ground crystal, covered with ruby and white, richly cut in three

centre of the lower group is a large alabaster VASE, nearly five feet high, elegantly and

opaque white, enamelled, heightened with gold in the ornament and handle; and in the left of the group is a VASE of dark, opaque blue, cut

shields; on one are the royal arms of England, and on the other two the monograms of the Queen and Prince Albert respectively. In the

tastefully ornamented with gilt scrolls; on either side stands a JUG and GOBLET, of

and scalloped, and ornamented with oak-leaves and acorns in silver. The whole of these works are executed in the highest degree of finish.

We have, on former occasions, made ourselves acquainted

with the manufactured works of Messrs. MESSENGER & SONS, of Birmingham, who are contributors to the great Exhibition

of an extensive variety of useful and ornamental productions

in iron, bronze, &c., distinguished by elegance and correctness of design, and excellent workmanship. Of these we might have

ful in form and character: the next is a GROUP, in bronze and or-morlu, of the Queen

is, in all respects, a good example of English casting. A stair-case BALUSTRADE, in or-

beneath it is equally entitled to commendation, and the VASE, of open-work, is both

selected a large number for illustration, if our space had been less limited. The CANDLE-STICK, which commences this page is grace-

and the Prince of Wales, modelled by Mr. John Bell,—the distinguished sculptor. It

morlu, is an admirable piece of work in form, colour, and casting. The INKSTAND

light and elegant. The firm of Messenger and Sons has amply sustained its reputation.

We should most assuredly have omitted one of the *greatest* features of the Exhibition had we neglected to introduce into our Catalogue the colossal statue of the renowned crusader, GODFREY OF BOUILLON, modelled by M. SIMONIS, of Brussels. It is a work conceived in a noble spirit, and as admirably carried out.

Some objects of manufacture, novel in this country but much practised by

the continental jewellers, are exhibited by Mr. F. ALLEN, of Birmingham; we engrave two FLOWER-VASES, of fillagree-

The SCROLL underneath is another of the many valuable contributions of Messrs. MESSENGER & SONS, of Birmingham; it is intended for a gas-bracket, and shows a very graceful arrangement of curved lines.

work, made of fine gold threads throughout; they are exquisitely delicate.

Messrs. JACKSON & GRAHAM, the eminent upholsterers, of London, are large contributors

to the Great Exhibition of many important articles of their manufacture. We engrave on

this column a portion of a BOOK-CASE, the panels of which are fitted with plate-glass, and the end

of a SOFA, showing a demi-figure, boldly carved. The SIDEBOARD and CHEVAL-GLASS, with their

underneath are good in their respective styles. The BOOK-CASE on the next page exhibits the best

taste in its design; the artist has evidently aimed to combine simplicity of idea with a due

bronze candlesticks and ornaments, are beautiful in design, and admirably carved; the CHAIRS

regard to richness of detail. The CARPET shows a bold and well-tilled pattern, arrayed in bright

and harmonious colours. It is quite evident, from the examples here shown, that Messrs.

Jackson & Graham employ artists of no common order to furnish them with designs for their manufactures; and to this circumstance may be traced the large amount of business carried ou

by the firm. Public taste has, of late years, increased to such an extent, that mediocre productions find little chance of sale; hence the best producer is certain of being recompensed in proportion to the spirit and taste with which he may conduct his manufacturing transactions.

The manufacture of the particular kind of earthenware generally known as "BEAUVAIS

WARE," is carried on in places far distant from that ancient town. The three objects occupying

this column are from the factory of M. DE BOISSIMON, of Langeais, in the Department of Indre et

Loire; he is also the producer of other objects, applicable to mere purposes of utility. The VASES are beautiful examples of the "ware."

The musical instrument shown in the appended engraving is from the manufactory of Messrs. LUFF & SON, of London; it is called by the exhibitors an "Albert Cottage Pianoforte HARMONIUM;" the design of the case is elegant, being carved with much elaborate workmanship.

The engraving underneath is from a printed cloth TABLE-COVER, commemorative of the Great Exhibition, manufactured and exhibited by Mr. W. UNDERWOOD, of London, from a design by Mr. Slocombe. It is exceedingly rich in its ornamental work, conspicuous among which are the

royal arms of England, surrounded, in the centre and border, by those of the principal nations contributing to the grand display of industrial art; appropriate mottoes enclose the whole.

From one of our most picturesque and fashionable provincial towns, we have a display of plate

and jewellery unsurpassed by places of greater celebrity. Messrs. MARTIN, BASKETT, & MARTIN, of Cheltenham, are the contributors of the objects introduced on this page. The first is a richly

chased CLARET-JUG, after Cellini, a sufficient guarantee for its beauty. The next is a SALT-CELLAR, showing great novelty and elegance in its design, and very skilful execution. The two

subjects heading the other columns are respectively termed a PORTE-MONTRE and CHATELAINE; they are made on such a principle as to suit watches of any size, besides having the advantage

of keeping the watch secure and steady. A BUTTER-COOLER succeeds; the dish for the butter is of white marble, the ornament, consisting of leaves and butter-cups, is of silver, the interior of the flowers being gilt; the combination of

these materials produces a very chaste effect. The last illustration is from a BRACELET, formed of gold, enamels, diamonds, and carbuncles, in the following style: the diamonds are placed

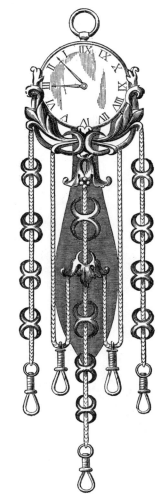

over the carbuncles; the gold cross-bands connecting the precious stones are slightly enamelled in scroll-work of a rich turquoise-blue colour, forming altogether a brilliant and perfect ornament. Other contributions of these tasteful manufacturers are some beautiful pearl ornaments, an ink-stand on which is modelled a group of Milton and his daughters, a silver-gilt toilette stand, tea-services, centre-pieces, and a

large variety of chronometers and watches. One would scarcely expect to see such productions emanating from a place having no manufacturing notoriety; but the call upon our national industry seems to have been answered from every quarter, even where the least expected.

M. REGOUT, of Maestricht, Holland, exhibits some tasteful FLOWER-STANDS of bronze; articles

of elegant luxury, which we are glad to know are becoming more generally adopted for the

decoration of our houses. We engrave two specimens, one in the form of an antique tripod, the other in a more free and fanciful style.

We have elsewhere found occasion to notice the great improvement visible in the papier-mâché works of the present day, as contrasted with those of a few years since; this improvement characterises the works of nearly every manufacturer in this branch of trade.

and gilding, on the dark ground usually adopted, cannot be by us represented. The DRESSING-TABLE beneath is a very light and tasteful production; the glass swings freely from scrolls which spring from each side, and thus the ordinary objectionable stand for this necessary

article is obviated, and a positive gain in the general appearance effected. The CHAIR has also the merit of grace and lightness, and the FOOTSTOOL is of a novel and agreeable form. Mr. Clay deserves this meed of praise for the skill he has displayed in the selection of designs

The PAPIER-MÂCHÉ works exhibited by Mr. H. CLAY, comprise tea-trays and articles of furniture of much lightness and elegance. An elaborate and beautiful design for one of these TEA-TRAYS we here engrave, premising that we can give the design only; the brilliancy of colour

for manufacture in this material. It is pleasant to know that manufacturers of such old standing are willing and able thus to exert their capital and ability in upholding the character they have obtained. It is a good and healthy tone of mind, which we are glad to recognise generally.

An EMBROIDERED VEST, manufactured and exhibited by Messrs. McGEE & Co., of Belfast, from a design by J. B. Wilkinson, of the School of Design in that town, combines neatness with elegance of pattern. The drawing gained the prize of 5*l.*, offered by the manufacturers for the best design.

This engraving is from a piece of SILK, manufactured by M. GABIAN, of Berlin, with whose establishment we were much interested on our recent tour of inspection through Germany. The pattern displays great boldness; the silk itself, we presume, is intended chiefly for Royal use, as explained by the black eagle of Prussia, with its spreading wings.

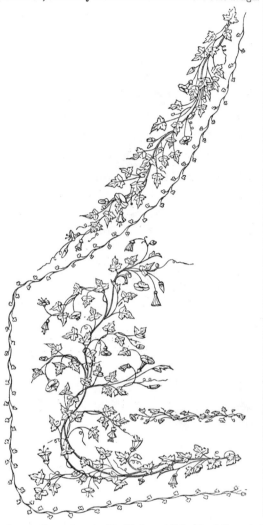

Among the various textile fabrics exhibited by Messrs. REDMAYNE & SON, of London, is a piece of RIBBON, the pattern of which we here introduce; the design is very graceful, consisting of floriated wreaths, in which is the passion-flower, one of the most beautiful productions of the garden.

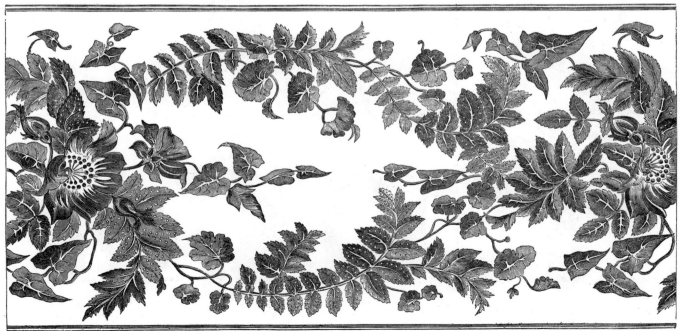

A small but well-selected display of silver work and jewellery is made by Mr. R. ATTEN-

BOROUGH, of London, from which we have chosen a few examples for introduction on this page.

The first is a SPOON, to which the manufacturer has given the title of the "Paxton Spoon," in

compliment to the gentleman whose name is so worthily associated with the vast undertaking in Hyde Park; the design of the spoon is in pure

leaves set with brilliants. The TAZZA with its top is excellent and novel in form, and exhibits some very elaborate engraving; it also shows

or Bachelor's Pattern," is worthy of commendation from its simple but pure form; the only attempt at ornament is in the handles, and

prize cup, &c., all of which are highly creditable to his taste, and to the skill of those whom he employs to work out his designs. He is one of

classic taste. The BRACELET that follows this is of very choice workmanship; the cable is of massive gold, and the pendent consists of vine-

the effect that can be produced by the various methods of working upon silver, gilding, and chasing. The TEA-SERVICE, called the "Albany,

the borders, or rims. Besides the objects we have engraved, Mr. Attenborough exhibits a silver centrepiece for the table, an agricultural

the many who uphold the reputation of England in a branch of the industrial arts, in which we are so rapidly advancing in every department.

Messrs. ELKINGTON, MASON, & Co., of London and Birmingham, are extensive contributors of their celebrated electro-plate manufactures, a

branch of industrial art which has made immense strides since the patent for the various processes of gilding and plating metals by the agency of

electricity was granted to this firm in 1840. Messrs. Elkington alone employ about five hundred work-people in their establishment, and about thirty other British manufacturers have

licences to use this process, which is also extensively adopted in foreign countries; thus some

dilate upon the advantages which electro-plating possesses, as there must be few persons who

selection from the numerous objects which the glass cases of Messrs. Elkington in the Exhibition contain, but we think our examples will

ornamented with subjects taken from English national games—cricket and archery; the figures on these objects are well modelled, and the composition of each is very effective. The COM-

idea may be formed of its importance to the trading community. It is unnecessary for us to

have not practically tested its use and excellence. We have found some difficulty in making a

sufficiently illustrate the variety and artistic qualities of their productions. We commence with two TABLE ORNAMENTS, or FRUIT-DISHES,

MUNION-SERVICE, commencing this page, is designed in the ornamented Gothic style. The TEA and COFFEE-SERVICE, which follows, is an elegant adaptation of the arabesque pattern;

and the lower one is of richly-engraved Gothic.

A Jug and three Vases appear on this

column, each excellent of its kind; as are also

the CANDLESTICK and FLOWER-VASE; the former shows much originality of design. The next

engraving is from a large CENTRE-PIECE for eight

lights, in the style of the fifteenth century, with winged figures supporting baskets for fruit. The

CRUET-FRAME has an arabesque pattern, and the

CENTRE-PIECE which follows it is modelled from the "Crown imperial" plant. A very elegant

CLARET-JUG completes the next column; its form

and enrichments are highly to be commended.

We come now to what must be considered, for

design and workmanship, the most important

contribution of Messrs. Elkington,—a VASE, intended to represent the triumph of Science and the Industrial Arts in the Great Exhibition; the style is Elizabethan enriched. Four statuettes on the body of the vase represent Newton, Bacon, Shakspeare, and

Watt, commemorating Astronomy, Philosophy, Poetry, and Mechanics respectively. On the four bas-reliefs, between these figures, the practical operations of Science and Art are displayed, and their influences typified by the figures on the base, indicating War,

Rebellion, Hatred, and Revenge, overthrown and chained. The recognition and the reward of peaceful industry are symbolised by the figure of Prince Albert surmounting the composition, who, as Patron of the Exhibition, is rewarding the successful contributors. The height of the vase is four feet; it was designed and modelled by Mr. W. Beattie. Among the other manufactures of this firm, is a group, in silver, representing "Queen Elizabeth entering Kenilworth Castle."

THE INDUSTRY OF ALL NATIONS.

The two CARRIAGES engraved below are contributed by Messrs. JONES, BROTHERS, of Brussels, extensive manufacturers and exporters of carriages of all descriptions; employing in their different departments upwards of a hundred men. They have obtained five medals

The appended STOVE, from the manufactory of Mr. MAUND, of London, in no degree detracts from the elegance of the most classically-furnished hall, or other apartment, in which it may be placed. The general form is that of an antique urn, and is another proof of

or their productions at various exhibitions in Belgium, and in 1847 they gained the "Gala" medal.

These medals have been found of the greatest use as a stimulus to inventive industry among continental manufacturers, but, until the present period, they have been unknown in our own country. The rewards of this kind intended to be bestowed on native ability contributed to the Great Exhibition, will test its applicability to our own land, and, we have very little doubt, will be found as effective here, as they have certainly been proved to be upon the continent.

the great and universal applicability of the graceful designs of antiquity,—forms studied with perfect truth and beauty, which are capable of being reproduced for new purposes, unthought of by the men who imagined them, but whose pure taste has rendered their ideas immortal.

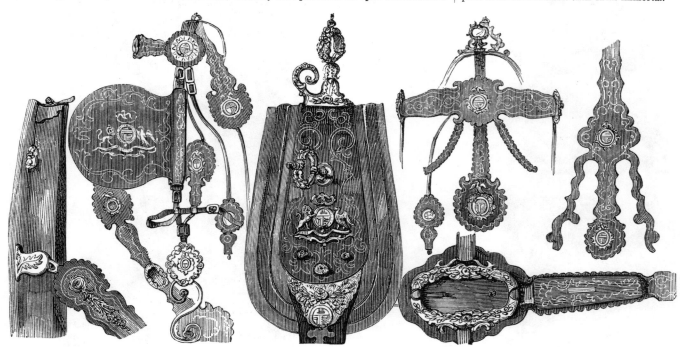

The various examples of decorative HARNESS, exhibited by Messrs. LACEY & PHILLIPS, of Philadelphia, exhibit manipulative skill, and are tasteful and elegant additions to the well-appointed equipage. The mountings are of silver, and the decoration is executed with very great care.

This is another of the CARPETS, manufactured by Messrs. T. SMITH & Co., of whose contributions we have inserted two examples in a former page. The pattern of this is very bold, and rich in colours, and the fabric itself is of the most luxurious character, uniting elegance of decoration with great warmth, the two grand desiderata requisite in manufactures of this description; we cannot possibly award them higher praise.

Our continental neighbours, on the other side of the Straits of Dover, have undoubtedly made a most excellent display in every kind of cabinet-work; this will not be thought singular by those who are acquainted with the demand which exists in France, and in Paris especially, for every description of decorative furniture. There is scarcely a house of public entertainment, of the better kind, in the French metropolis, that cannot show numerous articles in which the skill of the wood-carver and the taste of the designer, are not abundantly manifest; while the

private residences of the middle classes, and of the more wealthy, are supplied according to the means of each respectively. The CABINET engraved here is manufactured by M. RINGUET LEPRINCE; its chief interest, in our estimation, lies in the elegant simplicity of its ornament.

The Spoons and Sugar-ladle, manufactured and contributed by Mr. W. R. Smily, of London, will please exceedingly by their novelty, and a rich and graceful style of ornament; the running foliage on the handles of the spoons is a pretty idea, and the bowl of the sugar-ladle is good.

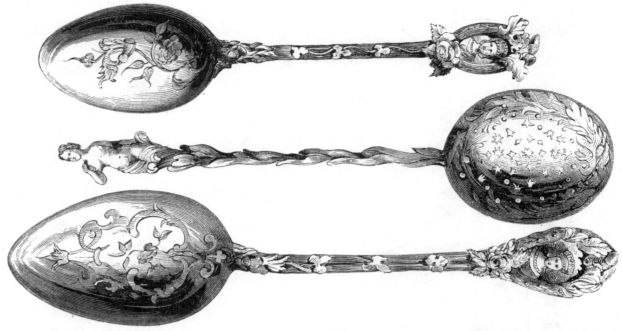

Mr. Jeakes, of London, is the manufacturer of the Stove and Fender which occupy the remainder of this page. The designs of the former object especially are most elaborate, and were, we are informed, supplied by Messrs. Lawford and Heneker, architects. The narrow

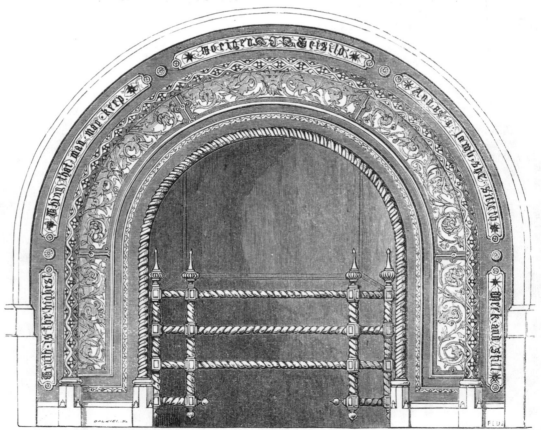

mouldings of the arch are fancifully varied, and form an agreeable contrast to the broader one, which shows a light, Raffaellesque kind of pattern.

The style and form of the twisted bars are uncommon, adding considerably to its novelty. The fender harmonises well with the stove.

The CHAIR is one of a set, manufactured by Messrs. W. & B. HILTON, of Montreal, in Canada, as a present to the Queen, from the ladies of that place, who have worked the tapestry.

The illustration underneath is from a damask TABLE-CLOTH, manufactured by Mr. BERRILL, of Dunfermline, especially for the American market. The medallion in the centre is intended for a portrait of Washington; it is surrounded by devices bearing reference to the part he acted in asserting the independence of his country. The border shows a bold and well-filled pattern.

From several CARPETS, manufactured and exhibited by Messrs. H. BRINTON & SONS, of Kidderminster, we have selected one for the purpose of engraving. It is a Brussels velvet, of an exceedingly bold and effective pattern, consisting of scrolls and the leaves of the palm-tree,

with some smaller floriated ornaments. There is infinite variety in the arrangement of the forms introduced, and great ingenuity and skill must have been exercised in combining them into an harmonious composition; notwithstanding which, the artist has succeeded in his object.

A set of polished steel FIRE-IRONS, with ormolu handles, by Messrs. H. & W. TURNER, of Sheffield, have as much elegance imparted to them as can be exhibited on objects affording but little scope for the exercise of the designer's taste.

Messrs. HANCOCK, RIXON, & DUNT, of London. exhibit a CHANDELIER, of cut glass, for thirty-two lights. The section of the body forms a star; the upper part is composed of drops, which are arranged in the shape of banners. It will present a brilliant appearance when lighted.

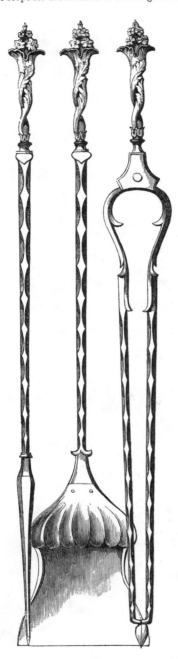

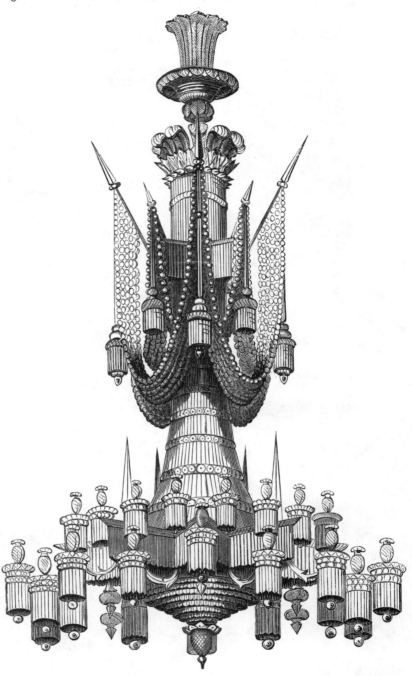

The illustration that fills the lower part of the page is from a piece of EMBROIDERED CLOTH, from the establishment of Messrs. HOULDSWORTH & Co., Manchester. The pattern is worked in what appears to be gold thread, on a deep moreen ground, presenting altogether an ex-

ceedingly rich effect, as the pattern stands out in bold relief. The cloth is intended for a table-cover, and a very splendid table-cover it makes.

Messrs. W. HARGREAVES & Co., of Sheffield, exhibit a large and well-selected assortment of cutlery, as table-knives, carvers, game-carvers, dessert-knives, from which we introduce here four examples of ornamental handles. The first two are of TABLE-KNIVES, in a bold style of workmanship, and carefully executed; the last is from a GAME CARVING-KNIFE, with a brace of birds at its termination; the third is an ivory-handled BREAD-KNIFE, which, in form, is a manifest improvement upon most of those in general use. All these handles are of fine ivory elaborately carved and mounted with silver ferules, and the blades are of the highest polished steel.

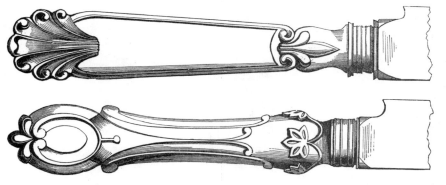

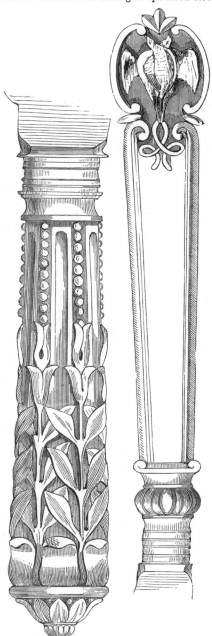

The engraving immediately underneath is from the hilt of a COUTEAU DE CHASSE, manufactured by M. DELACOUR, an extensive armourer, of Paris. The design is very elegant in all its details, but its merits are likely to be overlooked, without a close inspection of the work, which is of iron, bronzed and richly gilt.

A FRIEZE, modelled in plaster by Mr. J. HARMER, Jun., of Pentonville, shows considerable taste in the art of design as well as skill in the manipulation. The scroll is judiciously ornamented with flowers, leaves, and wheat-ears, and a variety of other natural objects, and it encloses some admirably arranged groups of fruit, &c.

The appended design is from a piece of SILK, exhibited by Messrs. REDMAYNE & SON, of London; it shows a graceful running pattern of natural objects—the rose, shamrock, and thistle.

Messrs. MESSENGER & SONS, of Birmingham, have a CANDELABRUM for ecclesiastical purposes.

A LIBRARY TABLE, manufactured by Messrs. GILLOW, of London, is worthy of the high position which the firm holds as cabinet-makers; it is of very simple construction, but elegant in its design: the *chimeræ* at the angles are boldly carved; the other ornaments are in excellent taste.

DANTE'S LOVERS are embodied by Mr. MUNRO in a touching and characteristic style; worthily depicting the simplicity and earnestness which the immortal poet has made the prevailing traits of those whose course of love "never did run smooth." The quaint costume gives an air of much truthfulness to the group, which is excellently composed.

A Rhenish legend has furnished M. ENGELHARD, of Hamburg, with the theme for a very lovely statue of LURLINE, the dangerously-beautiful resident of the Lurley-berg, who woos the boatmen to destruction.

The SIDEBOARD, by Mr. GILLOW, of London, is of bold design and spirited execution; it is an excellent specimen of the ability of our manufacturers in wood-carving, as well as of taste and fancy in composition. It shows a freedom from too great slavishness of idea, a determination to get rid of the trammels of conventional styles, which is very cheering to all who have felt its primary importance to native interests.

Messrs. MAPPIN, of Sheffield, some of whose contributions appeared in a former page of our Catalogue, are the manufacturers and exhibitors of the DESSERT KNIVES engraved underneath.

Mr. JAMES EDWARDS exhibits a gracefully-conceived bas-relief, which he terms "The Last Dream" in life, of a fair and delicate female, and illustrative of the passage, "her sun went down while it was yet day, but unto the upright there ariseth light in the darkness." The young girl has sunk to rest, peacefully and trustingly; the volume upon which her hope is founded rests on her bosom, and her last earthly imaginings are of the ever-living spirits who welcome her.

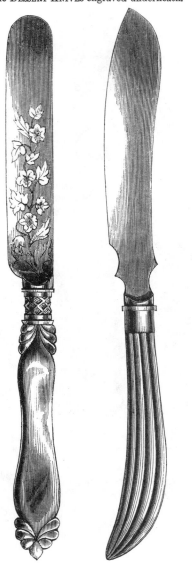

The manufacturers of BILLIARD-TABLES have recently introduced a great improvement into them, by the substitution of slate tops for wood.

That engraved is of this description; the frame is of Spanish mahogany, boldly carved. The manufacturers are Messrs. THURSTON & Co., of London.

The exquisitely beautiful Stove, enclosed in a mantel-piece of white statuary marble, is manufactured by Messrs. Yates, Haywood, & Co., of the Effingham Works, Rotherham, from the design of one of the artists of that establishment, Mr. George Wright. It is certainly one of the most superb objects of this kind which we remember to have seen. The hearth-plate slopes upwards, and is so contrived that the ashes, falling upon it, run through and are concealed. The andirons are composed of groups of foliage and rustic appendages, in the midst of

which are seated a shepherd and wood-nymph, charmingly modelled. The material of which it is made is steel, very highly polished, set with or-molu ornaments; we may add, that its construction is such as to require no fender. Messrs. Yates & Co. exhibit other articles—all designed and produced on their own premises, by their own workmen; a merit of no common value, and which augments the worth of their contributions.

The contributions from our fellow-countrymen in the Channel Islands are comparatively few, and of these, still fewer which attract attention as objects of manufacturing or decorative art. The only work we have found available for our purpose is a Cheffoniere, or sideboard, manufactured by Mr. G. C. Le Feuvre, of Jersey; it is made of oak, a portion of the wood being the produce of the island; the designs in the compartments are worked in tapestry. The upper part of the sideboard is omitted—as by no means so good as the portion we have engraved.

Messrs. H. C. McCREA, of Halifax, exhibit numerous specimens of FURNITURE DAMASKS, table-covers, poncho stuffs, &c.: we here engrave a piece of the first-named—the furniture-damask—of a bold and good pattern.

The CANDELABRUM is one of a pair formed of the purest crystal, by Messrs. F. & C. OSLER, of London and Birmingham, for her Majesty the Queen: each of them stands eight feet high, and is made to hold fifteen lights.

This engraving is also from a piece of FURNITURE DAMASK, manufactured by Mr. W. BROWN, of Halifax, an extensive producer of table-covers, &c.

The PEDIMENT of a fire-place, of bronzed iron, is from the foundry of M. EGELL, of Berlin, and is designed by Shinkel, after Thorwaldsen.

The engraving underneath represents a STAINED GLASS WINDOW, executed by Messrs. BALLANTINE & ALLAN, of Edinburgh. It is intended for the entrance-hall of Glenormiston, the property of Mr. W. Chambers. This estate is held direct from the Crown, on condition that the proprietor, when required, shall present the sovereign with a red rose on the festival of St. John. The design in the centre of the window represents this ceremony, which, according to local tradition, was last performed in 1529

Mr. W. HASLAM, of Derby, exhibits a specimen of IRON WORK, intended for the door of a church. It is, as far as can be ascertained, a fac-simile of that placed, in the year 1251, on the door of the chapel in which Prince Edward, afterwards Edward I., and his wife, Eleanor, attended divine service. This attempt on the part of Mr. Haslam to imitate the style of

the ancient church-wrought iron-work, which was carried to such high perfection during the period referred to, has been eminently successful.

an heiress of that period, supported by a knight, is offering a rose to the monarch; in the background, a retainer displays the banner of St. John. The picture, as well as the entire window, is surrounded by a rich border of ruby and gold, studded with imitations of gems. The background is pale blue, with gold bands, stencilled in white enamel, with the united national emblems—the rose, shamrock, and thistle. In the upper corners is the legend—"HE THAT THOLES (*i. e.* endures) OVERCOMES."

A WINE-COOLER, manufactured in terra-cotta, and exhibited by Mr. W. MARSH, of Longport, Staffordshire, merits commendation from the excellence of its design; in its form and ornament it displays taste of no ordinary kind. The chimeræ forming the handles are fanciful, but of a fashion which reminds us of some of the best antiques, both in mineral and metallic substances. The work is designed by one of the pupils of the Hanley school—an establishment that, with others of a similar character in the neighbouring locality, has done good service among the "potters."

Brussels Lace, that magnet of attraction to ladies, is contributed in great abundance and beauty, by many famed manufacturers of the Belgian capital. We have already engraved the contribution of one celebrated house; we now add another, by M. DELEHAYE, the successor to the well-known firm of Ducpetiaux & Co. It is a portion of the border of a LACE VEIL, and is remarkable for the delicacy and grace of its design, in which flowers, wreaths, and scrolls, are ingeniously combined to form an enriched pattern, through which a ribbon is entwined;

the line of this is prevented from becoming monotonous, by its combination with a leafy spray, introduced with the best possible taste. The same manufacturer exhibits some exquisite examples of handkerchiefs of equally graceful design, and remarkable for the extreme delicacy of their fabric. The patient labour and perseverance necessary to complete these exquisite additions to the toilette of beauty can scarcely be understood by those who have not witnessed their slow growth in the manufactory, in which years are consumed in the product of a single veil.

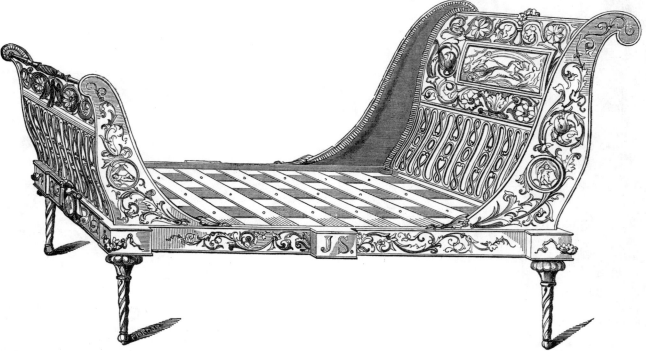

The IRON BEDSTEAD is a Spanish contribution, and is the work of TOMAS DE MEGNE, of Madrid. It presents some peculiar features of a graceful character, besides being well designed for its use. The great improvement in articles of this class, both at home and abroad, cannot fail to attract the notice of the most unreflective; the Crystal Palace alone contains a great and striking variety, both in construction and ornament.

The engravings on this column are from the papier-mâché contributions of Messrs. M'CULLUM and HODSON, of Birmingham, who have already

been noticed in one of the preceding pages of our Catalogue. The first is a LADIES' CABINET,

fitted with writing-desk, and drawers for various purposes, such as holding jewels, envelopes, &c.;

the second is a JEWEL-BOX of elegant form; underneath this is another LADIES' CABINET,

inlaid with pearl, containing work-box, &c.; and the last is a WORK-TABLE, also inlaid with pearl, with papier-mâché work-bag; the bag is somewhat of a novelty as regards its material.

The two subjects on this column are from the electro-silver-plate manufactory of Messrs. CARTWRIGHT & HIRONS, of Birmingham. Their establishment is, we are informed, of comparatively recent date, but there is no doubt, from the taste

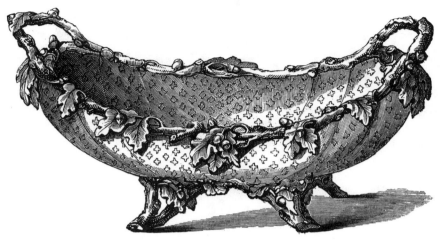

ornamented in a chaste style; it is mounted in a floriated pattern of carved oak. The other is

is entirely new in construction, the bottles and handle being made to revolve within the border, while the frame remains stationary; the orna-

exhibited in the few objects they have contributed to the great emporium of industry, that it will, ere long, become favourably and widely known. The first of our engravings is from a BASKET, for cake or fruit, of good form and

a large revolving LIQUEUR-STAND, to hold five bottles, with glasses between each. This frame

ment bears the same character with the preceding; the two objects, thus harmonising, being evidently intended to be used at the same time.

Messrs. GRAY & Co., of Birmingham, exhibit a variety of new designs for chandeliers and lamps,

constructed in the brass-work for which that city is famed. The free use of foliage in works

of this class is not without great value, in break-ing stiff and monotonous lines, and aiding the

general elegance of the entire composition. The only danger—and it is one, we confess, we often

see and regret—is the too free use of this ornamental adjunct; the *juste mileu* is not so easy to obtain as may be generally considered, and good taste only can ensure it; this is to be

acquired only by much study and experience, by a constant striving after a knowledge of the great leading principles which governed the art-manufacturers of past times. The CHANDELIER in the style of the renaissance, is a successful work, presenting an attractive general form, the

details being well studied from original authorities. We are most pleased, however, with the CARRIAGE-LAMP, an exceedingly graceful design, the leading lines of which are all good; and the elegance of its general form proves how a common-place article may be elevated into a tasteful and beautiful work. The small HAND-LAMP beneath is a quaint and not inelegant conception, greatly superior to the ordinary deformities,

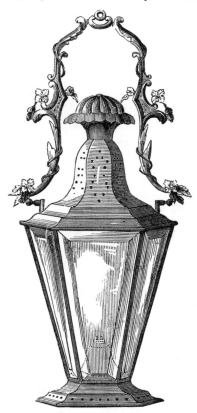

which, at one period, completely usurped the place of utility. Another graceful HANGING-LAMP appears on this column, uniting the necessary qualities of beauty and usefulness. The LAMP affixed to a scroll underneath is intended

for the interior of a carriage, and possesses also its own peculiar merit. The BRACKET-LIGHT and the lower half of a CHANDELIER, on the former page, are light and very elegantly decorated ornaments: the patterns of the two being *en suite*, we presume they are intended for the same room.

Mr. JAMES HEATH, of Bath, exhibits some of the INVALID CHAIRS which are named after that city, and universally welcomed by all who need their aid. We engrave two examples, the

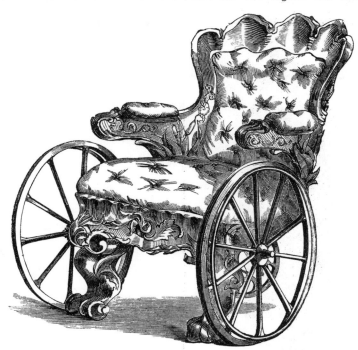

upper one constructed to move about a room at the pleasure of the sitter, unassisted by an attendant. The lower, for open air exercise, is very elaborately painted and gilt, combining an

amount of luxurious elegance by no means inapplicable to a work of the kind. On the side panels, and at the back, are paintings: the one indicated in our engraving is from the " Aurora " of Guido.

The SKATE, by Mr. LOY, of London, presents features of great novelty in form and construction. The spring across the instep secures it on the foot without screwing; and a simple contrivance of plug and socket does the same for the heel. It is made of satin wood, enriched by plates of gilded metal work; the swan's neck in front is a graceful and appropriate ornament.

The FISH SLICE and RAZOR which appear on this page are from the well-known manufactory of Messrs. JOSEPH RODGERS & SONS, Sheffield, whose cutlery goods have acquired a reputation for excellence throughout the world. Their

Two elegant examples of the Art-manufactures of America may be found in a pair of GAS CHANDELIERS, made and contributed by Messrs. CORNELIUS & BAKER, of Philadelphia. They stand about fifteen feet and a half high, by six

feet wide, having fifteen burners with plain glass globes, and are of brass lacquered. The design is very rich in ornament, and possesses some novelty in the succession of curves ingeniously and tastefully united: the gas-keys represent

show of knives, razors, scissors, &c., of all descriptions, is, as would be expected, commensurate with the extent of their establishment; and it embraces not only the finished articles, but the several processes or stages of manufacture, from the raw material to the polished blade.

bunches of fruit, thus combining beauty with utility. Besides these objects, the manufacturers exhibit a number of patent solar lamps, which they have named the "damask lamp," from the rich damask colour they have succeeded in imparting to the brass: the designs in these lamps can be varied at pleasure. Messrs. Corne-

lius & Baker are the most extensive manufacturers of lamps, chandeliers, gas-fixtures, &c., in the United States, employing upwards of seven hundred persons in the several departments of the establishment, which has been in existence for upwards of a quarter of a century; if we may judge from their contributions to the Exhibition their celebrity is not undeserved.

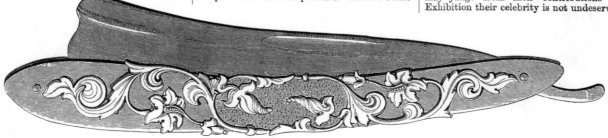

This engraving is from another of the admirably constructed and beautifully designed STOVES, manufactured for Messrs. Gray and Son, of Edinburgh, by Messrs. HOOLE & ROBSON, of Sheffield, the whole of whose works have been objects of very general admiration,—and of great attraction to all who desire to combine elegance with comfort "at home."

The CLOCK, for a table, or to be placed on a bracket in a hall, is manufactured by Mr. BENNETT, of London; the case shows some bold carving, executed with considerable taste. A large number of horological objects are exhibited by Mr. Bennett, particularly a model watch on a large scale, constructed to show the most compact form of the modern time-piece, with all its many recent improvements.

We have given in a former page of our Catalogue, one of the CARPETS contributed by WATSON, BELL, & CO., of London, we now introduce another equally worthy of attentive notice, and high estimation. It is made of a determinate shape, the centre being filled with a rich group of flowers; the double borders are very light and elegant; the outer one, by its delicacy, contrasting well with the dark ground-work.

The large engraving is from a FLOOR-CLOTH of a good, bold pattern, manufactured by Mr. R. Y. BARNES, of London. We introduce it no less as a correct and appropriate design, than from a desire to give examples, so far as they appear suitable, of every description of industrial art.

Mr. WOODRUFF, of Bakewell, in Derbyshire, has already been noticed by us, and some of his works engraved. We then stated that his ability had brought him to the notice of royalty, and that he had been commissioned to construct a CONSOLE TABLE-TOP, in coloured marbles of the county, from a design by Mr. Gruner; this beautiful work we here engrave; it is an excellent example of native talent and ingenuity.

The productions of Mr. HALL, of Derby, have been heretofore noticed in our pages as admirable examples of ability in a class of manufacture of great local interest; and by which

that interest has been extended far and wide as the result of the excellence of the works produced. Derbyshire is as much celebrated for the mineral spars it contains, as for the beauty

of its scenery, and within the shire live many ingenious workmen, who well know how to convert these natural advantages into objects which rival in attraction the productions of

Italy. The black marble, which forms, in most instances, the basis of their work, is nowhere found more pure in its colour and stratification, than in Derbyshire; while the

fluor spar is unsurpassed in its beauty of tint. The advantage of good material has, therefore, always been ready, in this favoured county, to the hands of its workmen; yet they have been,

ever, they have seen the necessity of progress; have studied the best examples of the antique; have called invention to their aid; and the consequence is, that they have found markets for

and may direct attention to the works of Mr. Hall as in all respects admirable. This page contains several of his contributions; they exhibit the taste and judgment by which he has been guided in the choice of appropriate and

for many years, too content with this alone, and have not paid the attention to elegance of form which the articles they produced only required, to insure universal appreciation. Of late, how-

their commodities in all parts of the world. We have already engraved some satisfactory proofs of the success which may attend works of this class, by native artists, from native products;

elegant "authorities." His establishment in Derby has been fully described in the *Art-Journal* for September, 1850; it is extensive, and admirably conducted, and sends forth a variety of works, chiefly of the marbles of Derbyshire.

We introduce here another of the CARPETS manufactured by Messrs. HARRIS & Co., of Stour-port. It is of the quality termed "Brussels velvet pile." The border is designed by Mr. I. K. Harvey,

Messrs. BLEWS & SONS, of Birmingham and London, are extensive manufacturers of brass candle and ship lamps, candlesticks, bells, imperial weights and measures, &c.

We engrave on this and the succeeding column four examples of their CANDLE-LAMPS: the first is called the "armorial

from the *Magnolia grandiflora*, with the flower-buds in their different stages of advancement, and the *Ipomœa*. The centre is a large wreath of exotic and other flowers, on a rich crimson ground, and the corners are occupied by the national emblems. The borders and corners are on a maroon ground.

lamp;" the second, termed the "vine-wreath foot," shows that graceful plant climbing up the shaft and over the shade; the leaves and fruit being coloured. In the third example the convolvulus forms the principal ornament at the base. The fourth has a very elegant pedestal of leaves, dogs' heads,

and birds; the pillar is of richly-cut ruby glass, with centre groups of flowers. The glass, it is

sufficient to say, is from the factory of Messrs. Richardson, of Stourbridge; the bronze and brass castings are exceedingly sharp and brilliant.

The engraving which occupies so large a portion of this page is from a STAINED GLASS WINDOW, manufactured and exhibited by the ST. HELEN'S GLASS COMPANY, Lancashire. The subject is "St. Michael casting out the great red Dragon,"

stiff lines of lead and metal that disfigure the ordinary pictures are avoided. It may be remarked that the colours themselves are all glass, and have been repeatedly fired to "flux" them;

from a design by Mr. Frank Howard; and instead of being produced on numerous pieces of glass, as is usually the case, it is painted upon one entire piece upwards of nine feet in height, by nearly five feet in width, whereby the dark

no varnish or other perishable colours are employed, but all have passed together through the fire. The establishment by which this work is contributed is of high repute and of great extent.

Messrs. T. & R. BOOTE, of Burslem, have attained considerable eminence as producers of earthenware of a fine order. We

have engraved on this and the succeeding

have attracted great and deserved attention: having placed their names high on the list of our best

manufacturers. The first, fourth, and fifth JUGS are

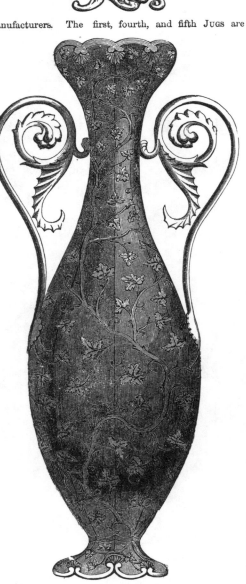

giving the effect of bas-reliefs, without being raised; the second JUG is of Parian,

with the bouquet in high relief; and the

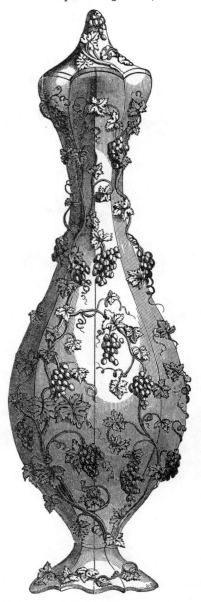

page several of their productions—which   made by mosaic process, the patterns being let in, and   third, also of Parian, of a fawn colour, with white figures, is of Gothic form. The two large VASES, somewhat similar in form, are of drab-coloured Parian, the flowers and fruit, which

are beautifully modelled in high relief, being white; the centre VASE, of mosaic character,

has a rich jet tint; the pattern is of a deep mazarine blue, traced in gold. The FLOWER

VASE on this column is in the Gothic style; stained glass is introduced on certain of the perforated parts. Our limited allotment of space prevents our rendering, by our remarks, full justice to this very admirable establishment.

The DAMASKS of Messrs. J. HOLDSWORTH & Co., of Halifax, are rich and beautiful fabrics.

The GROUP underneath is another of the contributions of Messrs. T. & W. BOOTE, for whom

symbolised by their attitudes. The work is well arranged; it stands nearly two feet high, and is of

We engrave one—which, for its combination of delicacy and boldness is worthy of especial notice.

it was modelled by Mr. Gillard; it represents Repentance, Faith, and Resignation, respectively

Parian. Another group—the Mother—is entitled to high praise. Both are original productions.

THE INDUSTRY OF ALL NATIONS.

The luxurious decoration of fire-arms may be said to have commenced when the practice of war declined as an exhibition of mere force, and became a science, whose principal stratagems and modes of operation were studied in military schools. Spain and Italy first adorned their weapons with artistic decoration, and many costly and elaborate works of the kind grace our museums. The PISTOL, by M. GAUVAIN, of Paris, here engraved, rivals in beauty of execution many of these old works, and is a good specimen of modern art applied to such purposes.

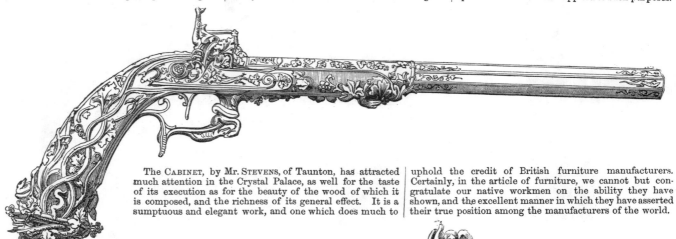

The CABINET, by Mr. STEVENS, of Taunton, has attracted much attention in the Crystal Palace, as well for the taste of its execution as for the beauty of the wood of which it is composed, and the richness of its general effect. It is a sumptuous and elegant work, and one which does much to uphold the credit of British furniture manufacturers. Certainly, in the article of furniture, we cannot but congratulate our native workmen on the ability they have shown, and the excellent manner in which they have asserted their true position among the manufacturers of the world.

Messrs. RETTIE & SONS, of Aberdeen, exhibit some curious specimens of persevering ingenuity successfully exerted in a material the most unpromising. The hard and impracticable character of GRANITE would seem to defy delicacy and

minutiæ of workmanship, and to preclude its becoming an article of personal decoration. Yet the BRACELETS here engraved are cut with much labour and patience from this material, the various parts being mounted and linked together

in silver. A choice of granite has been made from Aberdeen, Balmoral, &c. ; and, by dint of labour, a comparatively valueless article is elevated into the position of a precious stone, and placed among the fancy articles of a jewel case.

When Raffaelle was embellishing with his immortal pencil the walls of the Vatican, he, perhaps, had little idea what a legacy he was leaving for the use of future decorators, not alone for actual copyists, but for those to whom his beautiful designs serve as suggestions to be moulded

Messrs. ARROWSMITH, of London, exhibit their patent WINDOW-CURTAINS,—a novelty. It is an application on a net-work ground, giving it the effect of Brussels lace, and on moreen, or other common material, of velvet.

into whatever forms may be required. The two engravings on this page, which the reader will easily distinguish from the others,

The elegant carved zebra CABINET, which we also engrave, has its panels decorated with paintings, illustrating the phases of "Woman's History." It is a remarkably agreeable example of English furniture.

are from a decorative PANEL, exhibited by Messrs. HINCHLIFF & Co., of London; they are of the genuine Raffaellesque character, and that is sufficient to attest their excellence.

The number of hands employed upon the production of a single article, even of common use, is greater than would be supposed by one unacquainted with the art and mystery of manufacture; but when the object assumes a strictly ornamental character, it naturally embraces a wider range of operation. Sheffield, from the extent and variety of its decorative manufacturers, must employ no inconsiderable number of designers and artists on the knife-handles produced there. That here engraved is the HANDLE of a silver FISH-SLICE, from the establishment of Messrs. HILLIARD & THOMASON, of Birmingham.

The CONSOLE TABLE and GLASS are contributed by the GUTTA PERCHA COMPANY, of London, and, of course, the ornamental portions are manufactured of that material. The design of the frame shows an elaborate composition of fruit, leaves, and flowers, arranged with much elegance and artistic effect. The panels of the table are decorated with antique shields.

The RAZOR that terminates the illustrations on this page is from the manufactory of Messrs. HAWCROFT & SONS, of Sheffield, and is exhibited under the title of the "Sheffield Town Razor," from its having been made for the express purpose of showing the skill of the artisans of that place, in the production of such objects. The handle is fancifully inlaid with a design of no small excellence, and the blade has engraved upon it an exterior view of the "Crystal Palace."

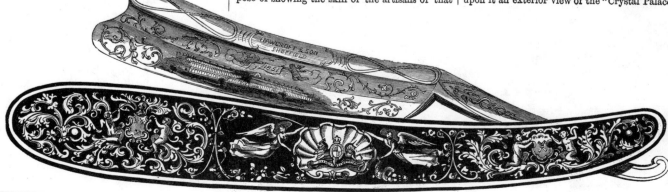

The continental manufacturers of fictile ware have not been slow in answering the demand upon their industrial classes; many of them have forwarded contributions which evince a large amount of artistic design and mechanical

The TABLE is from the manufactory of Messrs. | GILLOW & Co., of London. It is boldly carved.

skill. From some quarters these productions are adapted for ordinary use in the particular localities where they are manufactured, and other contributions may be designated as "for all nations," inasmuch as Art, by its high qualities,

The CONSOLE TABLE, and FRAME for a glass, with the BRACKET, are of gutta percha, contributed | by the company by which this novel material for manufacturing purposes has been introduced.

makes itself universal, and welcomed everywhere. The three objects on this column, are manufactured by MM. VILLEROY & BOCH, of Wallerfangen, near Mannheim; the first is a BEER-JUG, without a handle; it is made of brown clay, the figure in white; the profits arising from its sale

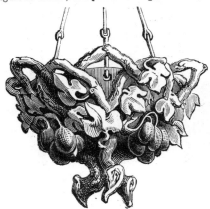

are to go towards defraying the cost of repairing the cathedral of Cologne. The next is another BEER-JUG, of variously-coloured clays, with some grotesque ornaments upon it; and the last a HANGING VASE, of terra cotta, silver mounted.

The stand of MESSRS. F. & R. PRATT, of Burslem, exhibits several excellent examples of earthenware, printed in a peculiar style, some of them after the pictures in the Vernon Gallery ; and also a dessert-

service with designs from the works of our best English painters. We have selected, from their more

miscellaneous contributions, four objects, engraved in this column, of a less decorative character, but never-

theless most excellent of their class ; the forms Messrs. Pratt have adapted to objects of general use, have

been, in some instances taken from the Etruscan, and exhibit, therefore, the good taste of the manufacturers in resorting for suggestions to the best sources.

Among the contributions of cabinet-work received from France, not the least excellent are some specimens forwarded by M. J. P. JEANSELME, of Paris, consisting of sideboard of oak, dressing-room furniture, arm-chairs, and chairs in the Louis Quatorze style, and the CABINET, which we have here engraved. It is manufactured of dark wood, highly polished, and inlaid with beautiful marbles and stones of different colours, which give to

the whole a rich and unique effect. The ornament exhibits, perhaps, little that is novel in design, but it is of the highest character and is executed with a delicacy and precision that show it to be the work of a well-practised craftsman. Nowhere has the general " breadth " been destroyed by an overlaying of decoration, as we sometimes see it.

The HERALDIC CHAIR, upon the surface of which are sculptured the arms borne by the ancestors of her most gracious Majesty in the Saxon line, was made by G. SHACK-

The graceful figure of ANDROMEDA, from the sculpture by Mr. J. A. Bell, has been excellently rendered by the COALBROOK DALE COMPANY, and is a work every way honourable to British Art-manufacture. As an example of casting, it may take rank with the best specimens in the Exhibition. The figure is very elegantly conceived,

LOCK of Bolsover, near Chesterfield, in Derbyshire. It is a work of considerable merit.

Professor RIETSCHEL of Dresden, exhibits his bas-relief of CUPID ON A PANTHER, whose headlong flight has alarmed the youthful god, and disarranged his arrows.

and has a charming simplicity of treatment. The pedestal is a work of much fancy, and is in the highly-wrought style of the Cellini period. It is emblematical throughout of the story connected with the figure it supports.

The manufacturers of Sheffield have contributed well and ably, asserting their due position, and maintaining it by their works in a marked manner. The reputation enjoyed by that town for plated goods has been of long duration, and we hope to see it of as long continuance. The group we engrave is from the manufactory of Messrs. HALL & Co., and consists of a series of graceful articles for the breakfast-table, executed with much care; a TEA and COFFEE-SERVICE, possessing the necessary requisites of utility, combined with elegance of form and delicacy of ornament. The TOAST-RACK beside it is a "registered" novelty; it occupies less space upon the table than the elongated form so generally adopted for such articles, and is better in every way. The bars, formed of the wheat-ear and leaf, are very graceful and most appropriate.

The group of the EAGLE AND CHILD, by M. AUG. LE CHESNE, the French sculptor, whose works have attracted much attention during their exhibition among us, is a powerfully-told story, but of somewhat too painful a kind. The mother has fallen in a deep and troubled sleep in the prairie, her infant clings to her side, holding an arum flower in his hand, and endeavouring to rouse her aid against the eagle, which, attracted by the hope of prey, has seized, and will speedily carry away, the alarmed infant. The work is characterised by strong expression, as well as great care in execution. It is the intention of the sculptor to continue the story in a bas-relief on its pedestal, representing the mother awakened, strangling the eagle, and saving her child.

The CAR engraved below is manufactured by Messrs. HUTTON, the celebrated carriage-builders of Dublin; in it a body of the shape of an ordinary Irish car is adapted so as to obviate some of the objections to that kind of carriage, while it has the effect of making it more commodious and better suited to general purposes. Messrs. HUTTON exhibit other descriptions of carriages.

The BASKET, in silver filagree, belongs to those delicate and beautiful works which must be seen to be fully appreciated. It is one of the contributions sent to us from Tunis, and exhibits all the patient manipulation and elaborate ornament which we associate more with eastern climes than with our own northern latitude.

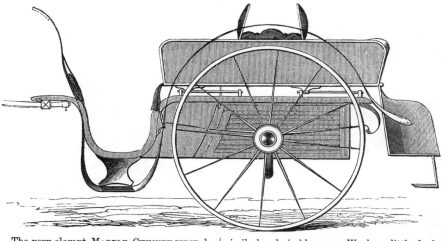

The very elegant MARBLE CHIMNEY-PIECE, by M. LECLERCQ, of Brussels, has been made expressly for his Majesty the King of the Belgians, and is one of the most chaste and beautiful works in the Exhibition; the excellence of its workmanship fully equals the taste of its design; the ornaments and figures are executed in a similarly admirable way. We have little doubt that this result is obtained through the constant connection preserved between artist and manufacturer on the continent. We perfectly remember, on the occasion of our visit to Brussels last year, calling on M. Leclercq while he was preparing this chimney-piece, and finding M. Simonis, the great sculptor of the principal

public work in Brussels—the statue of Godfrey de Bouillon—tendering his advice and assistance to M. Leclercq. The absence of this union of powers as supplied by the artist and artisan, so to speak, has long been felt in England, and has, doubtless, operated injuriously upon British manufacturing art: it will not long continue.

The annexed engraving and that which follows are cabinet-work, manufactured by M. TAHAN, of Paris; the first is a FLOWER-STAND, appropriately ornamented with leaves. The CABINET has

much florid ornament in dark walnut wood, which is agreeably relieved by the coloured paintings in the panels; copies of Ary Scheffer's popular pictures of Mignon reflecting on her country.

Mr. CRICHTON, of Edinburgh, exhibits the beautiful CLARET-JUG, in silver, decorated with enamel, which has been deservedly placed in the Fine-

Art Court of the Crystal Palace. The mantle of the famous silversmith, George Heriot, seems to have again descended on the city of his birth.

The illustration underneath represents the top of a carved rosewood WARDROBE, by M. JOLY-LECLERC, of Paris; the Italian style of furniture decoration has been here well applied.

The VASE by M. VITTOZ, of Paris, is an elaborate and artistic work, one which may bear comparison with its earlier prototypes, in design.

The KNIFE-HANDLES here introduced are from the manufactory of Mr. W. T. LOY, jun., of London. The first and fifth are from BREAD-KNIVES; they are of ivory, with small figures bearing wheat in their arms; the blades are of highly-polished steel, ornamented on each side with ears of wheat, in open-work. The second is from a DESSERT-KNIFE; it shows the figure of Silenus, carrying grapes and other fruits. The fourth, from a TABLE-KNIFE, exhibits a female dancing-figure; it has a gold ferule, and a richly embossed blade. The centre engraving is from a CHEESE-SCOOP; it shows a boy, supporting on his head a basket of fruit, &c.

The engraving underneath is from a BATH, manufactured of slate, by Mr. G. E. MAGNUS, of Pimlico; it is of large proportions, the two wings projecting to a sufficient extent to take in the basin between them, as seen in the shaded part of the engraving, at the base of the centre. The design is in the Italian style, and the slate is enamelled in

imitation of various beautiful marbles. In the establishment of Mr. Magnus we have seen many objects of this material, vases, chimney-pieces, &c.

There are many individuals too apt to entertain an idea that the manufacturers in provincial towns, excepting always those places especially distinguished for certain classes of productions, as Birmingham, Sheffield, Manchester, &c., are very far behind those of the metropolis. This opinion cannot justly be entertained after the display which the provinces have made in the Exhibition. Here, for instance, we have, in the CABINET of Mr. FREEMAN, of Norwich, a specimen of work that would do credit to the first house in London. It is made of walnut-wood and ebony, richly carved, from a bold and well-studied Italian design.

Mr. F. H. THOMSON, of Glasgow, exhibits some beautiful specimens of electro-plating, two of which we select for engraving—a CUP, supported by a figure of Cupid, and a TEA-URN by that of Time. There is much ability displayed in these

and other works exhibited by this firm; and it is something to find manufacturers forsaking the worn-out paths of their predecessors for new ones, even though they do not exactly reach those we should wish to see them pursuing.

The FENDER is manufactured and contributed by Messrs. ROBERTSON, CARR, & STEEL, of Sheffield, some of whose beautiful stoves have already been illustrated by us, and to which the present object is a suitable addition to the fireside. The curved outline flows gracefully from the centre.

The FONT is of terra-cotta, from Switzerland, made by J. ZIEGLER-PELLIS, of Winterthur, in the canton of Zurich. The general arrangement of the architectural ornament is in the best taste of the later Gothic style.

Among the Viennese manufacturers, few have exhibited more ability in designs for furniture than M. KITSCHELT, whose LADIES' WORK-TABLE we here engrave. The flow of line throughout its composition is very free and elegant; there is also much taste displayed in the arrangement of the draperies in the centre, which are of delicate and varied tints.

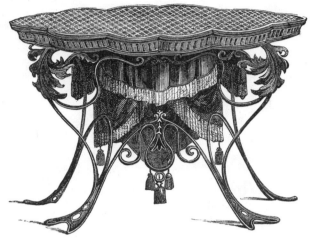

M. CARL LEISTLER, of Vienna, is the maker of the PRIE-DIEU below, which is remarkable for the finished elegance of its details; constructed of costly and beautiful woods, its value is enhanced by the artistic taste of its design; it possesses some claim to originality of style, following no

The ALMS-BASINS by Mr. J. WIPPELL, of Exeter, are carved from the wood of the walnut tree; they are lined with crimson or scarlet silk

velvet. Inscriptions in medieval characters surround the moveable lids, such as "All things come of thee, and of thine own have we given

thee,"—"Freely ye have received, freely give." The ornament appears of a very graceful and appropriate character for ecclesiastical purposes.

particular school of ornament. These devotional pieces of furniture are unknown among us, but are very common on the continent; the Exhibition furnishes several beautiful examples of this kind of manufacture.

Messrs. Doe, Hazleton, & Co., of Boston, U. S., exhibit an admirably carved Table of ebony.

Mr. Hopkins of Wimborne contributes a Door Handle of Gothic design, lined with coloured glass and china, a combination of new materials.

We introduce here two out of the numerous Carpets contributed by the distinguished firm of Messrs. Requillard, Roussel, & Choqueil, of Paris.

Messrs. BAILY & SONS, of London, exhibit a large number of artistic works

included in the general denomination

of "hardware," which are deserving of

high praise from the great amount of care bestowed upon their design and

execution. The ornamental cast-iron is particularly good; the DOOR-HANDLES, KNOCKERS, and BELL-PULLS, a few of which we

have selected for engraving, will testify fully to this fact; they embrace much variety of style, but each style is admirably

rendered. The HALL-STOVE is novel in design and bold in its details. The

wrought-iron BALCONY has been placed

by the Royal Commissioners in the Fine

Art court,—a very marked testimony to the merit of a really beautiful work.

The statue engraved on this column is by M. GEEFS, of Antwerp, and is entitled by the sculptor "THE FAITHFUL MESSENGER;" the story being told with graceful simplicity. It is that

of a young Greek girl separated from her lover, who is refreshing the carrier-pigeon, returned from conveying to him her missive of affection.

The Austrian department shows various examples of INLAID FLOORING, by MM. LEISTLER and SON, of Vienna; we introduce here one of their patterns—a star upon a ground of dark wood.

Messrs. M'ALPIN, STEAD, & Co., of Cummers- dale, near Carlisle, contribute several speciments

of CHINTZ-FURNITURE, manufactured of cotton- velvet and of cotton, and printed by blocks

and machinery. Two of their patterns are engraved on this page; they are both excellent.

The FOUNTAIN, which presents many features of novelty and gracefulness of general construction, is by Professor KALIDE, of Berlin, whose group of "The Boy and Swan," which forms the centre,

The three glass VASES are by Messrs. NEFFEN, of Winterburg, in Austria. They

principally differ from those by Hoffman, which we have already engraved, by a

more frequent use of polished surface, and the introduction of gold rims. Many of

appears in more instances than one in the Crystal Palace, and is a favourite work of the artist. The fountain ornaments the gardens of Charlottensberg, the summer residence of the King of Prussia.

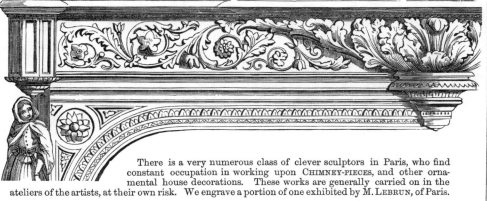

There is a very numerous class of clever sculptors in Paris, who find constant occupation in working upon CHIMNEY-PIECES, and other ornamental house decorations. These works are generally carried on in the ateliers of the artists, at their own risk. We engrave a portion of one exhibited by M. LEBRUN, of Paris.

the forms exhibit much elegance. The prevailing colours are pink, green, and white; some of them are richly engraved.

THE INDUSTRY OF ALL NATIONS.

Messrs. J. & M. P. Bell & Co., proprietors of the Pottery Works Glasgow, exhibit the various

objects illustrated in this column; they are made principally of Parian and terra-cotta,

and are designed after some of the best antique models. The Toilet Set is especially elegant.

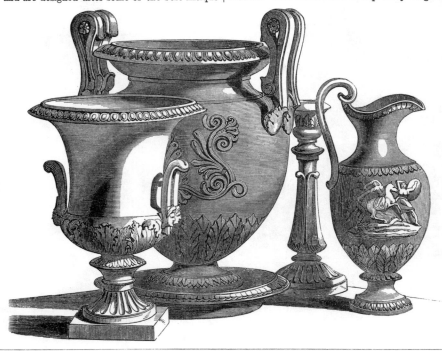

The Sculptor Rauch, of Berlin, exhibits the Statue of Victory—a work remarkable for its freedom from ordinary conventionalities of treatment, and for general vigour of conception. The action is that of the Genius suddenly awakened to the merit of the victor, and about

to raise the laurel crown for his due reward. The entire pose of the figure is original; she turns half round in her seat, the action being that of sudden thought and prompt attention, with a willing promptitude to acknowledge merit.

The above pattern exhibits that adopted for one of the Inlaid Floors of coloured woods, designed and executed by M. Leistler, of Vienna.

Messrs. JACKSON & SONS, of London, are ex- | tensive manufacturers of works in papier-mâché,

relief, the subject a dog attacking a duck's nest; the other, of a similar description, shows two

carton-pierre, and composition, for decoration | and furniture. We introduce on this page four

dogs fighting over the nest of a heron; these subjects are very cleverly modelled. A CANDE-

LABRUM exhibits a very pretty design; and the DECORATION that follows it is a bold example of of their contributions to the Exhibition, different | in character. The first is an ORNAMENT in high the Italian style, with its grotesque ornaments.

THE INDUSTRY OF ALL NATIONS.

Among the silver works manufactured and exhibited by Messrs. HILLIARD & THOMASON, of

The graceful statue of the youthful BACCHUS gazing on the inviting grape, is by LEOPOLD

NENCINI, of Florence, and is the production of one who has perfected his taste in the best school.

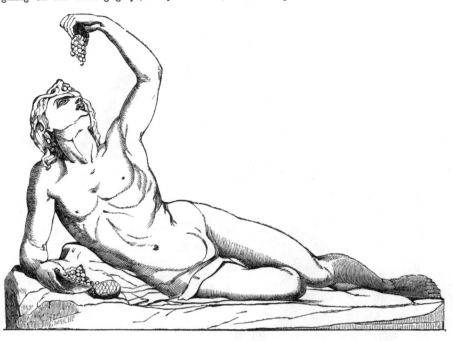

Birmingham, is a prettily designed INFANT'S CORAL, in which appears a child ringing a bell.

The appended engraving will be easily recognised by hundreds of visitors to the Exhibition, as the INTERIOR OF HER MAJESTY'S THEATRE,

drawn from a model made of card-board by Mr. T. D. DEIGHTON; the ornaments are painted by Mr. Powell. The representation is most accurate.

Among the large variety of objects in silver, manufactured and contributed by Mr. G. R. COLLIS, of Birmingham, are the CANDELABRUM and CENTRE-PIECE engraved on this page. Without any attempt at originality

of idea, the arrangement of the scrolls and floriated ornament in each is good and effective. In the lower object we should have preferred to see a less massive introduction of the scroll-work, which would give it a

greater degree of lightness. We notice, among the contributions of Mr. Collis, a solid silver table top, weighing nearly nine hundred ounces, for the Governor of Aleppo; and numerous other specimens of silver manufacture, many of which are deserving of illustration, had our space permitted.

The TABLE introduced underneath is from the manufactory of Mr. J. FLETCHER, of Cork; he terms it the "Gladiatorial Table," from the figure of a gladiator supporting the top. The idea exhibits great originality.

The most valuable contributions from the vast empire of Russia are, unquestionably, her mineral and other natural productions. Of manufactured objects we notice only a few specimens, except in textile fabrics.

The engraving above is from a small model of a CATHEDRAL-DOOR, executed in bronze by Count TOLSTOY, of St. Petersburg. The original of this, also in bronze, thirty feet in height, adorns the cathedral of Moscow.

The engraving which occupies so conspicuous a place on this page, is from a piece of exquisite WOOD-CARVING, executed and contributed by Mr. T. W. WALLIS, of Louth, in Lincolnshire. It is the first of a series of four that the sculptor purposes to execute, representing the four seasons. This is intended for "Spring," symbolised by flowers, the growth of that season, among which birds are introduced; these are arranged with an elegance and natural disposition

The manufactory of Messrs. CHARLES MEIGH & SON, of Hanley, is one of the largest and oldest in the pottery districts, having been established by the father of Mr. Meigh, Sen., about seventy years back; in proof of its extent,

we may remark that upwards of seven hundred hands are employed there in the various departments; that more than two hundred and fifty tons of coals are consumed every week; and

that, during the same short space of time, eighty tons of clay are made up into their various articles of manufacture. Of these, which consist exclusively of earthenware, Parian, and stone-

of their several forms that can scarcely be surpassed, and are carved with exceeding boldness of relief, some of the objects projecting twelve inches from the background. The work stands five and a half feet high, by nearly three feet wide; it contains forty-seven varieties of plants.

ware, about two-thirds are for the home market, and the remainder for exportation. We introduce on this column a CANDLESTICK, adapted from a celebrated wine-cup by Cellini, and two JUGS.

The subjects on this column are also from the contributions of Messrs. MEIGH & SON. The

JUG adorned with the vine exhibits a young Bacchanal imbibing the juice of the grape; the

BUTTER-COOLER is covered with a trellis-work, overgrown with creeping plants; the other two

objects are FLOWER-POTS, differing greatly in form and style of ornament, but both excellent

and appropriate to their purpose; the idea of the basket among the leaves, in the latter, is good.

The CENTRE-PIECE, serving the double purpose of an epergne and a candelabrum, is manufactured by Messrs. HAWKESWORTH, EYRE, & Co.,

the manly game of cricket, for which Sheffield has, within the last few years, become celebrated.

"melon pattern," with scroll handles and feet, &c., in the Louis Quatorze style; it is elegant

of Sheffield. It is a testimonial presented to Mr. M. J. Ellison, of that place, by his fellow-townsmen, for his exertions in promoting there

The TUREEN, by the same manufacturers, is an adaptation of what is generally known as the

in form, and far more consistent with our ideas of beauty than if more elaborately ornamented.

The contributions of Mr. W. WINFIELD, of the Cambridge-street Works, Birmingham, occupy a prominent position on one side of the "Birmingham Court" in the Exhibition. They consist

of articles of a similar kind, the majority of which are distinguished by tasteful design and most excellent workmanship. On this and the two following columns will be found illustrations from a few we have selected to demonstrate the variety and importance of the manufactures of this establishment. The first column exhibits three BED-PILLARS, good in design, and of a rich and handsome appearance. The GAS-LAMP and BRACKET is one which, we understand, has been purchased by the Queen, a fact that supersedes the necessity of any further reference, as it bears ample testimony to the excellence of

the work: the figures introduced are of parian.

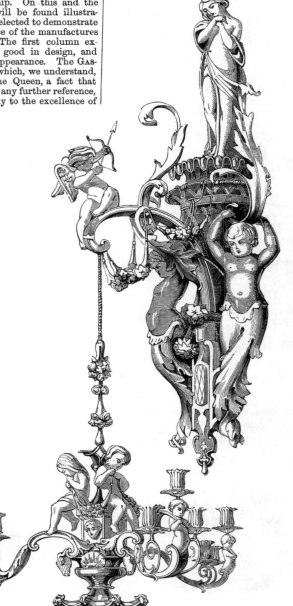

principally of metallic bedsteads, of which Mr. Winfield is one of the oldest and most extensive manufacturers, gas-fittings of every description, window-cornices, curtain-bands, and a multitude

The two CURTAIN-BANDS are graceful appendages

to the windows of the elegant drawing-room.

The two CLARET-JUGS on this column are manufactured by Messrs. LISTER & SONS, of Newcastle-upon-Tyne, silversmiths and jewellers.

These objects derive their value less from the metal of which they are made than from the taste displayed in the designs and the skilful work-

manship bestowed on them. They differ greatly in their styles, but the delicacy and boldness displayed in both are worthy of commendation.

Resuming here our notice of the works of Mr. WINFIELD, of Birmingham, we commence with a CHILD'S COT, which he terms the "Angel Cot," from the figure very happily introduced into it, suggested by the traditional idea that, in

these unseen beings are present to watch over and protect us; the body and frame of the cot are very elegant. The BEDSTEAD that follows is excellent in the character of its design; the fluted taper pillars are drawn by a new process,

LAMP, of more than ordinary excellence in the arrangement of its composition; while the superb BEDSTEAD that completes our illustrations is one

the earlier stages of our existence especially,

that enables a tube of this description to be made with the same facility as an ordinary parallel one. On the next page is a wall BRACKET, ornamented with the figure of "Dorothea," modelled by Mr. Bell: by its side is a

of the best objects of its kind ever brought before our notice. The style of this production is *renaissance*, and it abounds in all those rich features peculiar to that period of decorative

art; the figures on the pillars are modelled with

great care, but those on the head and foot-rails

are objectionable from their unartistic attitude.

The contributions of M. RUDOLPHI, the eminent jeweller of Paris, are so truly beautiful

that we cannot resist the temptation of adding another column of illustrations to those already

given in preceding pages. The three BROOCHES are exquisite in design, and of the most delicate

workmanship; and a close examination of the TABLE will show how much artistic taste and

skill have been expended on its production.

The PIANOFORTE engraved is an American contribution, the manufacture of Mr. J. PIRSSON, of New York; it is of extraordinary size, being intended for four performers, two at each end. Its instrumental qualities are spoken of in high terms; and it is said to have been used at the concerts of Mademoiselle Lind.

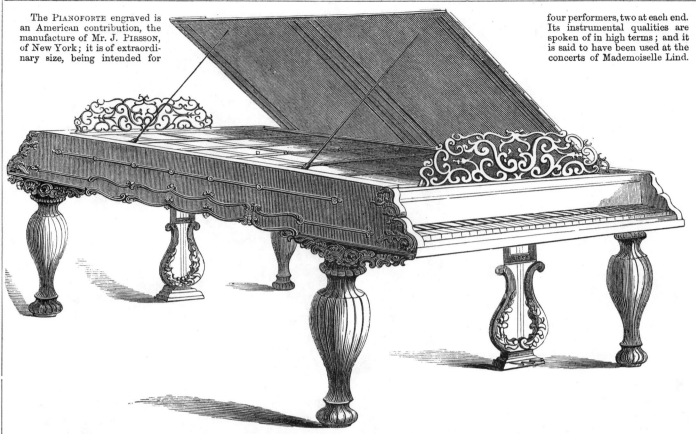

The very elegant BAPTISMAL FONT, sculptured in Caen stone, is designed and executed by Mr. J. CASTLE, of Oxford, and is one of the principal ornaments

The LOCK and KEY are exhibited by Mr. J. GIBBONS, Jun., of Wolverhampton; he terms it an improved lock for doors, park-gates, &c.

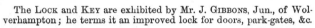

of the English Fine Art Court. Symbolical figures of angels decorate its sides, bearing emblematic devices, the entire being covered with foliage and fruit.

The BROOKLYN FLINT GLASS WORKS, situated at New York. U. S., contribute a well-filled

stand, which occupies a central position in the American de-

partment of the Great Exhibition. There is enough novelty of form in these works to

assure us that our transatlantic brethren are fully aware of the mercantile value of Art.

THE CRUSADER CHESS TABLE, is the work of Mr. GRAYDON, of Dublin; the pieces represent the chief characters of the Crusades, under Cœur-de-Lion. These pieces were carved in ivory by Mr. Slaight, of London.

Messrs. C. W. DOVE & Co, of Leeds, exhibit a number of beautiful velvet-pile Brussels, Kidderminster, and Threeply CARPETS; we engrave an elegant and exceedingly rich pattern, designed for them by Mr. Harvey.

Messrs. GOUGH of Sheffield exhibit articles of electro-plate, from which we select a group possessing much gracefulness of contour. The CANDLESTICK is of novel decoration, and the EPERGNE of light and elegant form, the ornament being well adapted to the objects manufactured.

Mr. BENNET, of Dublin, exhibits the very

Mr. BATTAM, of London, some of whose successful imitations of antique vases, &c., are engraved on a former page of our Catalogue, has adopted the appropriate and picturesque method of exhibiting his works, in a fac-simile of an ETRUSCAN TOMB, the various niches containing their urns, and the ground covered with pateræ and sacrificial vessels of a characteristic kind.

graceful CLARET-JUG, in silver, here engraved.

Mr. T. EARLE has embodied the story of JACOB AND RACHEL in a gracefully conceived group. The shepherd stands by the well where the maiden fills her water-vessel, and tells his tale with simple earnestness.

The VASE in Terra Cotta, is produced at the works of Messrs. FERGUSON, MILLER, & Co., of Neathfield, Glasgow, and contains figures typical of the great gathering in 1851. In colour and manipulation it is decidedly good.

Mr. WHITWELL of Dockray Hall Mills, Kendal, | a carpet manufacturer of eminence, contributes | among many other very excellent specimens, the

Kidderminster CARPET we here engrave. The fabric | is double cloth, not twilled in the warp, and the | colouring is produced by change of the shuttle.

This engraving is from a TABLE-COVER, de- | signed and executed by Messrs. Webb & Son, of | Spitalfields, for Messrs. DEWAR & Co., of London.

The two objects filling the lower part of this page are from examples of the cabinet work of Mr. J. M. LEVEIN, of London. The first is an ESCRITOIRE, of satin-wood, in the Louis Quatorze style, inlaid with tulip-wood in flowers and scroll-work. The other combines a JEWEL-CASE and STAND; it is made of the tulip and kingwoods, ornamented with or-molu, and inlaid

with Sèvres china. Another of the contributions | of M. Levein, which our space would not allow | us to illustrate, is a very beautiful sideboard | formed of a wood, the growth of New Zealand.

A TABLE, in papier-mâché, which, we presume, is intended for a ladies' work-table, is from the manufactory of Messrs. HALBEARD & WELLINGS, of Birmingham. Its vase-like form is a novelty in this description of cabinet manufacture.

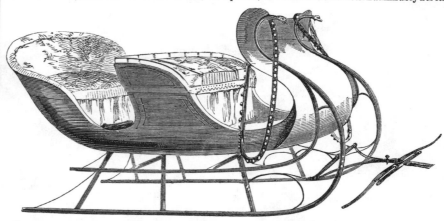

The SLEIGH, from which the engraving underneath is copied, is an American production, manufactured by Messrs. J. GOOLD & Co., of Albany, U.S. It is a double-bodied carriage, of excellent workmanship, to be drawn by two ponies, for which its construction admirably fits it.

The second engraving on this column is from the other contribution of Messrs. NEWTON, JONES, & WILLIS, to which allusion is elsewhere made.

From the numerous articles of merit in ALTAR-CLOTHS, hangings, &c., exhibited by Messrs. NEWTON, JONES, & WILLIS, of Birmingham, we select two—engravings of which occupy the lower part of this page. That underneath is a portion of the ORPHREY of an archbishop's cape, designed for the Anglican church; the whole of the enrichments are worked by hand in gold and silk.

It is a portion of an ALTAR-CLOTH, embroidered by hand, in gold and silk; in the design is a dove, drawn in the style of the ancient illuminators.

The simplicity of the worship of the English church is most striking, when compared with that of the church from which it sprung; even in our highest festivals, there is little room for that "outward adornment," to which the subjects here engraved are meant to be applied.

The original of the appended engraving is a CLOCK and INKSTAND for a library table; it is exhibited by Mr. J. HUX, of London, the manufacturer of the clock; the case and stand are beautifully carved by Mr. W. G. ROGERS, the eminent sculptor in wood, who has also executed several other clock-cases for Mr. Hux, that appear in the Exhibition, and which are well worthy of his high reputation. The work before us forms an elegant and useful ornament.

On the opposite page is an illustration from the papier-mâché TABLES of Messrs. HALBEARD & WELLINGS, of Birmingham; another, of a different character, appears underneath; both in its form, and its ornamentation, it exhibits a taste that qualifies it for a place in the boudoir.

One of the great defects we have frequently noticed in decorative furniture is the inapplicability of ornament to the purpose of the object on which it appears; and another is the combination of styles, sometimes the most distinct from each other, so as to form an incongruous mixture, showing how little of the true principles of decoration have been acquired by the designer; and also how much labour, time, and cost of workmanship, may be expended fruitlessly. The architecture, if the term may be permitted, of a piece of furniture should be as pure as that of an edifice, otherwise it offends rather than pleases the eye which can detect the slightest want of harmony. No such charge, however, can be brought against the splendid

SIDEBOARD of M. E. P. DURAND, of Paris, which, in design and execution, may compete with the best which the Exhibition has called forth. The leading idea of this work is eminently good, while the several details of which the ornaments are formed, at once declare its intended purpose.

THE INDUSTRY OF ALL NATIONS.

A GIRL AT A SPRING is a favourite subject with English painters and sculptors; Mr. W. F. WOODINGTON has here brought forward a figure which displays considerable elegance of attitude.

The PIANO FORTE is a contribution from the manufactory of Mr. CHICKERING, of Boston, United States; his instruments have obtained

The two engravings placed in this column are from an imperial quarto BIBLE, bound in morocco, by Mr. R. NEIL, of Edinburgh, and ornamented in a very costly manner, with the

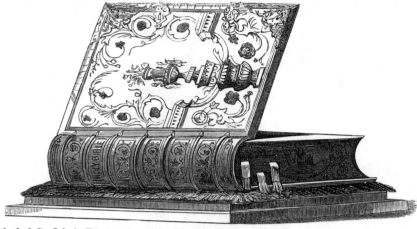

Cathedral, St. John's, Edinburgh, and St. Giles's, Edinburgh; the whole sketched from the buildings, and wrought with the hand. Mr. Neil is

high reputation, even among European professors who have tried them, for their brilliancy of tone

description of work known among bookbinders as "blind tooling," enriched with embossing and illuminated colouring. On the gilt edges are representations of three churches—Glasgow

almost self-taught, and he has executed the entire work by gas-light, after business hours : it is highly creditable to his industry and taste.

and their power. That which we have here

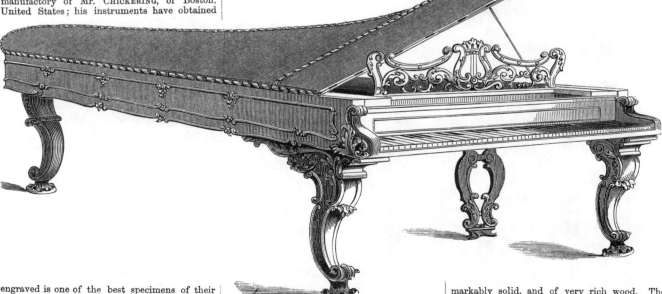

engraved is one of the best specimens of their manufacture, and will bear the test of comparison with those of the most celebrated pianoforte makers of London or Paris. The exterior of the instrument is designed with much taste.

It is simple in design, and by no means elaborately ornamented; in construction it is re-

markably solid, and of very rich wood. The climate of America compels the manufacturer of musical instruments to study solidity rather than lightness in most objects constructed principally of wood, such as piano-fortes, harps, &c.

The engraving underneath, stretching across the page, shows the top of a SOFA-BACK, manufactured by M. JEANSELME, of Paris, whose name has appeared in other parts of our Catalogue. The work is beautifully carved in the style of the best period of Italian sculptured art, and merits high praise for design and execution.

The contributions in papier mâché of Messrs. SPIERS & SON, of Oxford, are numerous; they consist of tables, work-tables, writing-desks,

being sufficiently subdued, and regard being had, generally, to harmony of composition. They derive much of their interest and attraction

The piece of EMBROIDERY intended to decorate the front of a waistcoat, is exhibited by Mdlles. DANIEL and CORSINS of Hoxton; the pattern exhibits a Cornucopia, round which flowers are clinging: the work is executed with great delicacy, and exhibits considerable taste in design.

tea-trays, albums, fire-screens, portfolios, &c., all of which are in good taste; the ornamentation lished, consisting of some of the most pic-

from the paintings with which they are embellished, consisting of some of the most pic-

The CHAIR is another of the contributions of Messrs. GILLOW, of London, to whose works we have frequently referred. It presents a solidity of construction that would have appeared too

turesque or celebrated edifices in Oxford, as well as sketches taken from its outskirts.

massive, if not lightened by the character of the ornament with which it is judiciously relieved.

The town of Paisley maintains the reputation it has long enjoyed for the manufacture of woollen and worsted textile fabrics, in shawls, plaids, tartans, &c. We here engrave one of the woven long SHAWLS, exhibited by Messrs. J. & A.

ROXBURGH, of this place; the design is a very elaborate composition of floriated forms, arranged in a most intricate pattern, yet exhibiting little or nothing of that confusion which might be looked for in such a multiplicity of details. The

On this and the succeeding column, are introduced illustrations of some of the silver goods manufactured by MM. CHRISTOFLE & Co., of

Paris, who are entitled to take rank with the best silversmiths of the French metropolis, for

purity of taste in the designs they have here furnished. Our first subject is a CREAM-JUG of

task of the engraver is rendered intelligible, without the aid of colour, although to combine such a variety of forms is by no means easy; and even with all his skill, a mere black and white

transcript of the pattern does but meagre justice to this rich and beautiful object of manufacturing art, one of the best among the many excellent productions emanating from Paisley.

very elegant form, slightly ornamented in a good style: the next is a FLOWER-STAND, showing much originality of design, as regards the combination of the two principal parts. The engraved work on the COFFEE-POT is executed with

great delicacy in the *Renaissance* style. The CANDELABRUM is gracefully modelled, and shows

considerable lightness in the design. The VASE, concluding the series, is a bold composition.

Occupying the central place in the Crystal Palace, the GLASS FOUNTAIN, by Messrs. OSLER, of Birmingham, is, perhaps, the most striking object in the Exhibition; the lightness and beauty, as by bars of iron, which are so completely embedded in the glass shafts, as to be invisible, and in no degree interfering with the purity and crystalline effect of the whole object.

well as the perfect novelty of its design, have rendered it the theme of admiration with all visitors. The ingenuity with which this has been effected is very perfect; it is supported

Many of the manufacturers of our country towns have succeeded in enforcing that general claim to notice, which, while awarded to them in their own locality, they might have failed to have obtained, but for the great and general

competition called forth by the invitation of 1851. The TABLE by Mr. PALMER, an eminent upholsterer of Bath, is an excellent example of provincial manufacture; it is very graceful in design, and the execution is of a most satisfactory kind.

The CHAIR is engraved from one manufactured by M. BALNY, of Paris, who contributes numerous articles of furniture, manifesting good taste, and no little ingenuity of workmanship. The style of this chair is Elizabethan, well carried out.

A terra-cotta VASE, from the works of Messrs. FERGUSON, MILLER, & Co., of Heathfield, near Glasgow, shows, among its other ornaments, a

Mr. C. J. RICHARDSON is well known by his excellent works on Elizabethan ornament and furniture, in which he has, with much perseverance and ability, pointed out the peculiarities, and rich fancies, visible in that school of design. He has now practically realised his knowledge,

by the production of various ARTICLES OF FURNITURE, possessing all the picturesque richness of the style, combined with the knowledge of its leading principles, which elevate these works.

nuptial procession, designed in the style of the antique. These figures are modelled with great accuracy, and are arranged in an artistic manner.

The CONSOLE-GLASS and TABLE combined, are designed and manufactured by Mr. S. LECAND, of London; the frames are carved in American pine and lime-tree woods, and double gilt in matted and burnished gold.

The style is a variation of the *Louis Quatorze*; birds, flowers, and winged horses being mingled with the other description of ornamental work, and giving to the whole more novelty than we are often accustomed to see.

These VASES are the productions of Captain BEAU-CLERC, and are formed in terra-cotta, of two tints. The

body of each vase is of deep red, the figures of a much

Among the numerous objects of cabinet-work manufactured by Messrs. GILLOW & Co., of London, is a SOFA, termed a "Wanstead Sofa." It has little carved work, but it is of a good order; the griffins at each end, forming the legs, are sculptured with boldness.

yellower clay, both being the production of Ireland.

The GOTHIC HINGE is manufactured and exhibited by Messrs. BARNARD and BISHOP, of Norwich. It is of wrought iron, and is a well-directed attempt to revive the ancient iron smith-work, of which many of our old ecclesiastical edifices and baronial mansions furnish fine examples.

The manufactory of Messrs. J. ROSE & Co., ot

A STATE-BED, designed and manufactured by Mr. T. FOX, of London, is a fine example of this description of furniture. The design is in the Elizabethan style, but showing greater lightness than we usually find in the carved works of that period. It is made of walnut, relieved by

Coleport, Shropshire, has obtained considerable

eminence for its productions in embossed porce-

gilding; the footboard is divided into panels, and in the centre is a shield, on which appears a Bacchanalian mask; carved figures are placed at each corner. The backboard is stuffed, and the furniture is of light blue silk with satin margin and white trimmings. It is of good workmanship.

lain, which bear comparison, for beauty of material and skill of workmanship, with the best of the Pottery districts of Staffordshire. Some idea of the

variety and originality of their patterns, combined with other good qualities, may be received from the examples

we have here introduced. The first column commences with a DESSERT-PLATE, the border of which shows a

pleasing novelty, while the groups of fruit are painted with much taste. The FLOWER-VASE that follows is also

new in design, and appropriate; and the EPERGNE is entitled to favourable notice. On this column we engrave

specimens of TEA and COFFEE-CUPS, all of which are characterised by novelty of design in their ornament;

a JUG in this column is justly entitled to a similar remark. The

group which follows is composed chiefly of FRUIT-DISHES, de-

signed in the character of the style known as the "Louis Quatorze." The GROUP OF

FIGURES—Puck throned on a mushroom

—is of Parian. It is a clever design and

the figures are capitally modelled: it is,

we believe, the work of the late admirable sculptor, Mr. Pitts, and finished by his son.

The figure placed on this column is from another of the models exhibited by Mr. F. M. MILLER. The sculptor has given it the title of SPRING, symbolising that season by the doves perched on the hand of the figure, and the plough, modelled after an antique agricultural implement, on which it rests. The embodiment of the idea is carried out in a graceful manner, and the pose of the figure is remarkably easy.

The illustration above is a portion of a Gothic | CHIMNEY-PIECE sculptured by M. LEBRUN, of Paris.

The engraving underneath is from a piece of EMBROIDERY TRIMMING, exhibited by Messrs. BENNOCH, TWENTYMAN, & Co., of London.

A CONSOLE CHEFFONIER is exhibited by Messrs. TRAPNELL & SON, of Bristol: it is made of English walnut-wood, the top is of statuary marble, set in a rich moulding of ebony and tortoisehell.

The CARRIAGE here introduced is manufactured by Messrs. R. & E. VEZEY, of Bath; it belongs to the class usually termed "sociables." The general appearance of this carriage is very elegant, and all the springs being fixed with india-rubber bearings, it "rides" very easily. The body, &c., is painted in rich ultra-marine blue, relieved with white and amber, in delicate lines; and it is lined with drab silk and lace.

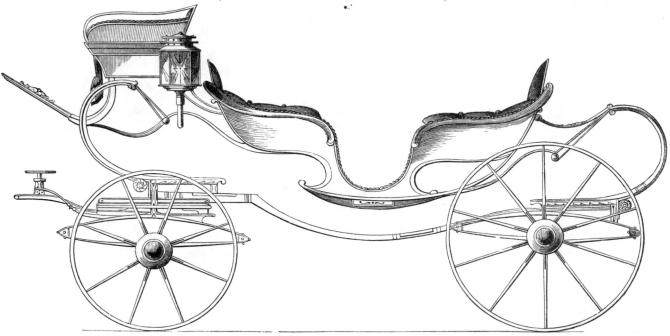

Messrs. HILLIARD & THOMASON, of Birmingham, are the contributors of fish-knives and forks,

The engraving underneath shows the pattern of a BRUSSELS CARPET, printed by patent machinery, at the factory of Messrs. J. BRIGHT & Co., of Crag, near Macclesfield. The composi-

taper-stands, &c. We engrave here the HANDLE OF A FISH-KNIFE, very excellent in design.

tion of this design is exceedingly bold, though we cannot assign to it much originality of invention. Messrs. Bright are also exhibitors of velvet pile carpets, tapestries, furniture-covers, &c.

We occupy this page with works by M. LEISTLER, who may be, with justice, considered the most important Austrian manufacturer; that he claims high rank, as well for the artistic taste as for the beauty with which his

works are executed, will be readily admitted by those who inspect the four palatial apartments he has furnished for the inspection of "the world," in its Exhibition. A very grace-

ful novelty is represented in our first cut; it is an ORNAMENTAL STAND, of a fanciful and original design, the large framed boards of rosewood being intended for the exhibition of small minia-

tures, and other objects of art, which may thus be conveniently and elegantly arranged over their surface. The figures who hold them, the

they are carved. The small SETTEE beneath is equally good in execution, but is less graceful in

of these articles of furniture, and many that might be passed by as ordinary looking, deserve

possesses elegance. The TABLE beneath is intended for a drawing-room; it is of the finest-coloured and most costly wood. The CHAIR is

fanciful foliage, and the equally fanciful group of horned serpents forming the base, are all remarkable for the vigour and delicacy with which

design, and is not redeemed from heaviness. In some instances, parts are better than the whole

study in detail; we engrave the central portion of a SOFA-BACK as an illustration of this, which

of sumptuous construction, whether its carved work, or its upholstery, be considered; it is constructed with the strictest attention to comfort.

The engravings on this page are from a *suite* of carved decorative furniture, consisting of about twenty objects; they are manufactured are made is Irish bog-yew. The FAUTEUIL, or arm-chair, shows at the back busts of ancient Irish warriors, supporting the ancient arms of chanalian busts at the angles; a figure of Hibernia surmounts the top, with the accessories of the wolf-dog, harp, &c. The POLE-SCREEN, one of a pair, stands on a tripod composed of three busts with helmeted heads; the looking-glass panels

by Mr. A. J. JONES, of Dublin, from his own designs, which are intended to illustrate Irish history and antiquities; the wood of which they Ireland; the elbows are represented by wolf-dogs, one in action, the other recumbent. The TEA-POY, being a receptacle for foreign produce,

is appropriately ornamented; its base exhibits the chase of the giant deer by wolf-dogs. A sarcophagus WINE-COOLER is elaborately sculptured on the four sides, and enriched with bac- form the field on which is sculptured, in demi-relief, an ancient Irish Kern, or light-armed warrior, on the one, and on the other, the Gallowglass, or heavy-armed Irish warrior.

THE INDUSTRY OF ALL NATIONS.

It was reasonably to be expected that Germany, so rich in musical talent, would furnish some examples of her skill in the manufacture of MUSICAL INSTRUMENTS. We have, therefore, engraved several from the establishment of Messrs. F. GLIER & SON, of Klingenthal, in Saxony.

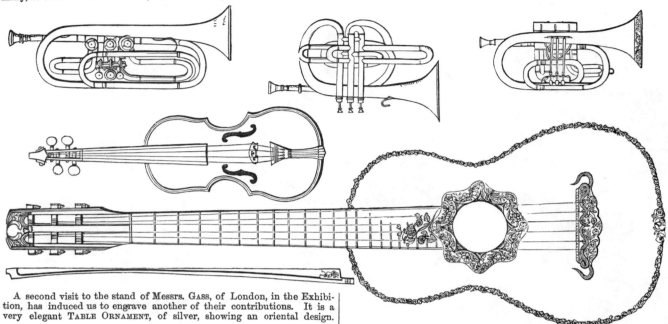

A second visit to the stand of Messrs. GASS, of London, in the Exhibition, has induced us to engrave another of their contributions. It is a very elegant TABLE ORNAMENT, of silver, showing an oriental design.

Two Indian water-bearers are placed beneath a palm-tree; at each corner of the triangular base is a sphynx, between which is a wreath of flowers.

The three engravings which complete this page are selected from a

large variety of useful and ornamental articles, manufactured by Mr. T.

HARRISON, of Sheffield, chiefly in electro-plate on imperial metal and

nickel silver; many of these are designed with very considerable taste.

On this column we introduce a VASE of silver for perfume, and a TANKARD of silver gilt, from

the manufactory of M. VITTOZ, of Paris; each of these objects are exquisite examples of the taste

displayed by the French designer in producing models for the manufacturer in costly metals.

A valuable auxiliary to the amateur sketcher

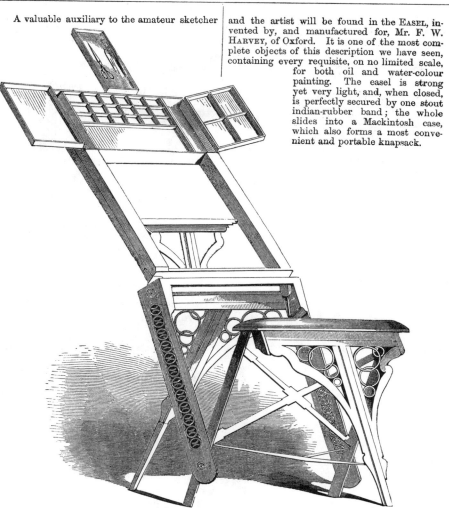

and the artist will be found in the EASEL, invented by, and manufactured for, Mr. F. W. HARVEY, of Oxford. It is one of the most complete objects of this description we have seen, containing every requisite, on no limited scale, for both oil and water-colour painting. The easel is strong yet very light, and, when closed, is perfectly secured by one stout indian-rubber band; the whole slides into a Mackintosh case, which also forms a most convenient and portable knapsack.

Mr. HANICQ, of Malines, has furnished a pyramid | of glazed cases, containing the important and beau-

tiful devotional books for which he is celebrated as | one of the most extensive continental publishers.

A CHIMNEY-PIECE of marble, designed and manufactured by Messrs. JOSEPH BROWNE & Co., of London, is a well-executed work, from a light and graceful composition, to which the two principal figures impart a novelty that is carried out by the ornamentation of the other parts.

The Russian contributions to the Crystal Palace evince a large amount of costly splendour combined with quaint and characteristic design,

The BRONZE FOUNTAIN is the production of Mr. JAMES, of Lambeth, and is of very appropriate design, inasmuch as all the accessories are really, or mythologically, connected with the element it is destined to display. It is a small work, a model, in fact, but all the details are carefully carried

showing much fancy in the Art-manufacturers who have been engaged in their fabrication. In other pages of our Catalogue, many of the

out, and it is worked by a miniature steam-engine, of singularly excellent construction.

larger Russian works appear; we here devote two columns to specimens of the silver cups which occupy so important a position in the department devoted to this great empire. There is a very free and fanciful taste prevalent in

these articles, which gives to them a strong individuality of character. This is particularly

visible in the first and second of our engravings; the others, however, call to mind the German

works of the fifteenth century, to which they are nearly allied. They are the productions of the goldsmith, PAUL SAZIKOFF, of Moscow.

A CONSOLE-TABLE, by M. JEANSELME, of Paris, is a good example of the Louis Quatorze style.

The engraving underneath is from the model of a SARCOPHAGUS with GOTHIC CANOPY, sculp-

tured by Mr. W. PLOWS, of Foss Bridge, York, in stone from the quarries at Heldenley, near Malton

The appended engraving is from a piece of EMBROIDERY, for a Priest's robe; it is manufac-tured by MM. LEMIRE & SON, of Lyons; the cross is worked in gold, upon a ground of purple.

A statuary group under the name of "THE SUPPLIANT" is exhibited, with other works, by Mr. WEEKES, the distinguished sculptor; the figure is presumed to represent a female in dis-tress, who, with her infant, is soliciting charity.

The CHAIR introduced below is made by MR. G. W. ENGLAND, of Leeds; it is manufactured

A TABLE, of walnut wood, is another of the contributions made by MR. PALMER, of Bath; it shows some bold carving, executed from a design of considerable novelty, especially in the

form of the cross-piece connecting the legs. The manufacturer is entitled to very high praise.

of mahogany, the grain of the wood running in one uniform direction: the design is good.

The sword here engraved is from the manufactory of Messrs. REEVES, GREAVES & Co., sword cutlers of Birmingham. It is a cavalry dress Sabre, the hilt, blade, and scabbard mountings of which are entirely of steel, elaborately engraved, in designs that show considerable ele-

The subject of the annexed illustration is a CARVED FRAME, for a looking-glass, manufactured by Messrs. GILLOW, of London; it is a very elegant production of its class. and a pleasing contrast to the *Louis Quatorze* style so much in vogue, and which we should be glad to see superseded by one of greater simplicity.

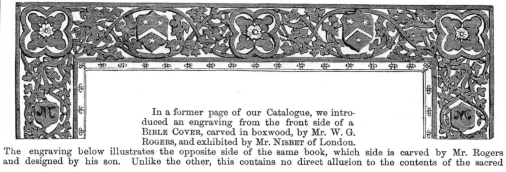

In a former page of our Catalogue, we introduced an engraving from the front side of a BIBLE COVER, carved in boxwood, by Mr. W. G. ROGERS, and exhibited by Mr. NISBET of London. The engraving below illustrates the opposite side of the same book, which side is carved by Mr. Rogers and designed by his son. Unlike the other, this contains no direct allusion to the contents of the sacred

gance of composition. The manufacture of these weapons from the rough metal to the finished object is highly interesting and curious, employing, as it does, a variety of workmen, each of whom must possess a greater or less amount of artistic skill and mechanical ingenuity to perfect his portion of work.

volume; the border is similar, but the centre ornament exhibits only a graceful arrangement of wheat, grapes, and other devices. The execution of this work is exceedingly delicate and masterly in all its parts.

The CABINET here introduced is manufactured by Mr. HARRISON, of the Wood-carving Company, Pimlico, whose operations are conducted by a process of burning the wood into the required

ornamented, while the latter possesses the pure outline of the antique without anything of a de-

corative character to detract from its simplicity

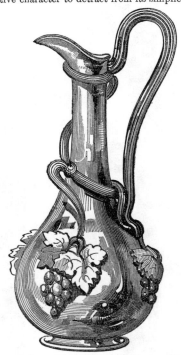

pattern, so as to imitate carving. The cabinet engraved is of oak, and it shows some excellent ornamental work: the contributions of this establishment are numerous and exceedingly varied.

the next is a WATER-JUG in the mediæval

MESSRS. LLOYD & SUMMERFIELD, of Birmingham, are the contributors of the productions in GLASS represented on this page. The group exhibits JUGS and a VASE; the former are richly style; the CLARET-JUG and decorated DRINKING-GLASSES show considerable novelty in design.

The FLOWER-STAND, one of a pair, and BRACKET, in this column, are by M. FLEISCH-MANN, of Sonneberg, in Germany; the latter object is of *papier mâché*, from a very bold

design. The flower-stand is chiefly constructed of iron, modelled in a new way, and combined with *papier mâché*, and covered with glass; it represents two vines, each with a bunch of

golden grapes. The pedestals consist of roots of trees thickly covered with grass and herbs.

The readers of the *Art-Journal* must be well aware of the interest we have always evinced in the welfare of the various schools of design established throughout the kingdom—institutions that we doubt not are destined to exercise an important influence on British Manufacturing

developed in the CABINET here engraved, which is the work of A. HAYBALL, a young woodcarver of Sheffield, and educated in the school of design attached to that town. It is made of English walnut-wood; the design is of the pure Italian style, abundantly rich in ornament, and free

Art. The fruits of the exertions which are made for sustaining these schools begin now to be manifested in a way that must be very gratifying to all who, like ourselves, have advocated their establishment, and augured their prosperity. One of these pleasing results is

from many of the monstrosities that too frequently deface similar productions; there is indeed scarcely a single part of the work open to reasonable objection. We understand that Mr. Hayball undertook the task from a desire to uphold the character of the Sheffield School.

Messrs. DIXON & SONS, of Sheffield, are extensive manufacturers of silver and plated goods,

articles they contribute to the Exhibition. In the TUREEN and DISH we have examples of the

a little refreshing to the eye, somewhat over-

elaborate and often over-decorated patterns of the Italian style, and those founded upon it.

and in what is known as Britannia metal; we have engraved on this page a few of the numerous

plain but truly elegant Grecian style adapted to objects of ordinary use; and it is certainly not

wearied with the constant recurrence of the

The absence of a *plethora* of ornament is amply atoned for by the simple beauty of that which

appears in these designs. The silver and gilt TEA AND COFFEE SERVICE possesses considerable novelty in form and composition; the various pieces are modelled from the pitcher-plant, and the waiter on which they are placed from a leaf

of the *Victoria Regia*. The COFFEE-POT on this column has a floral ornament in high relief; the CAKE-PLATE is modelled as from a single leaf, in

an elegant form; and the POWDER-FLASK, which concludes the page, shows an embossing in the Italian style, forming a frame and displaying in

the centre a group of dead game. The flask has a stopper, very ingeniously and effectively contrived to facilitate the sportsman in loading his gun.

The TABLE, manufactured by Messrs. JOHNSTONE & JEANES, of London, is circular, and made on the expanding principle; by a simple process, the quaternions of which the top is composed draw out, and sectional pieces being introduced, the table is increased to double its original size. The tripod is very massive; it looks disproportioned as seen in the engraving, but not so when the table is expanded.

A model, in bronze, of a FOUNTAIN is exhibited by M. GASSER, of Vienna; it would be highly effective on a large scale.

The GROUP OF FURNITURE introduced underneath is from the establishment of Messrs. SNELL & Co., of London. As might be expected, the invitations to exhibit have been answered by contributions from the most eminent cabinet-makers in Great Britain and on the continent, each of whom appears to have striven worthily in the production of works calculated to uphold their own individual reputation, and that of their respective countries. The CABINET and GLASS are much to our taste; the frame of the latter is especially good,

and possesses novelty. The oval TABLE has a rich marquetrie border, and the other objects that appear in our illustration deserve attention.

The Brooch engraved underneath is manufactured by M. Rudolphi, of Paris; the design of the beautiful setting is of the Renaissance period.

The city of Lyons, as might be expected, contributes a large, varied, and costly supply of the silk manufactures for which she has long been celebrated throughout Europe. It is not our province, here at least, to institute comparisons between the productions of France and those of our country; but we may nevertheless be permitted to add that, unfortunately for our own manufacturers, fashion has arbitrarily set a value upon the fabrics of the continent, to which they

The group, by M. Lechesne, of Paris, which he terms The Faithful Friend, is remarkable for the vigour with which the story is told by the

sculptor. A boy is accompanied by his dog, both are attacked by a serpent, but the faithful animal is on the defensive, and destroys the reptile.

are not always entitled. Of the two illustrations on the lower part of this page the first is from a piece of Ribbon, made by Messrs. Collard & Co., of St. Etienne; the pattern is simple, but

arranged with considerable grace. The second is from a silk Scarf, which presents a combination of elegant and novel forms most skilfully composed; it is a superb fabric from the manufactory of Messrs. Bertrand, Gayet, & Dumontal, of Lyons, an establishment of high reputation.

This group—THE DELIVERER—is a sequel, by M. LECHESNE, to that which we engrave on the opposite page. The dog has destroyed the aggressive serpent, and is receiving the caresses of the boy who has been saved by his prowess.

We introduce here another BROOCH by M. RUDOLPHI, of Paris; it is an exquisitely-delicate piece of workmanship; the mounting shows the leaves and bunches of grapes, elegantly arranged; the centre is a very charming enamel painting.

The engraving underneath is from a piece of SILK DAMASK, made by Messrs. MATHEVON & BOUVARD, of Lyons; the design is truly excellent.

The velvets of Lyons are no less distinguished by beauty of fabric than the silks manufactured in the same place; we engrave here one of the costly FIGURED VELVETS made by Messrs. MATHEVON & BOUVARD.

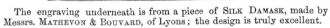

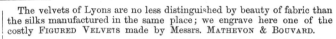

The CARRIAGE, or "Pilentum," as it is designated by the manufacturer, Mr. MULLINER, of Northampton, is an excellent specimen of provincial carriage-building, which may vie with the best of metropolitan manufacture; the panels are painted to resemble cane-work, and so successfully as almost to deceive the eye. The body of the vehicle is suspended on elliptical springs.

We introduce here two engravings from the manufactures of Lyons; the first is a cloth of silk, called "Drap d'Or," made by Messrs. MATHEVON & BOUVARD; it is an exquisitely beautiful fabric, in which the design and its arrangement are equally good, while the gold and colours weaved into it present a most rich appearance. The second is from the manufactory

of Messrs. LE MIRE & SON; it is a piece of gold brocade, showing great originality in the disposition of the pattern, which consists of flowers, both wild and cultivated, mingled with ears of rye-corn, bound together.

M. ROULÉ, of Antwerp, a wood-carver of emi- nence, who has been employed by his Govern- ment in the reconstruction of the ornamental Gothic wood-work of the stalls of Antwerp Cathedral, has sent some of his beautiful works in furniture to the Exhibition. A Gothic side- board is a fine specimen of his art, in which his knowledge of the style and power of treating it, fully prove how wisely the choice of his Govern- ment has fallen on him. The BEDSTEAD we en- grave is a more free and fanciful work in the Italian style; it is carved in ebony, and is very boldly and beautifully wrought,—a work that reflects the greatest honour on its fabricant.

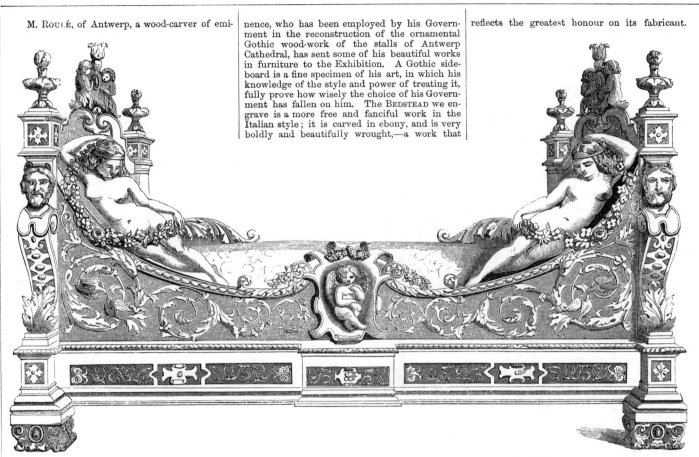

From the Sherwood Iron-Works, situated at Mansfield, Mr. F. WAKEFIELD, the proprietor, has sent a variety of stoves, and some other ex- amples of metallic work. We introduce here a specimen of his design for wrought-iron RAILING, exhibiting a pattern equally novel, artistic, and effective for its purpose. The STOVE-GRATE, as it is termed by the manufac- turer, is a laudable attempt, successfully carried out, to produce a chaste and simple style of ornament, in combination with a new and effective mode of diffusing heat throughout an

apartment, a desideratum too often lost sight of in the construction of stoves and grates; that here engraved is of highly polished steel, beau- tifully wrought. Among other manufactures contributed by Mr. Wakefield, but which are not altogether suitable for our pages, are various cooking apparatuses, adapted to the means of the three grades into which the community is generally divided, the higher, middle, and lower.

From the very few examples of Russian furniture, which appear in the Exhibition, we have selected a CABINET, manufactured by M. GAMBS, of

The CANDELABRUM is one of a pair, also from a Russian manufacturer, M. KRUMBIGEL, of Moscow. They are of bronze, gilt; the height of the

St. Petersburgh; it is made of tulip-wood, ornamented with bronze and inlaid with porcelain. The design is good, simple, and without pretension.

pedestal looks a little disproportioned to that of the shaft; in all its other parts the design is unexceptionable, and, in some respects, original.

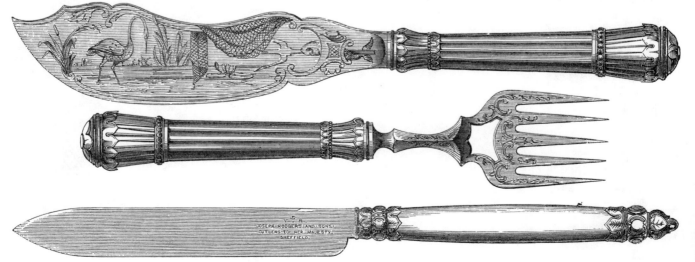

Messrs. J. RODGERS & SONS, of Sheffield, are the manufacturers of the FISH-SLICE and FORK, and DESSERT-KNIFE, which appear above. The blade of the first-named shows an engraving of a subject that is suggestive of the intended use of the article itself; a kingfisher is standing in a stream, surrounded by aqueous plants, while a fishing-net is tastefully brought into the composition. The handles are simply designed.

Mr. F. M. MILLER exhibits a bas-relief, the subject being from "Comus"—and exhibiting THE ATTENDANT SPIRIT descending on a glancing star. It is a grace- fully conceived rendering of a highly poetic image, and reflects honour on the young sculptor who has so successfully executed it. We hope to see it in marble.

Mr. J. E. JONES exhibits a portrait-statue which he terms "THE FAVOURITE," in allusion, we presume, to the dog, upon which the left hand of the lady reposes so trustingly, and which appears to return her confidence

The LUSTRE, engraved below, is intended for the display of sixty lights, and is manu- factured by BERNSTORFF & EICHWEDE of Hanover. It is very sumptuous in its en-

with a due amount of attachment on his part. There is a natural simplicity about the figure that renders it ex- tremely pleasing; the drapery is tastefully disposed, and the entire composition is altogether graceful and attractive.

richments, and good in general design. The contributions from Northern Germany are not large, but the present is one of the best, and may be suggestive to manufacturers at home, who sometimes display too much floral ornament in works of this class.

One of the parquetage FLOORS by M. LEISTLER of Vienna; the woods are of various tints, from the white lime to the dark rose-wood; they give variety and beauty to the pattern.

A STATUARY GROUP, modelled by Mr. JONES BARKER, of London, is a highly spirited production. We presume it to be the dying Marmion of Sir Walter Scott, shaking the "fragment of his blade." We have frequently thought this a good subject for the sculptor, and should like to see it carried out on a large scale. Mr. Barker's group is small, but it tells its story effectively.

A SILVER SCENT-BOTTLE is another of the contributions of M. RUDOLPHI, the eminent silversmith of Paris, and, like all the works produced by him, it manifests a pure feeling for art.

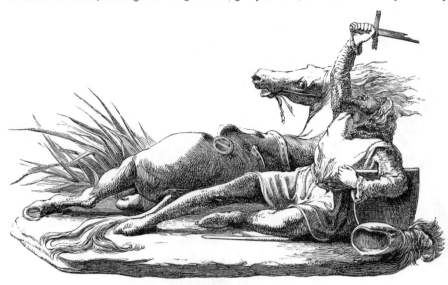

Every visitor to the Austrian department of the Exhibition, will at once recognise the annexed engraving as the magnificent oak BOOK CASE. manufactured by MM. LEISTLER & SON, as a present from the Emperor of Austria to the Queen of England. The work is well worthy of

the Imperial donor and the Royal recipient, while it does infinite credit to those who have produced it. The Gothic carving is beautifully decorated.

In a former page of the Catalogue we introduced several engravings from the jewellery manufactured by Messrs. WATHERSTON & BROGDEN, of London; we are induced to devote another page to the contributions of this firm, principally for the purpose of giving an illustration of the magnificent VASE of gold, jewelled and enamelled, which occupies so prominent a

festoons of diamonds, representing the rose, shamrock, and thistle; and, surrounding the body of the vase, are relievos, which express the ancient progenitors of the British nation; other appropriate devices are introduced. Still

lower are two figures of Fame, crowning England's most renowned warriors, poets, and men of science; while, on the lower part of the cup, as an expression of British character,

are the figures of Truth, Prudence, Industry, and Fortitude. The vase weighs ninety-five ounces, and is richly decorated with diamonds, pearls, rubies, carbuncles, sapphires, and eme-

position among their works in the Exhibition. It is designed by Mr. Alfred Brown: the group surmounting the cover represents the United Kingdom as symbolised by the figures of Britannia, Scotia, and Hibernia; around the edge of the cup are four heads emblematical of the four quarters of the globe, in all of which Great Britain possesses colonies. Below these are rands, relieved by a cinque-cento ornamental ground, in enamel. The work is surpassed by nothing in the Exhibition, in reference either to design or execution. The BROOCHES engraved on this column are elegant specimens of jewellery.

The Gallery of Art exhibited in the Austrian department has attracted great attention since the Exhibition first opened, and it has continued throughout to be one of the most crowded portions of the building. This is due as well to the excellence of the works exhibited, as to the striking peculiarities which some of them display; such as the "Veiled Vestal," purchased by the Duke of Devonshire, or the Bashful Beggar, by Gandolfi, of Milan, which we here engrave. The veil over the face is so rendered as to appear transparent; the fingers are also dimly seen through the thin drapery that covers the hands of the figure.

Messrs. Minton, & Co., of Stoke-upon-Trent, Staffordshire, exhibit some excellent Flower-Vases, coloured after the style of the old Majolica. The quiet tone of

colour he has adopted for their fanciful surfaces evinces the very best taste.

Mr. West, of Dublin, an eminent gold and silversmith of that

city, exhibits a variety of Brooches, made after the fashion of

those worn by "the daughters of Erin" some centuries ago.

That at the foot of our page is an entirely new design, and is the

brooch presented by the people of Dublin to Miss Helen Faucit.

Another of the most extensive silversmiths and jewellers of Paris, M. GUEYTON, contributes to the Exhibition a very large variety of his manufactures, consisting of almost every descrip-

tion of *bijouterie* and *virtu*. We engrave on this page a few we have selected from the many. The first is an unique ORNAMENT for the corner of a

book-cover; next follows a HAND LOOKING-GLASS of very elegant pattern. The BRACELET on the top of the page is a beautiful specimen of jewellery, with its winged figures supporting the

centre ornament. The large engraving is from a PERFUME VASE, in which the handles are not

the body is ornamented with an embossed

plants, and fish; the lid is surmounted by a

prey beneath. The CASKET is an admirable specimen of the cinque-cento style: the pattern

less distinguished by novelty than by good taste, though they may here seem somewhat too large:

running pattern of oak-leaves, acorns, aqueous

vulture, which seems ready to pounce on the

is engraved with much delicacy, while the figures of the key-escutcheon are in bold relief.

The OTTOMAN, exhibited by M. BALNY, of Paris, is a very elegant and novel mode of treating an article of furniture which, in general, has nothing to recommend it but unadorned utility.

M. Balny has shown how such objects may be made elegant and artistic, by using the centre of the ottoman as a pedestal for a statue; the idea has both novelty and ingenuity to recommend it.

M. VITTOZ of Paris contributes a BRONZE CLOCK, the design embracing a group of emblematical figures supporting a starry globe, upon which the hours are indicated by a serpent.

The establishment of Messrs. BROADWOOD of London has a reputation all over the world for its manufacture of pianos; and it would be superfluous to offer any observations as to their merited celebrity. Our business is less with the quality of the instrument than with the appearance of its case; and the GRAND PIANO we engrave is for this reason alone deserving of especial attention. The inlaid and ornamental work upon its surface is of the best

kind, and is very tastefully arranged; it is composed of ebony inlaid, the ornaments in gold relief; the legs are particularly novel and elegant.

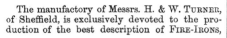

The manufactory of Messrs. H. & W. Turner, of Sheffield, is exclusively devoted to the production of the best description of Fire-Irons, for which it is famous in "the trade." We have, in former pages of our Catalogue, given some examples of their works; we now give one of a form equally novel and graceful. These fire-irons are termed by the makers "Cyma-Recta," and they certainly present in their curved lines a more elegant appearance than the old-fashioned straight irons now in common use. This will occur to all who examine the objects, which we expect to see very generally adopted.

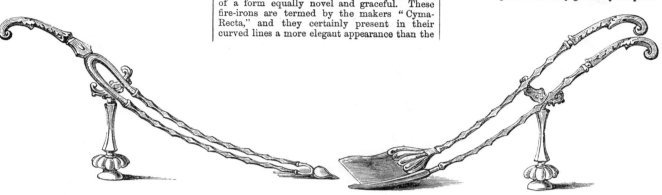

Undoubtedly one of the most superb specimens of cabinet-work to be seen in the Exhibition, is the Sideboard, of carved walnut-wood, by M. Fourdinois, of Paris. Whether we consider the elaborate richness of the design, or its skilful execution, we must award it the very highest merit. The multiplicity of details that make up the composition entirely preclude the possibility of our giving anything like a satisfactory description of the work; but the artist and engraver have each done his work so well, that our engraving amply supplies any deficiency of explanatory remark. The style of the Renaissance has certainly never been more successfully carried out in an article of furniture, than in this example of French taste and skill. It is beyond question one of the most meritorious articles of its class in the Exhibition, whether we regard the varied beauty of the design, or its execution.

From the manufactory of Count HAR-RACH, in Bohemia, many fine specimens of

the richly-coloured GLASS which gives the

country a peculiar reputation, are exhi-

bited. They show much quaintness of form as well as brilliancy of colour.

The bronze TABLE and VASE underneath are designed by Signor BERNARDI, of Milan, and are executed at the Prince of Salms' foundry, at Vienna; the FLOWER-STAND is executed by M. LEISTLER, in zebra-wood; the POTS are in coloured porcelain. The SIDEBOARD, also by M. LEISTLER, is magnificently carved in the wood of the locust tree; the top is a slab of *rosso antico*; the LAMPS on each side are designed by M. BERNARDI, and executed

by M. HOLLENBACH. The GLASS in the centre has a metal frame of rich design, and is by M. H. RATZERS-

DORFER, of Vienna. The Austrian department is one of the most attractive features of the Exhibition;

we have endeavoured to render it justice by the number and the quality of our various illustrations.

The establishment of M. ODIOT ranks among the largest of the silversmiths in Paris. The visit we paid to France in the autumn of the past year afforded us an opportunity of inspecting the immense stock of manufactured articles

displayed in his show-rooms; and we must do M. Odiot the justice to say that his productions do him infinite credit in every way. We fill this page with five engravings, selected from his important contributions to the Exhibition; the

reader will receive gratification from the novelty presented by the major part of them. Our first example is from a COFFEE-POT, of very elegant form and ornamentation. The CUP underneath is of exquisite workmanship; the figures on it are modelled with much freedom

and truthfulness; the floriated ornaments on the handles are novel. The next subject is

composed of fish, and objects appertaining to the sport of angling, and the sides of the ink-

illustrations are widely dissimilar, but each presenting features of beauty and novelty (we are

though richly engraved and sculptured, presents in its ornaments a unity of idea, that seems

an INKSTAND, which is altogether a novelty in design; the ornamental group on its top is

stand are in harmony with them. The two TUREENS and DISHES that make up the remaining

compelled to repeat the last word once more) that cannot fail to attract attention; the former,

wanting in the latter, which, nevertheless, is a magnificent piece of sculptured silver-work.

The group of DESSERT SERVICE is contributed by Messrs. DANIELL, of London : it is remarkable

not alone for much grace and elegance of design, but as a triumphant attempt to restore to fictile art the once famous rose colour, named after the favourite of Louis Quatorze, "Du Barry." In the works exhibited by Messrs. Daniell, and manufac-

tured at Coalbrookdale, this beautiful colour is unquestionably improved upon: it has a far finer and richer tint, and perhaps may be regarded as one of the triumphs of the Exhibition. The PARIAN VASE is also a contribution by Messrs. Daniell.

The figure engraved underneath is from the statue of the FISHER BOY, by HIRAM POWERS, the distinguished American sculptor ; it is a work in every way worthy of its high repute.

The eminent sculptor, GEEFS, of Antwerp, contributes a group designed from the old and

beautiful national legend of GENEVIEVE OF BRABANT ; who, wrongfully accused of infidelity, is

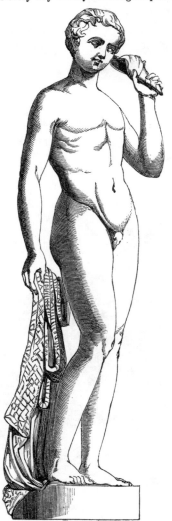

driven by her lord to the wilds of the forest, where she and her infant are succoured by a fawn until her innocence is established, and she

is again sought by her deceived husband. The story is simply and touchingly told, and the group well composed by the accomplished artist.

The two objects which form the illustrations on the upper portion of this page are produced by Messrs. WHITE & PARLBY, of London, who carry on an establishment for the manufacture of ornaments in composition, principally for the decoration of rooms, but also, as our engravings show, for the lighter description of furniture. They exhibit the model of a room, as prepared for the gilder, painter, and upholsterer, with

groups of other productions, which must be regarded more as models than as finished works. The TABLE is one of such; it has long pendent leaves

ornamenting the column. The LADIES' WORK-TABLE is very elegant in design; its style is Italian, well arranged in all its various details.

In an earlier page of the Catalogue we introduced two single examples of the BRONZES of M. PAILLARD, of Paris; we now bring forward a GROUP, composed from his numerous contributions in the Exhibition. In the centre is a noble VASE, of porcelain, in the Louis Quatorze style, with bronze ornaments, festoons of flowers, and

figures. To the right is the well-known group of the "CUPIDS STRUGGLING FOR THE HEART."

The remainder of the composition is made up of statuettes, candelabra, vases, and other objects.

One is so apt to associate the manufacturing productions of Manchester with cotton and calicoes, as to feel some surprise to see an exhibition of beautiful GLASS-WORK emanating from that busy town. The engravings introduced on this page sufficiently testify to the position which the "metropolis of the north" may assume in the manufacture of fictile objects; moreover, it is not generally known that not less than twenty-five tons of flint-glass are, at

the present time, produced weekly in Manchester, where the establishment of Messrs. MOLINEAUX, WEBB, & Co., takes the lead in this department of industrial art. This house has now existed for nearly a quarter of a century,

and its proprietors have paid such attention to the production of ornamental coloured glass,

that it may be affirmed, without prejudice to

other manufacturers in localities where such business is now carried on, that the Manchester

a SUGAR-BASIN, of cut prisms; by its side are a Grecian-shaped ruby JUG, and GOBLET to correspond, with richly-cut sunk diamonds; in the centre of the third column is a ruby gilt CHALICE,

in the mediæval style. The opalescent VASE at the bottom of the page is engraved after Flax-

man's design of "Diomed casting his spear at Mars;" and in the middle of the group to the

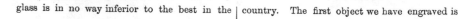

glass is in no way inferior to the best in the | country. The first object we have engraved is

left of this are a ruby antique JUG and GOBLET, on which has been engraved the lotus-plant.

The Duchy of Saxe-Coburg has made great exertions to be worthily represented in the Exhibition. This might be looked for from the connection existing between that country and the Prince who has rendered such efficient service in bringing the vast industrial display to its present satisfactory condition; the land of his birth would naturally feel a double interest in doing her best to second his laudable efforts.

Hence we find, among her numerous contributions, many valuable natural productions, and a large variety of manufactured objects, of a useful and a decorative character. We introduce on this page examples of the wood-carving of Messrs. T. HOFFMEISTER & Co., of Coburg, consisting of

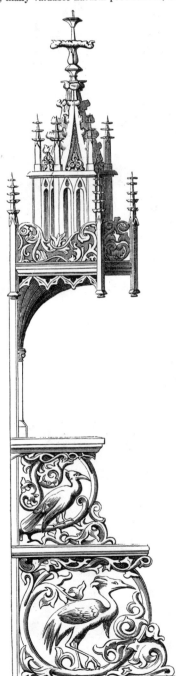

portions of an oak SIDEBOARD, executed in the German-Gothic style of the middle ages, and one of a series of four ARM-CHAIRS to match. The CROSS-PIECE at the top of the page is the upper part of the CANOPY seen underneath. The workmanship of these objects is exceedingly good.

The illustrations on this page form a portion

of the contributions from Malta, and are from

the sculptured works which have made the

Exhibition. The artists whose taste and skill have wrought out these truly beautiful productions are MM. Deccsaro, Dimech, Soler, S. and F.

particular description of each illustration; it will be sufficient to remark that the mantles of some of the old Italian masters seem to have fallen on the shoulders of these Maltese sculp-

column, the former by S. Testa, and the latter by J. Soler; while, in the whole of the illustrations, the elaborate ornamentation of the Italian school is abundantly manifest. While we con-

Testa; we place them together because we have selected our engravings almost indiscriminately from their contributions, and because we consider them of equal excellence. Our space, moreover, precludes us from entering upon any

tors, who exhibit so much "cunning workmanship" in their art. We would instance, as examples of rich and bold sculpture, the Vase with eagles, and the vine-leaf Jug, on the first

fess that our taste inclines more to the simplicity and elegance of the Greek compositions, we most readily award to these all the merit, and it is undoubtedly great, which belongs to them.

The gracefully-conceived group of EVE NURSING THE INFANTS CAIN AND ABEL, is by EUGENE LE RAY, a French sculptor of eminence; he has given it the title of "Le Premier Berceau," a

poetic term. appropriately applied to the group he has so tastefully designed and so well executed.

The RAZORS contributed by Mr. FENNEY, of Sheffield, are remarkable for the enriched character of the blade and handle; the former being a novelty with which we are but little

acquainted; it is an additional proof that our manufacturers are studying the beauty of ornament, and its general applicability to all purposes. The establishment of W. Fenney is one of the

most extensive and meritorious in the kingdom; the whole process of forming the razor, from the rude materials of iron, horn, ivory, and tortoise-shell, is there conducted, and few more interesting works are to be seen in the emporium of the steel fabricants with which Sheffield abounds.

The very elegant COLOUR-BOX engraved below is exhibited by Messrs. ACKERMANN, of London, whose names have been so long associated with the Fine Arts. The outer bands and outlines of the running decoration are of gold; the flowers pink; the ground pale blue. The darkest parts of the ornament are of a deep grape colour, producing a rich and chaste effect. The box contains an extensive assortment of drawing materials.

The STOVES by Messrs. JOBSON & Co., of Sheffield, are from designs by Mr. Walton, and manufactured for Messrs. Barton, of London. The first is especially designed to give due effect to

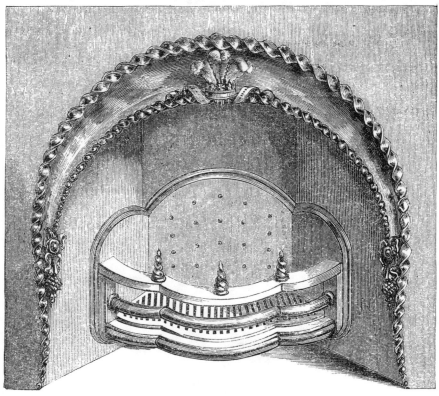

material in which it is to be constructed, that it is only fully to be appreciated by viewing it thus worked out. Our second cut exhibits a new

polished steel, and has a very brilliant appearance, owing to the twisted ornament adopted for its decoration. It is one of those designs so expressly adapted for the peculiarities of the

design for the patent light and heat-reflecting stoves, which have given Mr. Jobson a peculiar reputation; the power possessed by the circular

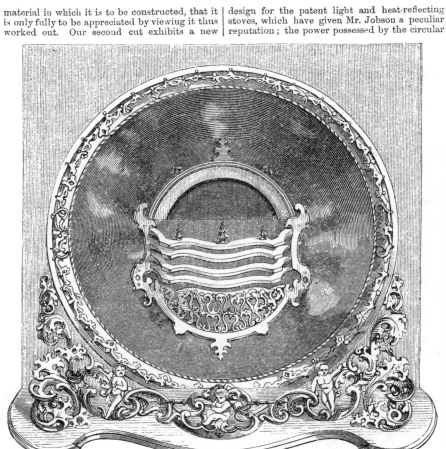

reflector which surrounds the fire-grate is very great, and more effective in throwing forward and economising heat, than any previous invention of the kind with which we have been made acquainted. It is also elegant in form, and the ornaments are judiciously connected with it.

Messrs. T. J. & J. MAYER, of the Dale-hall Pottery, near Burslem, exhibit, among numerous

other contributions, the TEA-URNS, VASES, and CUP, delineated on this and the succeeding

column. We are so accustomed to see the first-named objects manufactured in metal, that any of a ceramic substance must be regarded as a novelty: they are made, however, of a highly

vitrified stoneware that will resist the action of

extreme variations of temperature, and are,

consequently, well adapted to their purposes.

The DECORATIVE PANEL, in the style of Edward I., is designed by Mr. W. F. D'ALMAINE, of London. In the centre is a figure of Queen Eleanor, executed on a gold diapered ground.

Among the SILK manufactures of Messrs. WINKWORTH & PROCTERS, of Manchester, is a piece, from which we take the annexed engraving; the convolvulus and wheat are well arranged.

This artistic design for a LAMP, fitted for the court-yard of a palace, is by the architect BERNARDO DE BERNARDIS, and has been executed in bronze at the foundry of the Prince of Salms at Vienna. It is executed with considerable ability, as good an example of manufacture as of design, both being in their own way excellent. The TABLE on the upper portion of our page is by MICHAEL THONET, of Vienna, its top is elaborately inlaid with woods of various colours; we give one half of this to display the beauty and intricacy of the design. This top lifts and a receptacle beneath of a semi-spherical form is

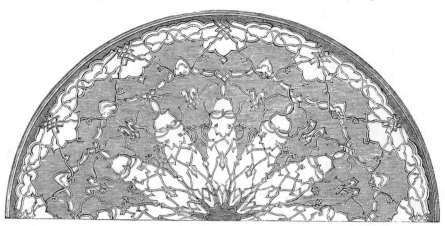

opened which has some peculiarities of construction: it is formed of rosewood, so bent that the grain of the wood invariably follows the line of the curve and shape required, by which means lightness and elasticity is gained, with the least possible material. The legs are similarly bent from the solid piece; the table. being entirely constructed of rosewood and walnut, slightly inlaid with delicate lines of brasswork, as an outline to the principal forms.

The large TABLE at the foot of the page is by M. LEISTLER, and is of rosewood and locust tree in the sumptuous style of later Venetian taste. We have engraved several other contributions by M. Leistler, in previous pages of our Catalogue, all of them testifying to the ability which

guides his hand-labour, and, more than all, to the right direction of taste in the primary forms of design exhibited in the varied works he has sent to England. The massive scrolls, forming the legs of this table, are carved with great boldness of execution combined with delicacy.

M. RINGUET LEPRINCE, of Paris, exhibits, with other objects of decorative furniture, one of which we have previously introduced, the large CABINET here engraved; it is designed by M. Lienard, whose name has also appeared in former pages of our Catalogue. The materials of which

The objects on this column are from the orna-

mental STONEWARE, contributed by M. MANSARD,

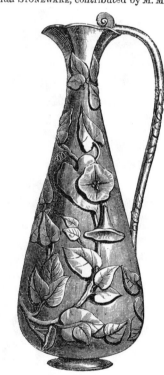

of Paris. They are similar to the Beauvais.

it is constructed are ebony and pear-tree wood : | the design and workmanship are excellent.

The CUP is by Mr. GARRARD. the eminent silversmith; its principal feature is a group of St. George and the Dragon.

M. SIMONIS, of Brussels. the distinguished sculptor, whose colossal figure of Godfrey de Bouillon has attracted such marked attention, has contributed some familiar transcripts of nature, which. although of much smaller dimensions, are to many equally attractive. "THE HAPPY CHILD" which we here engrave is one of these works; the infant is playing with a toy Punchinello. The statue is life-size, executed in marble.

Mr. J. E. CAREW, the eminent sculptor, realises very charmingly WHITTINGTON LISTENING TO THE BELLS OF LONDON.

Messrs. ACKROYD & SON, of Halifax, exhibit the elaborate DAMASK for hangings, a portion of which we engrave. It is designed in the style which pervades the Alhambra, and is carefully and exactly carried out, in strict accordance with its peculiarities. The pattern we have selected is red upon a ground of rich deep blue.

"THE UNHAPPY CHILD" below is the work of M. SIMONIS, of Brussels, a companion figure to "The Happy Child," which we have also engraved. The boy has broken his drum. and, in a violent fit of temper, has kicked his clothing about his feet till they have become entangled, and add to his ebullition of rage. The work is most truthful.

The TESTIMONIAL CUP, of silver, by Messrs. GARRARD, of London, is a most spirited and artistic work of its class.

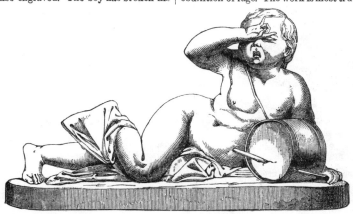

The DAMASK CURTAIN is also by MESSRS. T. ACKROYD & SON, of Halifax; it is very rich in colour, the flowers being white, the leaves and ornaments in various tints of

A graceful statue, by PUTTINATI, of Milan, which he

orange, on a ground of deep crimson. It is a very successful and artistic production, quite worthy of being placed beside the best works of this class in the Great Exhibition.

terms MORNING PRAYER, is full of the best feeling generated by the choice of a subject replete with sentiment.

THE INDUSTRY OF ALL NATIONS.

The importation of foreign WATCHES into England is carried on to a considerable extent,

A CHEVAL SCREEN, carved and gilt. is exhibited by Mr. T. NICOLL, of London; it is so

although, we believe, that since our manufacturers have learned to combine cheapness with

constructed that by a simple process it may be converted into a stand for lights, a music-stand,

excellence, a large diminution has taken place in the number imported. The watch-makers of Switzerland have long maintained their pre-

eminence in this branch of industrial art by the ingenuity and skill which they have brought to bear on their productions; so that the watches

of that country find a ready sale throughout the continents of Europe and America. We have engraved on this page six out of several which

M. PATEK, of Geneva, has contributed to the Exhibition. By a simple and ingenious mechanism, the use of watch-keys is rendered unnecessary in

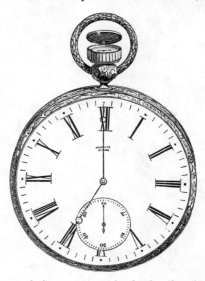

and a table. In the centre is a Pastil painting, by Mr. A. Blaikley, representing Peace and

Plenty; the composition of the picture is highly pleasing, while the design of the frame is good.

some of them; a screw in the handle, when turned, winds up the watch, and, by another movement, equally simple, regulates the hands.

A CHESS-BOARD and CHESS-MEN, in silver and gold, richly ornamented with jewels, enamels, &c., is exhibited by MESSRS. PHILLIPS, of London, but made by Messrs. C. M. Wieshaupt and Sons, of Hanau. Germany. The figures were modelled by M. E. Von Launitz, the sculptor, of Frankfort.

The female figure is from one of the "Queens" in the set of Chess-Men; she is habited in the costume worn in the early part of the sixteenth century by the royal princesses of Germany.

A Statue, in plaster, entitled "THE BATHER," is exhibited by Mr. J. LAWLOR, a clever sculptor, who has executed several excellent productions.

One of the "Kings" of the Chess-Men is here introduced, whose costume is in harmony with its companion on the opposite side. The whole of this work is singularly unique and beautiful.

The above engraving illustrates the lower portion of the CARVED FRAME, of which we gave the upper part in a preceding page. It is carved by Professor ALBERTY, of Berlin, from a design by M. Stüler.

Messrs. LITHGOW & PURDIE, of Edinburgh, exhibit the very chaste and beautiful design for

A carved MANTEL-PIECE, by M. CONTÉ, of London, deserves to be highly commended for its chaste style of ornament. M. Conté is an Italian

artist, who has long resided in London, where, in his atelier, we have seen very many most elegant works in marble, especially some statuettes.

The SIDEBOARD by Messrs. HINDLEY, of London, is in the later Gothic style, and is peculiarly appropriate for one of those mansions in which that form of decoration predominates. For a work of this kind, however, the style presents peculiar excellencies, as it has a singu-

the PANELLING of a saloon, indicative of "The Seasons." The style is Italian, of the best order.

larly solid character, and is capable of the boldest relief of light and shade. Floral decoration, in

conjunction with geometric form, has advantages which may be of great value to the designer.

A CARRIAGE, termed "The Diorapha" by the inventors and builders, Messrs. ROCK & SON, of | Hastings, possesses the advantage of being used either as a close carriage, a barouche, or entirely | open; it is therefore well adapted for all seasons and weathers. The transformations are easily made.

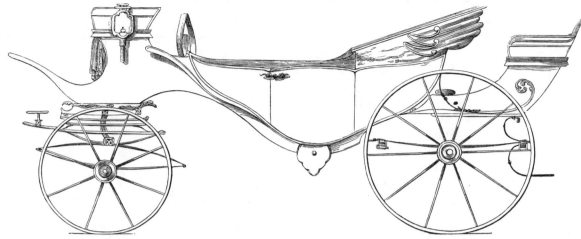

The VASE or Cup engraved underneath is sculptured in marble by M. VANLINDEN, of Antwerp. The body shows four bas-reliefs | A GOTHIC VASE of rich pale red terra-cotta, excellent in design, and of admirable workmanship, is modelled and exhibited by Mr. J. PULHAM, of

designed from Spenser's Faerie Queene, "Cupid trying his bow," "Cupid the conqueror of the mighty," "Fidelity," and "The end of his occupation;" at the top of the vase Cupid is represented as captive to Venus, who has bound the "mischievous boy" with roses. | Broxbourne, Hertfordshire. It stands on a granulated pedestal of similar character, which, like the vase, shows great sharpness and delicacy of execution.

Mr. BROOKER, of Maryport, exhibits the FIGURE-HEAD OF A SHIP, representing Ceres in search of Proserpine, discovering the veil she has dropped. It is a very meritorious attempt to elevate the character of such works.

The FOUNTAIN below is of iron, and is from the manufactory of Mr. HANDYSIDE, of Derby, whose beautiful vase we have already engraved.

Mr. WALLER, whose work on "Monumental Brasses" has rendered his name familiar to the antiquary, has exhibited a BRASS, exemplifying the adaptation of modern costume to monumental design. It represents a female figure, with a greyhound at her feet, beneath a canopy of enriched pointed architecture. In the shafts, which on either side support the canopy, are compartments, containing subjects from the six works of mercy, according to Matthew, xxv., 35, 36. The subject which occupies the centre of the Good Samaritan." That representing "Charity," each contain a subject "Mercy and truth are ness and peace have

canopy, is that of "The on the apex is a group and the two brackets from Psalm lxxxv., 10, met together; righteous-kissed each other."

The two knives are from the well-known establishment of Messrs. J. RODGERS & SONS, of Sheffield. The first is a silver-handled BOWIE-KNIFE, and the second a silver DESSERT-KNIFE with engraved blade; the designs of both are good. This firm well sustains its reputation.

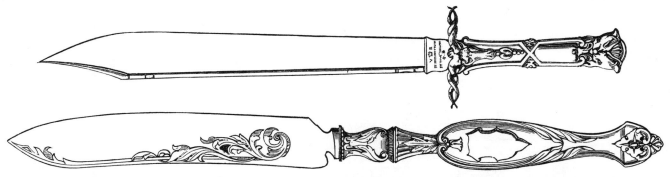

The Milanese sculptors, who, though under the political government of Austria, and exhibiting their productions in the Austrian department, have a closer affinity with the arts of Italy, contribute well and largely to the Exhibition. M. SANGIORGIO has sent four figures, from which we select one, called "L'ALMA," representing a soul ascending to heaven. The subject is one not easily susceptible of illustration; the figure is, nevertheless, very graceful.

We introduce here the central design of a COVER for a child's cradle or bassinet, manufactured and exhibited by Messrs. D. &. J. MAC-DONALD, of Glasgow. The material whereof it is made is cambric, the plain ground of which, by the ingenuity and skill wherewith the needle has been applied, is transformed into "point," most perfectly executed. The establishment of Messrs. Macdonald is among the most extensive in Glasgow, employing thirty thousand hands.

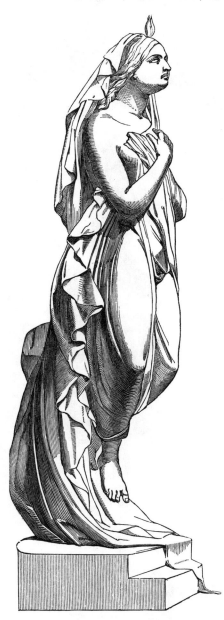

The manufactures of M. Van Kempen. of Utrecht, gold and silversmith to the King of the Netherlands, manifest great beauty of design. and very excellent workmanship; examples of

lands, William II.; in the niches are statues of six of the most famous princes of the houses of

some of his contributions appear on this and the next page. The first is a CASKET, in the pseudo-antique style of the Renaissance; it is bold in its design. The next is a table INKSTAND, in the

Orange and Nassau, from 752 to 1544; the lid is surmounted by that of Adolphus of Nassau,

style denominated Louis Quatorze; the attitude of the figure on each side is not less novel than pleasing. The TEA-SERVICE, in the same style, may claim a similar remark. The HAND-BELL

who became Emperor of Germany; this cup is a very beautiful specimen of silver-work. The

at the head of the next column also shows the Louis Quatorze ornaments and form. The VASE underneath is of Gothic style; it was made by M. Van Kempen for the late King of the Nether-

HAND-BELL on the next page is another example of the Louis Quatorze style, and the CUP that

follows it shows that of the Renaissance to great

advantage: it is exceedingly graceful in form.

The annexed engraving is from one of the few ornamental objects of industrial art contributed by the Swiss Cantons; it is a lady's ESCRITOIRE, manufactured of white wood by M. WETTLI, of Berne, and is so constructed that it may be used at pleasure for a writing-table in a sitting or a standing posture. The ornamentation is unique and characteristic; the figures which appear in the different parts represent the rustic economy and Alpine life of the inhabitants of Switzerland; many of whom, while tending their flocks, amuse themselves with carving various objects.

The CABINET underneath is manufactured by M. FOURDINOIS, of Paris; the material of which it is made is ebony, the moulding and ornaments are of brass gilt, the panels of tortoiseshell, inlaid with buhl. In this, as in many other objects of French cabinet-work, we cannot but

notice the purity of style that exists throughout the entire design, by which its true nature is so much enhanced. Ornament, like extravagant colouring in a picture, only attracts observation to its defects, unless it be accompanied by taste in its selection, and great skill in its adaptation.

The light PHAETON, by Messrs. BROWN, OWEN, & Co., of Birmingham, possesses all the requisites of convenience and elegance which characterise modern carriage-building, in England: the shafts are made of steel.

The noble old romance, the "Niebelungen Lied," has furnished FERN-

The SHAWL by Messrs. KEITH & SHOOBRIDGE, of London, is a tasteful and elaborate design, remarkable for harmony of colour, as well as for intricacy of composition. It is printed by Mr. Swaisland, of Crayford.

KORN with subjects for characteristic

statues, executed in bronze at the foundry of the Prince of Salms, at Vienna.

The MARLBOROUGH TESTIMONIAL, one of the striking groups by Messrs. HUNT & ROSKELL, represents John, Duke of Marlborough, writing the despatch of his great victory at Blenheim on the drum-head brought to him on the battle-field, as the only available desk on which to announce the important event to Englishmen at home. The note written on this occasion still exists among the family archives. The group surmounting the pedestal is modelled with great truth and spirit; the pedestal itself is a bold example of the Louis Quatorze style of ornament.

A SIDEBOARD, carved in walnut-wood, is the entire work—design and execution—of Mr. H. HOYLE, of Sheffield, a young man who is largely indebted to the Sheffield School of Design, of which he is a pupil, for the great ability displayed in this production. It has been executed under considerable difficulties, the producer having to labour at one of the manufactories in the town three days in the week for his maintenance, while he devoted the remaining three to the sideboard here engraved. It is a well-studied and very beautiful example of carved wood-work.

The CHAIR engraved below is made by Mr. G. COLLINSON, of Doncaster. Independent of its merits as an example of rustic furniture, there is a little history attaching to it, which enhances its interest. About three years since, two oak trees, measuring together two hundred feet of timber, were found below the floor of the river Dun out-fall drain, then being dug at Arksey, near Doncaster, by Mr. W. Chadwick, of that place, for whom, we believe, the chair has been manufactured. It is presumed, by those acquainted with the locality where these trees were found, that they must have been buried in the soil upwards of two thousand years.

Mr. AMOS HOLD, of Ardsley, near Barnsley, in Yorkshire, contributes an object of manufacture which proves the spread of artistic knowledge; it is a FRAME, elegantly carved in pine-wood.

The engraving underneath represents a portion of a CARPET, manufactured by Mr. B. H. WOODWARD & Co., of Kidderminster, and designated a "five-frame carpet." The advantages which we understand this peculiar fabric offers, are warmth, cleanliness, and durability; the capability of being made either in Brussels, Tournay, Wilton, or velvet-pile qualities; and facilities

for change of colours in the same design. The pattern we have engraved is one especially adapted for effecting these desirable results.

The illustration placed across the top of this page represents the upper part of a FRAME, carved by Professor ALBERTY, Member of the Berlin Academy of Arts, from a design by M. Stüler, principal architect to the King of Prussia. The design is successfully executed.

The CABINET, which appears beneath, is engraved from one manufactured and exhibited by Mr. J. W. INGRAM, of Islington, Birmingham; it is made of wood, decorated by the enamel process, with electro-gilt metal mouldings, forming a chaste and somewhat unique object of cabinet-work. The decorations are of a description to tell more effectively in the original, than in any illustration, however carefully executed.

The FENDER is another of those exhibited by Messrs. ROBERTSON, CARR, & STEEL, of Sheffield, and, like most of the productions of this firm, is characterised by a judicious combination of elegance with utility: it is of polished steel.

A WINDOW of stained and painted glass is exhibited by Mr. G. HEDGELAND, of London; its style harmonises with the decorated period of Gothic architecture; the background is executed with reference to the peculiar character-

The engraving underneath is somewhat of a deviation from the plan we have adopted with reference to machinery of every description; but the MILL here represented may be accepted as proof, that even to machinery may be given elegance of form and character. The manufacturers are Messrs. S. ADAMS & Co.,

of Oldbury, near Birmingham, whose object has been, in their invention, to construct a mill, more durable, yet not more expensive, than those in ordinary use.

istics of that style, as existing in the best examples of ecclesiastical decoration. The work is, in all respects, one of considerable merit.

A LACE SHAWL is manufactured by Mr. W. VICKERS, of Nottingham, from what is termed the "pusher bobbin net machine;" the work is exceedingly delicate.

Mr. PENNY, of London, whose mountings for carriage harness we have engraved elsewhere, exhibits some elegant heraldic SKEWERS; the handle of one is seen illustrated underneath.

Among the beautiful shawls and scarves exhibited by Mr. BLAKELEY, of Norwich, of whose contributions by the way, we gave specimens in an earlier number of our Catalogue, is an elegant SCARF of Cashmere, of which a portion is here engraved: in its simple yet elegant design, and

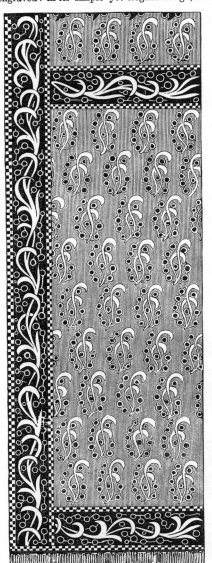

in tasteful arrangement of colour, it is every thing to be desired. We understand the scarf has been purchased at the Exhibition by the Queen.

Mr. SANGSTER, of London, exhibits some very beautiful WHIP-HANDLES, displaying an amount

of fancy and picturesque applicability to their uses which evince a well directed taste and

judgment, and show how thoroughly artistic the most ordinary article of use may be made. An

UMBRELLA-HANDLE and PARASOL-TOP concludes our series, which exhibit much originality.

The exhibition of LADIES FANS by M. DU-VILLEROI, of London and Paris, is unique; all that taste and ingenuity can devise in the way

of ornament may be seen among the variety contributed, any one of which is worthy of the ladies who graced the courts of Queen Anne or Louis XIV., to whom fans were always indispensable.

THE INDUSTRY OF ALL NATIONS.

A decorative picture for a CEILING is exhibited by Mr. HERVIEU, of London. Britannia is personified in her Sovereign leaning on Peace, and supported by Religion. She presides at the convention of Agriculture, Commerce, Science, and the Arts, and has called around her the representatives of all nations. The genius of Immortality bears a crown to Britannia, and other genii offer palms to the various representatives of the Industrial Arts: it is a spirited composition.

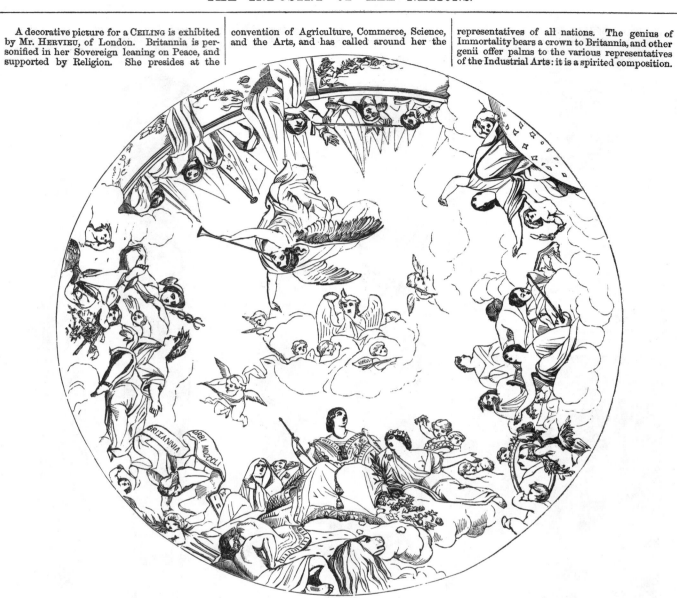

The two objects underneath are from the productions of Messrs. MARREL, Frères, of Paris: one is a MINIATURE FRAME, in gold and oxydised

silver; the other a large VASE with silver ornaments, executed for the Duc d'Aumale.

The annexed illustration is from a CASHMERE DRESS, manufactured by Messrs. T. GREGORY, Brothers, of Halifax, by direction of Prince Albert, for the Queen. It is made from the wool of a favourite goat, belonging to her Majesty. The design, which is simple but elegant, is by Mr. G. Odely.

Mr. THORNYCROFT has realised the tale of the youthful KING ALFRED TAUGHT BY HIS MOTHER, who places the illuminated book before him as an inducement to cultivate that knowledge, for which he ultimately became conspicuous; the composition of the group is spirited and clever.

The PIANOFORTE here introduced is manufactured by M. PAPE, of Lon-

Messrs. CLABBURN & Co., of Norwich, exhibit a large variety of the textile fabrics for which this city is famous; shawls, poplins, brocades,

hunting-wrappers, &c. We engrave here one of their POPLIN patterns, of an exceedingly neat and pretty design, that is most effective in the fabric.

don, Paris, and Brussels; it is made to serve as a table when shut down.

A SALVER is termed by Messrs. R. & S. GARRARD, the manufacturers, "The Great Railway Salver;" it being a testimonial presented to Mr. Brassey, (the famous and universally-respected railway contractor) by the sub-contractors and workmen in his employ. It is of silver, and in the compartments around are enamel portraits of the chief railway engineers; above each, respectively, is a view of his principal work.

The GROUP OF STATUARY is a most spirited production, by M. JERICHAU, of Copenhagen. It represents a man

We have already had occasion to notice the contributions of Messrs. FEETHAM, of London, who exhibit various works in iron of a very artistic kind; we here engrave one of their principal works, a FIRE-PLACE of great beauty, displaying a large amount of ornament of a well-studied character. The sides are decorated with slabs

defending himself from a tigress, whose cub he has taken.

of china designed in an elaborate interlaced pattern, enriched with coloured studs in raised work, similar to the old jewelled porcelain.

The group of ECCLESIASTICAL VESSELS, &c., are | selected from a large variety of those quaint and | beautiful works, designed by Mr. Pugin, and exe-

cuted by Messrs. J. HARDMAN & Co., of Birming- | ham. They fully realise the style and artistic | feeling of the best works of the middle ages

The CABINET here engraved is one of the most | important pieces of furniture in the Medieval | Court; it is executed by Mr. CRACE, of London.

The furniture of the Medieval Court forms one of the most striking portions of the Exhibition, and has attracted a large amount of attention. The design and superintendence of these articles are by Mr. PUGIN,

an artist who has studied the leading principles of medieval composition, and ornamental design, until his works are identified whenever they are seen. He has been ably seconded by Mr. CRACE, who has

executed his designs. The two specimens on this page are their joint productions. The PRIE-DIEU is very elegant, and is enriched with painting and gilding. The CABINET is of oak, richly carved, and is decorated with characteristic brass-work of exceedingly bold design.

On this and the succeeding page are engravings from the MONUMENTAL CROSS, designed and executed by the Hon. Mrs. Ross of Bladensburg, Ireland. It is sixteen feet high, and measures more than six feet across the arms. The object of this lady's design has been to illustrate, on one side of the

cross, the chief features of the Gospel, as typified in the Old Testament. The subjects selected for this purpose are "Moses and the Brazen Serpent," "The Translation of Elijah," "Noah entering the Ark," "Abel's Sacrifice," with busts of the prophets Isaiah, Jeremiah, Ezekiel, and Daniel, from each one of whose writings an appropriate text is introduced. On the opposite side, the same idea is maintained, by sculptures selected from New Testament history; "The Crucifixion," "The Resurrection," "The Return of the Prodigal," "The Good Shepherd," accompanied by busts of St. Peter, St. John, St. James, and

The LECTERN, of bronze, is the work of Messrs. HARDMAN, of Birmingham. It is an exceedingly beautiful production; a truthful rendering of the best antique style in all its varied enrichments.

The CABINET of oak, decorated with carving of the richest descrip-

St. Paul, with texts from their writings also. The north and south elevations of the cross are ornamented with busts, and the circle with emblematic grapes and wheat. The design, object, and execution of the entire work are equally honourable to the accomplished lady by whom it has been produced.

tion, is by Mr. MYERS, of Lambeth, who has contributed a large number of the finest articles in wood and stone to the Medieval Court.

The CHANDELIERS and LECTERN are executed

by Messrs. HARDMAN, of Birmingham, in brass-

work. They are excellent examples of modern

manufacture, unsurpassed in careful fabrication.

Mr. MYERS, of Lambeth, has contributed the very beautiful FONT which forms the centre of the group of Ecclesiastical Objects gathered in the Great Exhibition. The Font is sculptured

in stone, and stands on three steps. It is elaborately and beautifully enriched; the canopy above is of wood; the cover to the font rising into it when the sacred ceremony is performed.

The canopied STATUE OF THE VIRGIN AND SAVIOUR is entirely of stone, also executed by Mr. MYERS,

of Lambeth. We engrave beneath it the top of a

Gothic SCREEN, of the Flamboyant style, in oak.

The engraving on this column is from an ornamental GOBLET, modelled by M. CONRAD KNOLL, of Munich, and intended to be cast in bronze. It is in the true German style of the earlier period.

The merits of Mr. W. HARRY ROGERS as a designer we have long recognised, and have repeatedly availed ourselves of his talents in connection with our Journal; we were, therefore, pleased to see in the Exhibition a large number of ornamental works, manufactured from the designs he has furnished to the producers, as well as many subjects from his pencil applicable to future manufactures. Whatever Mr. Rogers puts forth is characterised by the purest taste, a taste which is fostered by an intimate acquaintance with the best works of the medieval ages. We introduce here a design for a KEY, in the Italian style; other illustrations from his hand will be found on the last page of our Catalogue.

The annexed illustration is also from a GOBLET, modelled in plaster of Paris, by M. J. HALBIG, of Munich; it is in the German Gothic style.

The contributions of M. FROMENT-MEURICE, of Paris, include a magnificent BRACELET, presented by subscription to her Royal Highness the Countess of Chambord, one of the old Bourbon family, by the ladies of Marseilles. In the centre are the arms of the city, surmounted by a mural crown; on each side are portraits, in enamel, of characters celebrated in the history of Marseilles, supporting a warrior in the

costume of the period, and a female, also accoutred, as indicative of the courage displayed by the women of the city when it was besieged in 1524. This unique article of jewellery is executed in the highest style of ornamental Art.

The engraving underneath represents a CHILD'S ROBE, of muslin, richly embroidered, from the extensive manufactory of Messrs. S. & T. BROWN, of Glasgow; the pattern is elaborate and beautiful.

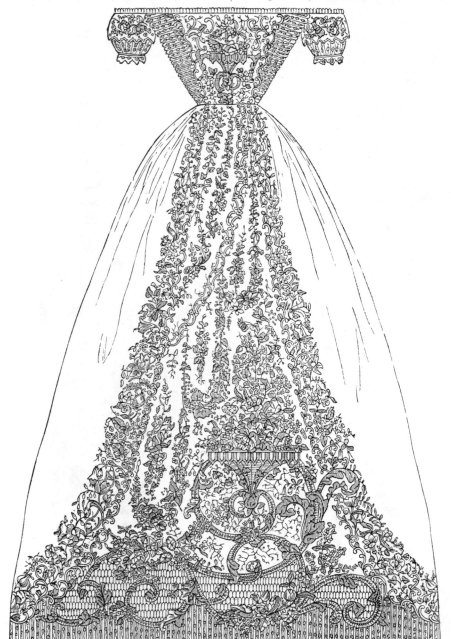

A DRESSING-CASE, made of yew-tree wood, is exhibited by Mr. STRUDWICK, of London. The

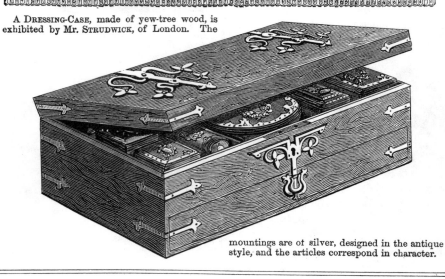

mountings are of silver, designed in the antique style, and the articles correspond in character.

Among the statuary in the Sculpture Court, stands Mr. THEED's life-size statue of NARCISSUS; he is represented leaning on his hunting-spear, and contemplating his reflection in the stream.

Messrs. MARREL, Frères, of Paris, exhibit, among other objects, a beautiful VASE, of gold

and enamel, designed in the purest Venetian style, and most artistically executed throughout.

The Jewels of the Queen of Spain are exhibited by M. LEMONIER, of Paris: we have engraved such of them as we consider most suitable for

illustration; it is almost unnecessary to add that all are of the most costly

description, and exquisitely set. Our first illustration is a TIARA, or

head-dress, of sapphires and diamonds; the next is an ORNAMENT for the

head, of emeralds and diamonds. most elegantly arranged as a bouquet; an AIGUILLETTE, or shoulder-knot, of diamonds, pearls, and a large emerald follows, by the side of which is a BROOCH, of pink pearls and diamonds; a BRACELET, of emeralds, and diamonds, completes the series.

Among the most successful productions in decorative furniture contributed by continental artisans may be classed the TABLE AND CHAIR we here engrave, and which are designed and executed in strict accordance with classic models; indeed there is no portion of these articles without

strict adherence in form and enrichment to antique authority. Ebony and ivory enter into their material as lavishly as they did into the furniture of the higher classes of Greece and Rome. They have been executed for the King of Sardinia by G. CAPELLO, of Turin, and are deserving of a

place in the palace of any sovereign. The Curule Chair is a really fine work, graceful in its general form, and enriched by the ornament of the best period of Grecian taste; when decorative Art received from that wonderful people an impetus and an ultimate perfection which has stamped it with an individual character of the most unmistakeable kind.

The proprietors of the GRANGE-MOUTH COAL AND FIRECLAY WORKS exhibit a large number of useful

articles, constructed in their improved material, which contains a

large amount of silica and alumina, both of the most essential use in the

production of an infusible fireclay. The VASES which fill our column are

made from this material. and are, therefore, well adapted for gardens.

The elegant CASKET we have here engraved. is of ivory, with or-molu mountings, by M. MATIFAT, of Paris.

An octagon TABLE, of which the top is here engraved. is an elaborate specimen of marquetrie, executed by Mr. G. WATSON, of Paddington, who has exhibited extraordinary taste and perseverance in its production.

M. GASSER, of Vienna, exhibits a FLOWER-VASE of metal.

Mr. J. BELL, the sculptor, exhibits the group engraved underneath; the subject is "Una and the Lion," to which the title of PURITY is given. It is a highly poetical work.

The figure in a devotional attitude is by Mr. P. MAC-

A rich and costly BEDSTEAD, carved in walnut | wood, is exhibited by Messrs. ROGERS & DEAR,

DOWELL, R.A., who calls it "MORNING PRAYER."

of London; with its magnificent and costly | hangings, it presents a most splendid appearance.

The display of jewellery in the Exhibition, whether of English or of foreign manufacture, naturally attracts no little attention. Whatever

is costly in itself, without any especial reference to the amount of human ingenuity expended upon adding to its primary value, is generally a matter of interest; thus the great Koh-i-noor

diamond finds crowds of admirers, though its brilliancy is unaided by the hand of the goldsmith; still it must be acknowledged that precious stones of every description lose much

of their splendour when seen apart from their settings; and on the taste of the jeweller, his knowledge of the qualities each jewel possesses, and his capability to draw out these qualities to

We introduce on this page an engraving from a rich figured CASHMERE SHAWL, manufactured by Messrs. CLABBURN, SONS, & CRISP, of Norwich, which, we understand, was purchased by the Queen. It is a first attempt, in Norwich, at shawl-weaving in a Jacquard loom. For fineness of texture, variety and beauty of colours, and elegance of pattern, it cannot be surpassed.

the best advantage, mainly depends the beauty of the stone, presuming it to be properly cut, which also is an operation requiring considerable skill and judgment. The jewellery engraved on this page is contributed by Messrs. PHILLIPS, Brothers, of London, and is very elegant. Of the BROOCHES, the first consists of diamonds set in gold and green enamel; the next is a cameo

surrounded with diamonds, on blue enamel; the eagle is also of diamonds; the third is of diamonds alone. The first BRACELET has diamonds and amethysts set in green enamel, with golden links; the other is of blue and white enamel, on which musical notes are represented.

An INKSTAND, in the cinque-cento style, is exhibited by M. F. SCHNEIDER, of Berlin. It is an elaborately ornamented and most beautiful work of art, full of subject which would occupy a large space to describe fully; our explanation, therefore, must necessarily be brief. It is made partly of gold, and partly of silver, gilt and enamelled; the extended wings of the Prussian eagle in front serve as pen-holders; the bird is overcoming the dragon, the source of all evil; behind this is the vessel for ink, over which preside two winged figures, emblematical of Peace and Happiness. The groups in the framework at the back signify the moral and Christian Virtues, and scenes of a domestic character, &c.: the design and execution are alike excellent.

The magnificent JEWEL-CASE engraved underneath is exhibited by the QUEEN, whose property it is, and who has, with great kindness and condescension, permitted it to be placed in the Crystal Palace. Like the preceding object on this page, it is in the cinque-cento style, and executed by Messrs. Elkington, of Birmingham, from a design by Mr. L. Grüner. The material is bronze, gilt and silvered by the electrotype process; upon the front of the case are enamel portraits, by Bone, of her Majesty, Prince Albert, and the Prince of Wales, copied from miniatures by R. Thorburn, A.R.A., besides small medallions, representing profiles of the other juvenile branches of the Royal Family, modelled from life by Mr. Leonard Wyon. At the top are two

Cupids, bearing the royal crown, surmounted by the British lion. On the back, which is represented in our engraving, are the royal arms, and those of Prince Albert, surrounded by wreaths of laurel, &c.; the caryatides at the angles of the case are novelties in an object of this description, but they impart great elegance to it. The whole of the ornamental work is in the purest taste, and most exquisitely engraved.

From the designs exhibited by Mr. W. HARRY ROGERS we select three specimens exhibiting much ability in their composition, and an intimate knowledge of the peculiarities of the Italian

artist, of thorough applicability to the uses of the workman and the necessities of the fabric he

and another, the centre one, of a similar character. The remaining designs for manufacturers by this artist are for bookclasps, encaustic tiles, pipes, gold spoons, keys, a crozier, and a

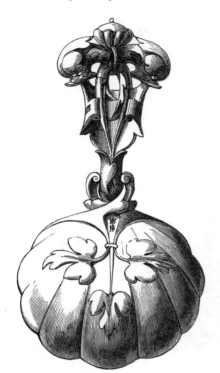  

style of the sixteenth century, in which some of his happiest efforts appear, and to which few have given so much attention and study. There is the great advantage in the designs by this

employs. We engrave two views of a SPOON for a tea-caddy intended to be carved in box-wood,

royal cradle. We may add, the head and tail-pieces which decorate our present Catalogue, are from the pencil of Mr. Rogers; they manifest his fertility of invention and the suitability of his designs.